# ESSENTIALS

# ESSENTIALS

## A liberal-evangelical dialogue

*by*
## David L. Edwards
*with*
## John Stott

## Hodder & Stoughton
LONDON  SYDNEY  AUCKLAND  TORONTO

**British Library Cataloguing in Publication Data**

Edwards, David L. (David Lawrence), *1929–*
Essentials.
1. Christian church. Evangelism
I. Title   II. Stott, John R. W. (John
Robert Walmsley), 1921–
269'.2

ISBN 0 340 42623 3

Heavenly Father, we bow in your presence.
May your Word be our rule,
your Spirit our teacher,
and your greater glory our supreme concern,
through Jesus Christ our Lord.


*a prayer used by John Stott before preaching*

# Contents

# Preface

David Edwards asked John Stott if he might write a book based on his published works. As a Church historian, he wanted to explore the dynamics of the current worldwide Evangelical revival. He also hoped to persuade his liberal friends to read Evangelical books, and his Evangelical friends to face liberal criticisms. More specifically, he wished to pose a question and invite John's reply: how 'conservative' do Evangelicals have to be, if they are to be faithful to the truth, including the Gospel?

John agreed that a liberal–Evangelical dialogue would be useful, and eventually acquiesced in the proposal that he should be the Evangelical under question.

David then studied most of John's publications and wrote an appreciation and criticism of them. Having recovered, John wrote a response chapter by chapter. It amounts to a restatement of aspects of Evangelical belief. David has not changed his own material; it stands as a collection of difficulties felt about the Evangelical tradition. But he has added a few questions which may be found useful by individuals or groups who wish to make this book the basis of reflection and discussion, growing into a greater Christian unity in the truth. That the book, despite all its limitations, may be such a basis is the prayer of its authors.

*London*

D.L.E.
J.R.W.S.

# Abbreviations

This is not a complete bibliography, but it indicates the books by John Stott to which reference is made in the text by way of letter and page number. UK and US publishers are given in that order. IVP is Inter-Varsity Press, which publishes both in the UK and in the USA.

AJ        *The Authentic Jesus* (Marshall, Morgan & Scott, 1985; American IVP, 1985)

ARBMW     *The Authority and Relevance of the Bible in the Modern World*. The Olivier Béguin Memorial Lecture (Bible Society in Australia, 1979)

B         *The Bible: Book for Today* (IVP, 1982)

BC1       *Basic Christianity* (first published 1958; revised edition IVP, 1971; Eerdmans/IVP, 1971)

BC2       *Balanced Christianity* (Hodder & Stoughton, 1975)

BF        *Baptism and Fullness: The Work of the Holy Spirit Today* (first published 1964; revised edition British IVP, 1975)

CtC       *Christ the Controversialist* (Tyndale Press, 1970; American IVP, 1972)

CoC       *The Cross of Christ* (IVP, 1986)

CCC       *Christian Counter-Culture: The Message of the Sermon on the Mount* (IVP, 1978)

CMMW      *Christian Mission in the Modern World* (first published 1975; Kingsway, 1986; American IVP, 1975)

CSP       *The Canticles and Selected Psalms* (Hodder & Stoughton, 1966)

CYS       *Confess Your Sins* (Hodder & Stoughton, 1964; Word Books, 1974)

EJ        *The Epistles of John* (first published 1964; British IVP, 1987)

ELC     *Explaining the Lausanne Covenant* (Scripture Union, 1975; as *The Lausanne Covenant: An Exposition and Commentary* by World Wide, 1975)

ESR     *Evangelism and Social Responsibility: An Evangelical Commitment* (Paternoster Press, 1982)

FC     *Focus on Christ* (Collins, 1979; as *Understanding Christ* by Zondervan, 1980)

FE     *Fundamentalism and Evangelism* (Evangelical Alliance, 1956; Eerdmans, 1959)

GG     *Guard the Gospel: The Message of 2 Timothy* (IVP, 1973)

GNS     *God's New Society: The Message of Ephesians* (IVP, 1979)

IBP     *I Believe in Preaching* (Hodder & Stoughton, 1982; as *Between Two Worlds*, Eerdmans, 1982)

IFCT     *Issues Facing Christians Today* (Marshall, Morgan & Scott, 1984; as *Involvement*, 2 vols, by Revell, 1985)

MMN     *Men Made New: An Exposition of Romans 5–8* (IVP, 1966)

OC     *Obeying Christ in a Changing World* (Collins Fount, 1977)

OGS     *Our Guilty Silence* (Hodder & Stoughton, 1967; Eerdmans/IVP, 1969)

OOW     *Only One Way: The Message of Galatians* (IVP, 1968)

OP     *One People* (Falcon, 1968; revised edition, Revell, 1982)

PP     *The Preacher's Portrait* (Tyndale Press, 1961; Eerdmans/IVP, 1961)

UB     *Understanding the Bible* (first published 1972; revised edition, Scripture Union, 1984; Zondervan, 1980)

WCTC     *What Christ Thinks of the Church* (Lutterworth, 1958; Eerdmans/IVP, 1959)

WR     *The Willowbank Report: Gospel and Culture* (Lausanne Committee for World Evangelisation, 1978)

YMM     *Your Mind Matters* (IVP, 1972)

# ESSENTIALS

# 1 The Power of the Gospel

## A Leader's Life

A young Englishman knelt at his bedside in a dormitory in Rugby School one Sunday night in February 1938. He later recalled his silent prayer. 'In a simple, matter-of-fact but definite way he told Christ that he had made rather a mess of his life so far; he confessed his sins; he thanked Christ for dying for him; and he asked him to come into his life.' Next day he wrote in his diary: 'He has come into my house and now rules in it.'

John Stott was then aged seventeen. He had been impressed by an evangelist visiting the Christian Union in his school, Eric Nash. During the next fifty years he became a loved and trusted leader, teacher and spokesman of the world-wide Evangelical movement – and apart from William Temple (who died as Archbishop of Canterbury in 1944) the most influential clergyman in the Church of England during the twentieth century. The author of more than twenty books, he told the story of his conversion as a schoolboy in *Basic Christianity* (BC1, p. 128). That book has sold more than a million copies in thirty-six languages.

He earned this influence by building up a spectacularly effective parish church and preaching centre. Born in 1921, he was the son of a leading physician, Sir Arnold Stott, who practised in Harley Street in London's West End. He grew up in the geographical parish of All Souls, Langham Place, near the BBC's Broadcasting House and the famous shops of Oxford Street. Having left Lodon during the war years, he returned to that parish as a curate in 1945 after completing his education in Cambridge (at Trinity College and Ridley Hall). He became Rector in 1950. So began a triumph, drawing congregations which were very large by British standards (about a thousand on an average Sunday) but also reaching out to the geographical parish (which had about nine thousand inhabitants) and influencing many visitors who did not go to All Souls regularly. This church became, more than any other in Britain, the shop window of the conservative Evangelical revival – which became, more than any other religious movement in Britain since the second world war, a success. Many students in Christian Unions and other Evangelical societies across Britain listened eagerly to John Stott as a guest speaker and university missioner, as did thousands of young Americans, particularly in the great student missionary conferences in Urbana, Illinois. Contacts with African, Asian and other students in London made him compare All Souls church with the international transit lounge of an airport and gradually made him an airport figure himself, with many journeys at the invitation of friends. This growing international work as a speaker and writer persuaded him to hand over the leadership of All Souls as Vicar to Michael Baughen (later Bishop of Chester) in 1970. He remained 'Rector' then and became 'Rector Emeritus' five years later. Most of those who knew him well thought this a sensible decision, for back in Cambridge in the 1940s he had been exempted from time-consuming attendance at the committee meetings of the Cambridge Inter-Collegiate Christian Union in order that he might 'get on with the evangelistic and pastoral work in which he was exercising an outstanding ministry'. (That story was told in Oliver Barclay's book about the CICCU, *Whatever Happened to the Jesus Lane Lot?*, 1977, p. 111.) But he has continued to keep a foot in London both as a frequent preacher in the church he had revitalised and as an animating teacher in the London Institute for Contemporary Christianity, which he and his friends founded in 1982 with a home in the nearby church of St Peter, Vere

Street. He has been appointed by the Queen an Honorary Chaplain and by the Archbishop of Canterbury a Lambeth Doctor of Divinity.

One reason why he has been admired and honoured in the Church of England is that he has remained loyal to it. His public disagreement with Dr Martyn Lloyd-Jones at a meeting of the Evangelical Alliance in 1966 was a turning point. Lloyd-Jones, often regarded as the greatest preacher of his age, urged Evangelicals to come out of their denominations and together form their own new association, if not an actual church; and John Stott, who was in the chair, resolutely opposed him. His chairmanship of the National Evangelical Anglican Congresses at Keele in 1967 and at Nottingham in 1977 was the most influential centre of advocacy of the alternative to separation – and that, too, brought him some criticism. There and later he urged the development of an Evangelicalism actively participating in church life at every level, in touch with the scholarship and culture of the day, in dialogue with other Christians of all sorts, determined to make the Christian gospel heard by youth and others unfamiliar with the conventional language of the churches, determined also to be thoroughly involved in discussion and action responding to contemporary social problems. As he summed it up while introducing the three pre-Nottingham books on *Obeying Christ in a Changing World* (1977), 'we publicly repented of that withdrawal from the visible Church and secular world which is often termed "pietism"'. And this development in England has had an impact on Evangelicals in many other nations. Around the world, the name of John Stott has been associated not only with the conservative Evangelical revival but also with some definite and creative answers to the growing problem of Evangelical identity.

Although Billy Graham was the host, John Stott has often been regarded as a key figure in the historic Lausanne Congress on World Evangelisation in 1974. He was chairman of the group which drafted the Lausanne Covenant. He wrote the official commentary on that agreed statement and chaired several international conferences developing its insights. Essentially what happened at Lausanne was that world-wide Evangelicalism publicly ceased to be identified with the culture of conservative, English-speaking Protestantism. Billy Graham, the most famous spokesman and symbol of American Evangelicalism since the second world war, himself pleaded for the distinction between that one culture and the everlasting, universal gospel. The cultures of Latin America, Africa, Asia and other regions were seen to be clothing in which a dynamically alive Christianity must advance into the twenty-first century. The social problems of what is best called the 'Two Thirds World' were seen to occupy by right a high position in the Church's agenda. Those problems, Lausanne demonstrated, are a matter of life or death to Christians in those regions and no Christian anywhere should be aloof. And this awareness of the cultures and problems of all the continents encouraged a much greater sensitivity to the fact that the Bible, too, belongs to a culture – in its case, to a Middle Eastern or Mediterranean culture which has been dead for many centuries. So Evangelicals took up the task of proclaiming the Bible's message to the individual and to society in ways which would be understood to the ends of the earth. In so doing they began to face the questions about the Bible's truth which had been asked most insistently in John Stott's own continent, Europe, as well as in the USA. 'Sensitivity to the real questions of the modern world,' he wrote in 1985, 'is essential to Christian maturity. And evangelism is impossible without it. We shall not win people to Christ by ignoring their problems' (AJ, p. 15).

This is the great teacher of the Church with whom I am entering into dialogue. I am honoured that he has consented to reply to the comments I shall submit. But since I am in every way his junior (in age, by eight years) I had better say why I hope for a fruitful conversation.

For all our differences John Stott and I ought to be able to understand each other. We are fellow-Anglicans, fellow-Englishmen, fellow-Londoners. We are fellow-priests of the Church of England and fellow-writers of popular theology whose writing has had to be done in the intervals of pastoral work or administration. My journey through life has not been totally different, although I have never belonged to an exclusively Evangelical fellowship. I knew Cambridge as a theological student and as Dean of King's College and a lecturer (in church history). I knew students elsewhere while Editor or General Secretary of the Student Christian Movement. I know central London, having spent many years as a curate of St Martin-in-the-Fields, as a canon of Westminster Abbey and now as Provost of Southwark Cathedral. And I have had to keep up with the life of the Church of England, partly because I am a weekly contributor to its leading newspaper, the *Church Times*. I have also done some international travelling and listening. For example, I remember John Stott's brave protest against the neglect of the biblical call to evangelism at the Assembly of the World Council of Churches in Uppsala in 1966.

In many ways I am by conviction a 'liberal'. I accept such science as I know. I am indebted to critical scholars for much of such understanding of the Bible as I have. I do not believe that the Bible provides a complete system of theology which all Christians ought to accept, or a comprehensive guide to how all Christians ought to believe and behave. The first person who tried to teach me theology was Professor Leonard Hodgson, whose key question has often been quoted: 'What must the truth have been if it appeared like this to men who thought like that?' I believe that as they answer that question Christians are given freedom to make up their own minds on many matters in the light of the vision or principle taught by the Bible – and are given reason and conscience to help them. And I think that God, who has a parent-like mercy for all humanity, has given many good gifts to all (not only to Christians) in order that everyone may choose to know his love, do his will and enter the joy of his salvation. His light shines on everyone in the world.

I am also, I believe, a 'Catholic' although many Roman

and other Catholics would suspect or exclude me. As a priest of the Church of England I am conscious day by day of the Catholic heritage. I have been conscious of that heritage ever since I was a schoolboy – even before I went to a school in the shadow of Canterbury Cathedral. That inspired me to write the three volumes of my history of *Christian England* while I was Dean of Norwich and I am nowadays glad that the church where I serve is one of the oldest in London. Baptism means much to me and it is almost true to say that the Eucharist means everything. I am sure that church buildings, the sacraments and liturgical worship which they house, and above all the personalities of the saints, can speak to the soul. They have spoken to me about Christ.

But in common with many 'liberal' and 'Catholic' Christians I should also like to be treated as an Evangelical if by 'Evangelical' is meant one who believes the gospel revealed in the Bible. With all my heart and mind I believe that the eternal God has communicated with us – has 'acted' and 'spoken', to use traditional language – supremely and uniquely in Jesus Christ. This was necessary because so much ignorance and so much evil are parts of the human situation, along with the human glories. I agree completely with John Stott when he writes in *Basic Christianity*:

> The history of the last hundred years or so has convinced many people that the problem of evil is located in man himself, not merely his society . . . We need more than an example; we need a Saviour. An example can stir our imagination, kindle our idealism and strengthen our resolve, but it cannot cleanse the defilement of our past sins, bring peace to our troubled conscience or reconcile us to God . . . No religious observances or good deeds of ours could ever earn our forgiveness. (BC1, pp. 61, 89, 96)

The gospel which I believe is the good news that in Jesus humanity has a Saviour, who lived and died for us all, delivering us from ignorance and evil, enabling us to know, love and obey God as our Father, releasing the divine Spirit to be our comfort, our teacher and our guide. Yes, I question and I criticise – but I, too, believe in basic Christianity. I, too, have been converted and in my weakness I have received the Holy Spirit (although my youthful religious awakening had no moment of crisis that I can recall apart from my confirmation by a bishop who undramatically admitted me to receive Holy Communion). I confess my sins. I thank Christ for dying for me and all sinners. I accept him as my Lord and Saviour and I ask him to rule in my life.

I have not undergone a recent conversion to being polite about conservative Evangelicals. Reviewing a book about *The Evangelicals* by John King, I wrote in the *Church Times* in 1969:

> In an age of widespread nihilism, they have a burning and shining sense of mission. In an age of religious famine, they know God through Christ. In an age of the unhappy cult of fun (or, to be franker, lust), their lives are given a shape by their prayers and the purity and joy of their homes are conspicuous. In an age of selfishness, they care. In an age of mass entertainment, they think. In an age of brash vulgarity, they are in touch with the great tradition of the life of the Spirit, which is the true glory of man. They actually read the Bible. In an age when so many softer options are available, many of them are willing to spend and be spent throughout their adult lives in the work of the sacred ministry. If laymen, they do go to church. They appeal to the young in considerable numbers.

## The Evangelical Success

Among the Evangelicals whom I know, John Stott has for many years been a hero to me. Of course I recognise that the exact nature of his success has been due to factors which can be analysed sociologically, psychologically and even genetically. Born into the English upper middle class, he started with an able mind which was developed by an excellent education. He won first class honours in his Cambridge examinations in modern languages and theology, during years when the lives of many men of his age were being laid waste by the war. After ordination he has always been encouraged to study, reflect and express himself copiously by the spoken and written word. He has been provided with eager young study assistants and skilled and devoted secretarial help. He has a remote country cottage (in Pembrokeshire in South-West Wales) where he can get peace. To these privileges has been added the incalculable asset of a calm and sunny temperament, and his confidence in his own mission has been combined with the courtesy of a diplomat. Not for nothing was it his father's hope that he might enter the British diplomatic service.

Instead he has become an ambassador for Christ. But he has not had to minister or teach in a strange and hostile environment, except perhaps among critical students during university missions. It is extraordinary that as child, curate, rector and rector emeritus he has always been based on the same London parish. It is also notable that although some of the parish consists of a multiracial, working-class overspill from Soho, this is a largely 'professional' or 'residential' neighbourhood, the nearest approach to industry being the great department stores. When he opened a parochial community centre in 1958, with a full range of clubs for all ages but with the emphasis on young people, this church-sponsored clubhouse received a good and continuing response. When he began the annual Training School at All Souls in 1950, it was in order to recruit and equip 'commissioned workers' who, going out two by two, could be lay evangelists in house-to-house visitation and other activities in the parish. He was able to insist that they should attend twelve lectures (half on theology and half on evangelism) and pass a written examination in addition to a personal interview at the end, returning for three or four meetings a year. An average of forty-three a year were commissioned. Their purpose was defined 'almost exclusively in terms of witness', we are told, concentrating on the spoken word about Jesus Christ, although these visitors always tried to lend a helping hand in situations of social need and their responsibility in that field was 'clarified' in the late 1960s (OP, p. 65).

Sometimes a city district like his parish still presents great problems to a clergyman. Most of those who work there commute from homes which are far distant and most of those who live there are either temporary residents or else rich enough to afford to be 'out of town' during the weekend. And those have been problems for All Souls, Langham Place. But the church is strategically placed. Designed by John Nash as the focal point of Regent Street in the 1820s, it is a landmark surrounded by other well-known buildings and by heavily used transport routes. Just as the nearby stores are the Mecca of shoppers in London, so this elegant church could quite easily become a magnet to churchgoers visiting London or coming into the centre from all over the metropolis. It seems that while John Stott was Rector many of the commissioned workers and other active laity at All Souls did not live in the geographical parish and that most of the congregation on a Sunday would not have been there had they gone to their parish churches. In particular All Souls attracted overseas students (of whom there were then large numbers in London) recommended by Evangelicals. John Stott explained in 1968: 'Being a London church, we receive a steady stream of letters from all over the world, from grannies and aunties, parents and cousins, clergy and friends, telling us that someone is arriving in London and asking us if we will make contact with them.' But that is not true of the average London church! In my mind I compare John Stott's ministry at All Souls with that of another Evangelical, Dick Lucas, in St Helen, Bishopsgate, in recent years; or with that of the liberal preacher and pastor, Dick Sheppard, at St Martin-in-the-Fields in Trafalgar Square in the 1920s (not forgetting his successors); or with that of a radical activist, Donald Reeves, at St James, Piccadilly, in the 1980s; or with the Anglo-Catholic ministry of successive vicars at All Saints, Margaret Street; or with the preachers to great congregations of tourists in St Paul's Cathedral and Westminster

Abbey; or with the pulpit eminence of famous Methodists in Westminster Central Hall or of famous conservative Evangelicals in the Free Church tradition in Westminster Chapel; or with the influence of the Roman Catholic priests of Westminster Cathedral or the Brompton Oratory. All these men have been given great opportunities in strategically placed London churches – opportunities not given to clergymen in more normal situations. I am not saying that no clergyman can be a 'success' outside London. The name of David Watson, who was based on York, is one of those that immediately spring to the mind. But London is London.

We may ask why John Stott's brand of Anglican Evangelicalism has had the power to draw crowds and to win a great number of committed adherents, remembering that even in the parish of All Souls, Langham Place, the clearest impression gained by the commissioned workers in their house-to-house visitation was 'the size of the gulf in contemporary England which separates the masses from the Church' (OP, p. 66). I believe that we have to remember also the date and character of his own conversion. Europe was about to be devastated by the Second World War, and although a schoolboy in February 1938 was presumably not a close student of international politics the young John Stott must have sensed that there was a widespread sense of insecurity. Many people felt, however dimly, that the Utopian optimism which had launched the League of Nations had led only to economic recession, to the rise of Communism, Nazism and Fascism, and to the return of the horrors of total war. There was no brave new world – only a world where science was not a credible saviour; where bourgeois respectability was not a strong enough moral code; where liberalism was worm-eaten; where the waste land seemed near. In such a world many turned to a political gospel for salvation. If neither the Left nor the Right offered enough to feed their souls, many found the answer in a religious movement which offered a revealed certainty and authoritative guidance. This was the time of the Catholicism of Pius XII and, among Protestants in Continental Europe, of the 'crisis theology' and 'neo-orthodoxy' associated with Karl Barth. In England these were the years when C. S. Lewis had a large audience for his defence of what he called 'mere' (in practice, a largely conservative version of) Christianity. In 1943 the Archbishop of Canterbury, William Temple, was encouraged by the Church Assembly's recognition of 'the urgent necessity for definite action' to appoint an impressive Commission which two years later produced a report, *Towards the Conversion of England*.

The young John Stott encountered conservative Evangelicalism in the small Christian Union in his school – and when he went on to Cambridge and back to London he met the fellowship and loving friendship of many who also gained spiritual strength from this source. In Christopher Catherwood's *Five Evangelical Leaders* (1984) it is on record that the young man rebelled against the science-based agnosticism of his father and for many years had a spiritual director (although that term is too Catholic to be fully appropriate here) in the shape of the evangelist to whom, humanly speaking, he owed his conversion. This second father, Eric Nash, was known as 'Bash' to generations of schoolboys. For about five years he wrote to John Stott with advice every week. He specialised in that kind of ministry to boys in England's top public schools ('key boys in key schools' was his unofficial motto). And he kept in touch with them in the universities or elsewhere. Many of the prominent men in the Cambridge Inter-Collegiate Christian Union at that time were, like John Stott, 'Bash campers'; they shared with Nash in the leadership of camps where the Evangelical influence on these boys could be strengthened. Christopher Catherwood speculates that it was partly Nash's untrammelled dedication to Christian service that encouraged John Stott to remain a bachelor, but that he deviated from Nash's style by becoming a scholar. At any rate his background in Cambridge Evangelicalism, and his continuing contacts with other Christian Unions of students, do something to explain his success in London. The monthly 'guest services' which he instituted in order to attract newcomers to All Souls (and to much more) were modelled on the challenging evangelistic services of the CICCU and probably most of those attending would not have felt ill at ease sitting among Cambridge University students. Many of the 'commissioned workers' who acted as counsellors when enquirers stayed behind in church after the main 'guest services' had been drawn to All Souls by John Stott's fame in student Evangelical circles.

However, it is obviously not the case that the appeal of conservative Evangelicalism has been confined either to the world of the 1940s or to elite English circles. On the contrary, Evangelical movements founded in the 1940s in the USA have flourished in very different periods since then and have fed a massively popular revival of this form of Christianity, organised in the World Evangelical Fellowship since 1951. The numbers of Americans who assure pollsters that they have been 'born again', and who have welcomed the public piety of Presidents Carter and Reagan, demonstrate conclusively that here is a phenomenon at the centre of American life. Much of this phenomenon is continuous with the old fundamentalism but many American Evangelicals occupy a position close to, or identical with, John Stott's – a position at home in the historic denominations and in touch both with biblical scholarship and with the big moral and social issues of the day. That is why many Americans have been enthusiastic in their welcome to his visits and initiatives.

Partly because of the emotional and financial strength of these Americans, the Evangelical movement is now powerfully at work in all the continents. It flourishes in Australia and elsewhere in the old Commonwealth. In Latin America and Africa it has swept through the historic Protestant denominations and the newer Pentecostal churches alike, and has brought many who were previously nominal Catholics or non-Christians into a living faith. It is less numerous in Asia, but in centres of capitalism on the rim of that continent – in Singapore, Hong Kong, Taiwan and South Korea – it has achieved much and it is certainly present in India, Indonesia, China and Japan. The world-wide Evangelical movement should not be thought of as being entirely dependent on English-speaking leadership. No such leadership has been decisive for the Evangelicals who have vigorously survived persecution within Communist China and the Soviet Union – or who have revitalised the old Protestant traditions of Scandinavia, Germany and other European countries. The emerging Evangelical leaders of Third World churches, anxious to affirm their national cultures, have felt more free than did their predecessors to be independent – and even critical – of the West. But the kind of Evangelicalism for which John Stott is a spokesman is clearly acceptable internationally.

The sociological explanation of this influence is, I suggest, that the impact of modernity on these societies (which are of course very different from each other) has produced sizeable numbers of people who are able to read the Christian Bible for themselves and who are potentially interested in a teaching which constantly refers to the Bible. Ceremonies performed by priests cannot satisfy them – not even when the priests are Christians. These people are often also aware of the intellectual and social questions of our age. Indeed, they are often deeply aware of the disintegration of their traditional cultures, leaving a spiritual vacuum. The second world war has receded into history, but the feeling of insecurity has not gone away. Economic progress has in some places brought a 'postmodern' technology but has not diminished the modern problems – the breakdown of family life, unemployment, urban stress, the addictions to the various drugs, the fear of nuclear war. Elsewhere the end of the European empires has not ended oppression, poverty and the fear of famine. And the political creeds of the 1940s – Communism as well as Nazism and Fascism – are discredited. 'I sometimes wonder', John Stott wrote in 1979, 'if good and thoughtful people have ever been more depressed about the human predicament than they are today' (GNS, p. 69). In many places around this unhappy globe the kind of faith and fellowship that appealed to John Stott in Rugby School and Cambridge University in the 1940s have (if adapted locally) much to offer. They attract not only simple 'Bible believers' but also literate, educated and sensitive people, uneasily aware that they live amid many revolutions and many anxieties yet need to build the house of life on rock.

It is also, I believe, possible to explain sociologically why English-speaking leadership has been more acceptable in international Evangelicalism than in any other world-wide Christian movement. The contrast is great with the recent history of the World Council of Churches, for example. There it would be difficult, or even impossible, for an Englishman, or even an American, to be the main spokesman. This is because the protests and hopes of the Two Thirds World dominate the agenda. In the churches of the Southern hemisphere and Asia the official and intellectual leadership, although often still indebted to American or European encouragement, is vocally determined to end anything that smacks of control by missionaries, of the old European imperialism or of the economic neocolonialism which has its centre in the USA. Those whose mother tongue is English are therefore heard with difficulty unless they loudly denounce the sins of their own peoples. For much the same reason it is highly unlikely that the Roman Catholic Church would choose a Pope with English as his mother tongue. And these pressures are felt in the world-wide Evangelical movement, as the proceedings of many conferences show. In his contribution to *The New Face of Evangelicalism* (1976) edited by C. René Padilla after the Lausanne Congress of 1974, John Stott remarked:

Those of us who come from the West assume too readily that the best teachers in the Church are westerners. But the bubble of our arrogant assumption is easily pricked when we are exposed to the openness and integrity of the brother from the East African revival area, or the mystical mind of a Chinese expositor, or the imagination and enthusiasm of a Latin American Christian. (p. 46)

However, Evangelicalism depends on the Bible and it requires and reveres speakers who have become in one sense masters, and in another sense, servants of the Bible. Most of the leading speakers in this category have so far come from the English-speaking world. That fact explains why at the popular level Billy Graham and other evangelists from the USA have been given an international hearing. It also does much to explain the more scholarly influence of John Stott, reaching out from his base near the old headquarters of the BBC.

However, when all such explanations of the Evangelical success have been given they remain unable to account for all John Stott's effectiveness. I am sure that many elements in his ministry would have made a deep impression on those in contact with him, even under conditions less favourable to numerical success and international influence. For there are things about him which appeal in all times and places – and which appeal to many people who are repelled by the kind of fundamentalism that owes its success and influence to quite different characteristics.

## A Man of God

He has been a man of God, able to draw others into God's presence. I need quote only two passages from his books which are all the more suggestive for being modest sidelights. In his exposition *Only One Way: The Message of Galatians* he mentioned that some difficult verses 'concern the central issue of religion, which is how to come into a right relationship with God' (OOW, p. 77). And when discussing the Holy Spirit in Christian experience he wrote that

sometimes we experience a quickening of our spiritual pulse, a leaping of our heart, a kindling of our love of God and man, a pervading sense of peace and well-being. Sometimes in the dignified reverence of public worship, or in the spontaneous fellowship of a home meeting, or at the Lord's Table, or in private prayer, invisible reality overwhelms us. Time stands still. We step into a new dimension of eternity. We become still and *know* that God is God. We fall down before him and worship. (BF, p. 69)

He has had a vision of the Church as it should be and deep down is. At the end of a book based on sermons on the letters of another John, to the seven churches of Asia, he summed up the marks of the Church – 'love for Christ and willingness to suffer for him, truth of doctrine and holiness of life, inward reality and an evangelistic outreach to others, with an uncompromising wholeheartedness in everything' (WCTC, p. 127). And he has been enabled by experience to describe the 'fruit of the Spirit' in the lives of Christians – 'love, joy, peace' because of our relationship with God; 'patience, kindness, goodness' in our relation-ship with others; 'trustworthiness, gentleness, self-control' in our relationship with ourselves (BF, pp. 76–85). He described the ground out of which that harvest grows in his *Focus on Christ*, sermons delivered in All Souls church in 1978. He presented the Christian life as life 'through, on, in, under, for, with, unto and like' Christ.

In accordance with the whole tradition of healthy Chris-tianity, he gives the spiritual and the moral priority over the intellectual. But it has been one of his great strengths that he has consistently taught a religion which claims to be true and not merely enjoyable or useful; which asks people to think, not merely to tremble or glow; which bases itself on a book which can be argued about, not on 'experience' which convinces only the individual who has had it. In a booklet published in 1972 he reminded his fellow-Evangelicals that *Your Mind Matters*. He regretted that 'the spirit of anti-intellectualism is prevalent today' – and he diplomatically softened any criticism of his audience by pointing out the dangers of the Catholic emphasis on ritual, the 'radical' Christian emphasis on social and political action and the

Pentecostal or charismatic tendency to make another kind of 'experience the major criterion of truth'. These, he said, are 'escape routes by which to avoid our God-given responsibility to use our minds Christianly' (YMM, pp. 7–10).

He has used his mind in the work that properly belongs to an ordained minister. In *The New Face of Evangelicalism* he urged fellow-Evangelicals to

> spare no pains to study Scripture in order to expound it accurately and meaningfully. This calls for a greater measure of integrity than we often display. If the Bible is God's Word written, we must pray over it and pore over it until it yields its message. We have no liberty to falsify the Word of God, twisting it to suit our prejudice or to conceal our laziness. (p. 42)

He has been the New Testament editor of and a fertile contributor to the series *The Bible Speaks Today* published by the Inter-Varsity Press – a series which shows what message Bible study has yielded to him. And in *I Believe in Preaching* he has given us glimpses of the trouble which he has himself taken to be a faithful preacher of the Bible's message. He tells us that he reads four chapters of Scripture every day but has no time for a daily newspaper (although he does attend to broadcast news and read the weekly *Guardian*). He advises people beginning to preach to spend ten to twelve hours on the preparation of every sermon. Even 'experienced preachers are not likely to reduce this to less than half' (IBP, p. 259). Still more impressive is the fact that he sounds convincing as he writes about the sincerity and earnestness, courage and humility, which must mark the preacher and pastor.

I am impressed in particular by his humility. Quite apart from some American TV evangelists who are sensationally ego-publicists, it is not unknown for preachers who are sincere, earnest and courageous to be also arrogant. Somehow there has been a failure to learn from the Bible to be sensitive to other people's sincerities, earnest about their importance rather than the preacher's, and courageous in serving their interests – although I am not surprised, since these are problems for me. I am struck by the emphasis on humility in John Stott's collection of New Testament word studies, *The Preacher's Portrait*:

> I cannot help wondering why there are so few preachers whom God is using today. There are plenty of popular preachers, but not many powerful ones, who preach in the power of the Spirit. Is it because the cost of such preaching is too great? It seems that the only preaching God honours, through which his wisdom and power are expressed, is the preaching of a man who is willing in himself to be both a weakling and a fool. (PP, p. 122)

In his chapter called 'A Father' he renounces a father's authority, rejecting the whole massive tradition – as much Protestant or Pentecostal as Catholic – which makes a congregation too dependent on an authoritarian pastor. But he advocates for the pastor paternal affection, understanding, gentleness, simplicity, personal example and conscientious prayers. It must be a self-portrait. I find it very attractive. It is all the more attractive because here we do not meet the humility of a weak personality. Here is a man whom other men follow and even imitate. In *David Watson: A Portrait by His Friends*, which Edward England edited in 1985, David MacInnes refers to the custom of hero-copying, strong among conservative Evangelicals:

> It used to be said of All Souls, Langham Place, during the fifties, that on any Sunday you liked you could hear the famous rector, John Stott, conducting the service, John Stott reading the lesson, John Stott leading the prayers, John Stott preaching, while John Stott was actually conducting a mission in Canada, having left all in the hands of his curates! (pp. 18–19)

I am struck also by John Stott's humility which enables him to see new light 'break forth from God's Holy Word', just as Pastor John Robinson promised the *Mayflower* pilgrims. As I read or hear about the Cambridge Inter-Collegiate Christian Union in the 1940s, I am appalled by its insensitivity to most of the movements which were to shape the post-war world. For example, its historian Oliver Barclay has recorded (p. 119) that its senior counsellor, Basil Atkinson, who was on the staff of the University Library, discouraged social work or a keen interest in politics. In 1933 Atkinson had edited and reissued *Old Paths in Perilous Times*, a booklet already twenty years old, justifying the separate existence of the CICCU. In the very year when the times had become more 'perilous' through Hitler's entry into power in Germany, he had added these words:

> While believing that it is always a part of Christian duty to ameliorate distress, the CICCU cannot be enthusiastic about schemes for bringing world peace by means of political bodies such as the League of Nations, or social uplift by methods of reform. It holds that in the Gospel of Christ alone lies the only hope for the world by the regeneration of the individual. All else consists merely of dead works without permanent value before God and may be written down as 'vanity'.

How large is the contrast with the mature John Stott!

In *I Believe in Preaching* he has painted another self-portrait. We can see it in his words about John the golden-mouthed (*Chrysostomos*), preacher to Antioch and Constantinople at the turn of the fourth and fifth centuries: 'He was biblical . . . His interpretation of the Scriptures was simple and straightforward . . . His moral applications were down to earth . . . He was fearless in his condemnations' (IBP, p. 21). 'A man of the Word *and* a man of the world' is a tribute to John Chrysostom (IBP, p. 147) which applies equally well to John Stott. He loves the image of the preacher as *pontifex*, 'bridge-builder'. He has praised Max Warren's definition of communication as a preacher: 'Thinking out what I have to say, then thinking out how the other man will understand what I say, and then re-thinking what I have to say, so that, when I say it, he will think what I am thinking' (IBP, p. 64).

In particular he has been sensitive to the problems of communicating as a Bible-based preacher. He asks: 'How can I, who have been brought up in one culture, take a particular biblical text which was given in a second culture, and expound it to people who belong to a third culture, without either falsifying the message or rendering it unintelligible?' (IBP, p. 185). And he has graciously indicated regret that this was not always his attitude. 'Although I hope that in recent years I have begun to mend my ways', he has written, 'yet previously both my theory and my practice were to expound the biblical text and leave the application largely to the Holy Spirit' (IBP, p. 141). He has been helped by watching contemporary films and plays, although previously he was one of those who 'received their spiritual nurture in a Christian subculture which frowns on the cinema and the theatre' (IBP, p. 193). He has come to see that 'in comparison with the big moral and social issues of the day', questions of smoking, drinking, clothing, coiffure and cosmetics are 'minuscule'. These questions are important but nowadays he thinks it pitiful that 'there is an Evangelical subculture which is obsessed' by them (IBP, pp. 155–6). Those are the words of a Bible-rooted man with the courage to be humble and therefore to grow.

This courage has made him an enthusiast about the place of the laity in the Church and – what is even more remarkable in so successful a clergyman – a great advertiser of the achievements of his successors at All Souls in training and releasing the laity. In 1968 he delivered lectures in Durham University on the 'theology of the laity'. Fourteen years later he updated them. The book was called *One People*. It insisted that 'the true and proper relationship of clergy to laity is a *serving* relationship', that 'it is not the clergyman who is the really important person and the lay person a rather inferior brand of churchman, but the other way round' (OP, pp. 19, 51). This was no new idea. (Archbishop William Temple said that 'the main duty of the clergy must be to train the lay members of the congregation in their work of witness'.) But John Stott found it necessary to confess that 'there must be many of us in the Church, both clergy and laity, who need to perform a complete mental somersault' – and he also found it possible to proclaim that 'the real reason for expecting the laity to be responsible, active and constructive church members is biblical not pragmatic, grounded on theological principle not expediency' (OP, pp. 51, 18). It was submission to the Bible that inspired him to believe that the laity must not be asked to submit to a dictator in the pulpit. He has quoted Calvin: 'If ministers wish to do any good, let them labour to form christ, not to form themselves, in their hearers' (OOW, p. 118). And at this John Stott has been rather more successful than was John Calvin.

With this firm belief in the laity he made experiments in All Souls which were very unusual at that time. Not only did he start the scheme for commissioned workers. He also made the church council a spiritual fellowship, where 'our policy has been to go on talking and praying together until we reach agreement rather than to act precipitately and force division' (OP, p. 38). In 1965 this council decided to replace the weekly Hour of Prayer in the church with fortnightly Fellowship Groups in different homes and (in the alternate weeks) Parish Evenings to which the groups would be urged to come together. These groups studied the Bible and offered intercessions in accordance with a parish plan. Once a year they celebrated Holy Communion in the room where they normally met (the minister not being robed and using a simplified service), and once a year they went away together to a spiritual conference.

Even more unusual is the graciousness with which John Stott paid tributes to his successors in the 1982 edition of *One People*. The numbers of laity involved in the life of All Souls church have grown and he gladly gave the enlarged figures. His successors have managed also to intensify the proceedings to which they invite busy laity. Thus the training for commissioned workers now lasts for thirty evenings, although it no longer consists mainly of lectures and there is homework instead of a written examination. And the fellowship groups meet for three hours an evening and much more attention is given to the pastoral care of their leaders. Rejoicing in these advances after his own achievements, John Stott has been able to show us why his successors were able to raise nearly a million pounds for the improvement of audibility and visibility in this historic church and for the construction and equipment of meeting rooms under it.

Such a man of God with a strong vision of the Church, an honest labourer in the pulpit but humble enough to grow in understanding of the laity's world and in the willingness to serve the laity, and generous enough to praise his successors, would eventually be loved and heard in any situation. In those respects the unique life of John Stott provides a model for all ministers – indeed, for all followers – of Christ. All of us are challenged by words near the end of his book on *Our Guilty Silence*:

> Our motive must be concern for the glory of God, not the glory of the Church or our own glory. Our message must be the gospel of God, as given by Christ and his apostles, not the traditions of men or our own opinions. Our manpower must be the Church of God, and every member of it, not a privileged few who want to retain evangelism as their own prerogative. Our dynamic must be the Spirit of God, not the power of human personality, organisation or eloquence. (OGS, pp. 117–18)

## What is Essential?

It is, however, not my sole purpose to pay compliments! I want to offer a critical commentary on the key themes in John Stott's teaching. I am trying to write on behalf of those who, while rejoicing that the power of the gospel of Christ has been displayed in his ministry, have not been willing or able to identify themselves completely with those who have heard him most gladly. For I want to argue that conservative Evangelicals do not monopolise the understanding of the Christian gospel. John Stott has himself criticised the exclusive claims of some Christians who are not conservative Evangelicals – and in the course of dialogue with them has grown in understanding of their positions. I believe that this shows that dialogue, if conducted with honesty and humility, is spiritually creative.

He has often criticised the exclusive claims of the Roman Catholic Church and of the Anglo-Catholic movement in the Church of England. He has attacked some of their traditional teachings as being false to the Church's only proper message, which is the message of the Bible. In *Confess Your Sins*, published for the Evangelical Fellowship in the Anglican Communion in 1964, he criticised the practice of 'auricular' confession of sins in private to a priest. He claimed that such a practice 'is neither recognised nor recommended in Scripture', which teaches that a sin against a person must be confessed to that person; 'if the sin has been committed against God it should be confessed to God secretly; if it has been committed against the Church it should be confessed to the Church publicly'. And he demonstrated the danger of making a penitent unhealthily dependent on a priest. These points will seem valid to many Christians – including the many Roman Catholics who in the years immediately after the publication of *Confess Your Sins*, the years of the Second Vatican Council and its turbulent aftermath, widely abandoned this practice. But it is significant that in 1964 John Stott saw no need to enter into any real dialogue with Roman Catholics or with Catholic-minded fellow-Anglicans. To him someone who had not been personally offended was simply 'not in a position to forgive the sin' and confessing sins against God and the Church to a priest 'is not right' (CYS, p. 84). He mentioned but did not stress the provision for the relief of a troubled conscience by confession to a priest made by (for example) the Book of Common Prayer of the Church of England in its service for the visitation of the sick. While of course accepting occasional consultation with a pastor, he showed little understanding of the motives which have led many Christians seeking holiness to make regular use of private confession and spiritual direction. As late as 1970 he wrote: 'I find it distressing to see Protestants and Roman Catholics united in some common acts of worship and witness. Why? Because it gives outsiders the impression that their disagreements are virtually over' (CtC, p. 22). He then protested against the *Credo of the People of God* issued by Pope Paul VI in 1968. This insisted on the perpetual virginity, immaculate conception and bodily assumption of Mary, the mother of Jesus and the mother of the Church; on the infallibility of the Pope and other bishops when teaching *ex cathedra*; and on the Mass which renders the Sacrifice of Calvary 'sacramentally present' and which makes the bread and wine cease to exist in 'reality' after the Consecration. He called for 'candid and serious dialogue' about such dogmas, but also described them as 'entirely unbiblical'.

John Stott has, however, patiently taken part in a number of careful theological discussions with Catholic-minded Christians of the Roman and Anglican communions during the 1970s and 1980s. In 1987 he was joint editor of the report of *The Evangelical-Roman Catholic Dialogue on Mission* and one of the contributors to *Stepping Stones* (edited by Christina Baxter), a book of essays which resulted from the dialogues of a group of Anglican Catholics and Evangelicals which he had jointly convened; he wrote on 'Mission Agenda for the People of God'. He drafted the Anglican Evangelical response which, while still criticising, warmly welcomed the progress in mutual understanding embodied in the reports of the Anglican-Roman Catholic International Commission. This progress has been achieved largely as a result of willingness to go together to the Bible. Not all disagreements are over even now – but the change since the 1960s, at least at this high theological level, has been dramatic. The reason why I do not dwell on it in this book (I discussed it in my *The Futures of Christianity*,

1987) is that Dr Stott has not so far written extensively under his own name in this field which many others are currently exploring.

With the charismatics – the advocates of a 'second blessing' bestowed by the 'baptism of the Spirit' – he has had a relationship which has to some extent been similar to his dialogue with the Catholics. He has condemned their exclusive claims – but has not been afraid to grow in his appreciation of their virtues. His own church saw some of the beginnings of the current charismatic revival in England. Michael Harper, who went on to become a charismatic leader, was a curate of All Souls asked to specialise in a chaplaincy to the Oxford Street stores. He found himself involved more and more deeply in the charismatic movement and he resigned his curacy to become Director of the Fountain Trust. That was in 1964. But the charismatics' challenge to the conservative Evangelical tradition did not go away when Michael Harper left John Stott's staff. Considerable numbers of Christians who had been attracted to that tradition now became critical of it. In their shining eyes the 'new wine' offered by the charismatics demanded new wineskins. In the new movement they found most or all of the Evangelical doctrines but in addition a quality of spiritual life to which John Stott paid tribute in the Preface to the 1975 edition of his *Baptism and Fullness*. 'Many Christians', he wrote,

testify to having experienced a new liberty and love, an inward release from the bondage of inhibitions, an overflowing joy and peace in believing, a warmth of Christian fellowship unknown before, and a fresh zeal for evangelism. The movement constitutes a healthy challenge to all mediocre Christian living and all stuffy church life.

In the same Preface, however, he confessed 'my own immaturity both in having been too negative towards the charismatic movement and in having been too reluctant to meet its leaders and talk with them'. Such hesitations no doubt deserved this very gracious apology, but they arose out of what was perceived as the charismatics' own tendency to exclusiveness. 'Some Christians', he wrote, 'give the impression that they hold a kind of "Jesus plus" doctrine, namely, "You have come to Jesus, which is fine; but now you need something extra to complete your initiation"' (BF, p. 10). He replied: 'Growth in Christ, yes! Additions to Christ, never!' (BF, p. 46). He insisted that according to the New Testament 'the gift of the Holy Spirit is a *universal* Christian experience because it is an initial Christian experience. All Christians receive the Spirit at the very beginning of their Christian life' (BF, p. 96). So he firmly associated the gift of the Spirit with conversion to Christ, of which the sacrament or sign is baptism by water. With equal firmness he denied that the gifts of tongue-speaking, miraculous healing and 'prophecy' which claimed to be directly inspired by God were essential to receiving the Spirit fully at, or after, water baptism. 'What worries me,' he wrote, 'is the wooden stereotype which a few zealous souls try to impose on everybody, when they insist on a so-called "baptism of the Spirit" subsequent to conversion, which must take a certain shape and be accompanied, or followed, by certain signs' (BF, p. 71). Pastoral experience had taught him that 'both those who claim exciting spiritual experiences and those who do not can fail in moral duties, in honesty, purity and unselfishness' (BF, p. 66). It had also shown him that God 'has made an almost endless variety of fascinating creatures, and among human beings there is an intricate pattern of racial and temperamental types' (BF, p. 89). Amid this variety, the often slow growth of the moral 'fruit of the Spirit' is far more important than any excitements. And such growth in its various forms can be expected, as baptised Christians are increasingly filled with the Spirit, for their various responsibilities. 'The fact that every Christian has a gift and therefore a responsibility, and that no Christian is passed by and left without endowment, is fundamental to the New Testament doctrine of the Church' (BF, p. 105).

To me, the condemnation of exclusiveness and divisiveness is very welcome. I cannot, however, accept all John Stott's criticisms of the charismatic movement. I do not feel that he quite answers the point which he makes himself: 'If all Christians have been baptised with the Spirit, the majority do not appear to have been! Some Christians claim to have received a further and distinct experience of the Holy Spirit, and *their* claim does appear to be true!' (BP, p. 63). In this movement, no less than in conservative Evangelicalism, I see the work of God, on a large scale, giving love amid lukewarmness, joy amid secular despair and peace amid the endless discussion of problems and dangers. In particular I do not think that John Stott has quite done justice to the experience of 'speaking in tongues' (in Greek *glossolalia*).

I have never had this experience of ecstatic utterance, babbling or singing uncensored by the conscious mind, and I do not want to have it, being far more interested in the struggles to be rational and to communicate intelligibly. But I gather that some good Christians have found this experience decisive in their entry to the new liberty and love which John Stott has finely described. Both Paul's letters and the Acts of the Apostles (10:46; 19:6) show that it was an experience common in the early Church, so common that it did not need to be explained. It seems certain that Paul gave instructions about the danger of disorder connected with it (1 Corinthians 14) and highly probable that this was the experience which new converts in Samaria lacked before Peter and John laid their hands on them (Acts 8:14–17) and the experience at the heart of Luke's story of the day of Pentecost (Acts 2:1–13). James Dunn analysed these texts persuasively in his *Jesus and the Spirit* (1975). In contrast, Dr Stott insists that because Luke explains the *glossolalia* on the day of Pentecost as the miraculous speaking of foreign languages, this is likely to have been the case in Corinth also (BF, p. 112). Nowhere in the New Testament, however, are we given a clear example of a Christian communicating in another person's language without learning that language, apart from this Acts story of Pentecost. The true explanation of the story may be that Luke composed it freely in order to make the theological point that the Holy Spirit has removed the curse of 'Babel' of divided languages (Genesis 11:1–9). Or he may have accepted as history a tradition which had been begun in order to make this point by a legend. Or the explanation may be that suggested by Professor Cyril Williams in the symposium *Strange Gifts?* edited by David Martin and Peter Mullen (1984), which incidentally contains a good bibliography of many years of British discussion of the charismatic movement:

> Some of the sounds may have evoked memories of words in known languages or dialects identified by some listeners as languages of their homeland. In the ecstatic atmosphere such claims multiplied and the miracle was enlarged. We must not forget, however, those who were not so impressed and heard only the babblings of drunken persons. (p. 79)

I am aware that it has been claimed that miraculous speaking in unlearned foreign languages has been experienced in the twentieth century, but I am unconvinced. What I am sure of is that the ecstasy of *glossolalia* has been experienced. It has had parallels in non-Christian environments, where excitements of this sort have frequently occurred and have been prized highly. For Christians who have had this experience after baptism in infancy and after many years when their religion was superficial or formal, joyless or loveless, *glossolalia* certainly *has* been a 'second blessing'. But I am equally clear that those charismatics who have claimed that only those who have 'received the Spirit' in that particular way have received it 'fully' are open to John Stott's criticism. They are being more exclusive than the New Testament. Many charismatic teachers (Michael Harper among them) have not made this mistake but have had a truly biblical understanding of the diversity of the Spirit's gifts.

On many occasions John Stott has also taken 'liberal' or 'radical' Christians to task. For example, in 1970 he wrote:

The Evangelical quarrel with the modern fashion of radical theology, which boasts of a 'new Reformation', a 'new' theology, a 'new morality', even a 'new Christianity', is precisely that, alas, it is what it claims to be! It is 'new'. It is not a legitimate reinterpretation of old first-century Christianity, for from this it deviates at many vital points. (CtC, p. 41)

And I have to admit that a good many criticisms are justified. Too often the 'liberal' Christian's enthusiasm has been for political or social movements which were naively identified with the kingdom of God before they brought disillusionment. The religion of any 'new Reformation' which may have appeared in the twentieth century has often been shallow in comparison with the gospel of the grace of God proclaimed by the great Reformers of the sixteenth. The 'new' theology of our age has often taken up old positions which in their time proved to be intellectually very questionable and religiously sterile, for example the belief in a non-interventionist Creator or Supreme Being of the eighteenth-century Deists. And the 'new' morality, when it has not been a cloak for the old immorality, has had to come to terms with the necessity of 'law' if 'love' is to seek the welfare of the other in any profound and permanent way. In comparison 'biblical' Christianity can be presented as a deeply spiritual love for God and man, 'new' in the sense that it – or, rather, its Saviour – is perennially able to make new men and women with a new love, joy and peace. At any rate it is clear that 'liberal' or 'radical' Christians cannot justify any claim to be the only real Christians. Indeed, it is to be hoped that very few have ever made any such claim, so alien is it to the liberal temperament.

But I base my hope of a fruitful dialogue in this field chiefly on John Stott's own generous commitment. In *I Believe in Preaching* (1982) he has written that 'one of the greatest tragedies of our time' is the contrast that 'conservatives are biblical but not contemporary while liberals and radicals are contemporary but not biblical'. 'Why', he asks, 'must we polarise in this naive way?' He regrets that those of us who criticise and condemn liberal theologians for their abandonment of historic Christianity do not always honour their motivation or give them credit for what they are trying to do. The heart of their concern is not destruction but reconstruction. They know that large numbers of their contemporaries are contemptuously dismissive of Christianity, because they find its beliefs untenable, its formulations archaic and its vocabulary meaningless. This fact causes the best liberals profound pain, and it is this which lies behind their theologising. They are anxious to restate the Christian faith in terms which are intelligible, meaningful and credible to their secular colleagues and friends. All honour to them in so far as they are genuinely wrestling with the need to discover the modern gospel for the modern world. I wish we conservatives shared this incentive, and were ourselves neither so entrenched in antique clichés, nor so offensively complacent about our failure to communicate. (IBP, pp. 143–4)

The questions and criticisms which I shall submit as a contribution to this dialogue will boil down to the suggestion that there are some conservative Evangelical ideas which, whether or not they are valid, are *not* essential if one is to believe the gospel revealed in the Bible. Obviously these ideas are much more important than the old Evangelical traditions which, for example, frowned on the cinema and the theatre. They are religious convictions which have often been thought to be the 'God-breathed' truth and to be absolutely essential, fundamental, 'non-negotiable' in any dialogue. When I explore them, I hope I shall be sensitive enough to realise that I am treading on sacred ground. These convictions, I feel, are in John Stott's mind when he passionately defends

the contemporary Evangelical emphasis on the Bible and the cross, and on the finality of both. It is not because we are ultra-conservative, or obscurantist, or reactionary or other horrid things we are sometimes said to be. It is because we love Jesus Christ and are determined, God helping us, to bear witness to his unique glory and absolute sufficiency. (FC, p. 32)

Nevertheless, I am compelled to ask whether the insistence on these ideas has not become a handicap in the communication of the gospel. Rightly or wrongly, these ideas are widely believed to belong not to the gospel itself, not to Christ's glory and sufficiency, but to a dead or dying culture. I long to persuade conservative Evangelicals that if only they can regard these ideas as optional (not necessarily as wrong) they will find that they can communicate the biblical gospel in terms which are far more intelligible, meaningful and credible. They can build bridges between the word and the world, so that their hearers, who at present are puzzled or repelled, will think what in their hearts Evangelicals are thinking about God, Jesus and the human situation. Evangelicals have the spiritual strength to do this, with very great benefit to the Church and the world. They have the holiness, the determination and the energy which we liberals often lack; we are better at criticising.

Yes, a great sacrifice will be required, for the ideas which I shall criticise are very dear to many conservatives. I shall be asking whether the Hebrew and Christian Scriptures are infallible or inerrant; whether Christ died in order to propitiate the wrath of God by enduring as a substitute for us the punishment we deserved; whether in order to believe in God as a Christian it is necessary to believe in all the miracles reported in the Bible; whether the Bible authoritatively offers us detailed teaching about our behaviour or about the future; and whether it is necessary to respond to the Christian gospel before death in order to be saved by God. That is asking a lot! But if this sacrifice of some ideas is seen to be for the sake of evangelism, I hope to appeal to Evangelicals. I echo Donald Bloesch: 'It is my position that the future belongs to that branch of Christendom that is willing to make itself expendable for the sake of the evangelisation of the world to the greater glory of God' (*The Future of Evangelical Christianity*, 1983, p. 7).

# John Stott's Response to Chapter 1

My dear David,

I hope you will not mind if my response to each of your chapters is couched in direct speech. It seems to me that it will help to ensure that our hearts and minds engage with one another. It may also help our readers to be drawn into the dialogue between us.

But first I want to thank you for having undertaken the task of wading through so many of my books in order to ask your important question, what is essential for Evangelicals? You will remember my embarrassed incredulity when you first approached me with your idea. For, although you describe yourself as my 'junior', I have never thought of you thus, except in years. On the contrary, I have always admired your scholarly brilliance as an author. I read your *Religion and Change* when it was published in 1967, and fully agreed with Bishop (now Lord) Michael Ramsey, who reviewed it in *Frontier*, that it is an outstanding assessment of modernity's challenge to all ancient religions. Your *The Futures of Christianity*, published earlier this year, is another *tour de force*, revealing your phenomenal range of reading and understanding, while your three-volume *Christian England* has confirmed your reputation as an extremely able church historian. Every week I read your latest book review in the *Church Times* and wonder how on earth you manage to keep it up. In all your writings, what impresses me most is your combination of gifts – the breadth of your learning, your recall of earlier views and events which lesser mortals would long since have forgotten, your tolerant and appreciative spirit (not least in relation to Evangelicals) and your

sharp, critical judgement. Often I find myself in agreement
with your comments. But now you turn your great intellectual powers on me! I tremble, even wince. The prospect of
having my published works scrutinised by your penetrat-
ing mind alarms me. It is not that I think you have combed
through my books merely in order to find sticks to beat me
with. Yet I hope you have recognised that my writing has
spanned more than thirty years and that during this period
my mind has not stood still. True, you begin with flattery
(not intentionally, I'm sure, although that's how it sounds
to me), but it is only the prelude to your wide-ranging
critique. First the butter; then the dagger! Still, I am grateful. For you open up a liberal-Evangelical dialogue which,
at the very least, will increase our mutual understanding
and respect.

## Methodology

There are two aspects of the way this book has been
conceived and brought to birth, to which I feel the need to
draw attention.

First, you ask: What is essential for Evangelicals?, but
confine your text to a critical evaluation of my books. To be
sure, sometimes (especially in chapter 2 on Scripture and
chapter 4 on miracles) you do not seem to be engaging with
me so much as with what you perceive to be characteristic
of Evangelicalism. On that account, I occasionally feel that
what you are attacking is not the real me, but a very
inflammable straw man of your own creation! Generally
speaking, however, you stick to what I have written. That
is, you treat me as a (even the) representative of the
contemporary Evangelical movement. I tried to persuade
you (remember?) to choose somebody else as your target,
and went on to make a suggestion or two. But you insisted,
and I gave in. Yet no one person can represent the full
spectrum of Evangelical thought and life. I think it was
Colin Craston who first remarked (at or after the 1977

Nottingham Congress) that the Evangelical Anglican constituency was now 'more a coalition than a party'. He was right. It is even more evident today than yesterday, and outside the Church of England than in it. I fear, therefore, that many Evangelical Anglicans will not be at all pleased to have me appointed as their voice. Some on the right wing have already dismissed me as a quasi-liberal (though you may be astonished to hear it!), while others to the left of me regard me as much too conservative for their liking. I often find myself caught in the cross-fire between these groupings. As I respond to you I shall endeavour to remember the breadth of contemporary Evangelicalism, not only in the Church of England, but in the Free Churches too. In the end, however, I can speak only for myself.[1]

Secondly, I honour you for having striven to be scrupulously fair to me by reading and quoting what I have written. And you have succeeded remarkably well. Nevertheless, what our readers are given are your selections and summaries, with my responses to these; most will not have read the originals. Sometimes, and inevitably so because of shortage of space, I feel that your presentation has not done full justice to what I have written. This is specially apparent in your third chapter, in which you evaluate *The Cross of Christ*. In addition, this way of developing our dialogue casts me in a defensive role, reacting to your criticisms. It will be easy for people to forget that I began with a positive witness to different aspects of Evangelical faith and life, and that it is to your reactions that I am now reacting. I do not labour the point, and I am not complaining, but the methodology puts me at a disadvantage, which I hope our readers may remember. You may of course retort that it is *you* who have the disadvantage because you have no chance to respond to my responses. Perhaps after all, then,

---

[1] At the same time I would like specially to thank my friends Roger Beckwith, Timothy Dudley-Smith and Dick France for reading the text of my six responses and making valuable suggestions for its improvement, together with Sam Berry and Ernest Lucas for answering one or two scientific questions which I put to them.

we are quits, since, if I have the last word, you have the first!

## 'The Evangelical Success'

You were generous in the appreciation of Evangelicals which you expressed in your review of the symposium John King edited, *The Evangelicals* (1969), and you have been much too generous to me. I have been particularly interested to read your analysis of the causes of what you call 'the Evangelical success'. You are entirely right to draw attention to the privileges which I have personally enjoyed in terms of endowment and temperament, upbringing and education, friends and assistants, early training in Christian service (especially in evangelism) at both 'Bash camps' and Cambridge, and the strategic situation of All Souls church. I fully recognise these initial advantages and am very grateful for them. At the same time, I think you paint rather too rosy a picture of my early life. Perhaps I may be allowed to mention (since you do not) that during the war my father, who was a Major-General in the Army Medical Service, declined to speak to me for two years, because he could not come to terms with my conviction that my call to the pastorate overrode even my duty to fight; that during three years of reading theology at Cambridge I wrestled painfully with the challenges of liberalism; that I struggled with the rival claims of marriage and singleness, of an academic life and a pastoral ministry; and that, after my ordination in 1945, the Evangelicals to whom I belonged were a small and despised minority.

I have no difficulty with your psychological and sociological explanations. For God surely works through – and not in spite of – social trends. Why, for example, has church growth among Kampucheans in Thailand far exceeded the slow advance of the gospel in Kampuchea itself? Is it not because these refugees, uprooted from their ancestral home and culture, are open as never before to finding new roots in Christ? I agree, therefore, that the widespread disillusionment with the liberal optimism of the 1920s and 1930s, the realisation that radical evils like war demand a radical remedy, the prevailing sense of insecurity, and the impact of modernity with its consequent intellectual and spiritual vacuum, all contributed to a fertile soil ready to receive the gospel.

What I miss in your reconstruction, however, is any reference to the attractiveness of Jesus Christ himself. Even self-conscious human needs cannot account for conversions to Christ unless he is clearly and persuasively presented as the fulfilment of all human aspirations. *Basic Christianity* begins with the words 'hostile to the church, friendly to Jesus Christ'. I still believe that this describes many people today. I have spoken over the years with large numbers of university students. In these conversations I have encountered severe, even bitter, criticism of the Church; but I have yet to hear any criticism of Christ. 'For one thing, he was himself an anti-establishment figure, and some of his words had revolutionary overtones. His ideals appear to have been incorruptible. He breathed love and peace wherever he went. And, for another thing, he invariably practised what he preached' (BC1, p. 7). So let's agree that, although personal privileges and social circumstances were on my side, yet these things only prepared the way. The decisive factor was the magnetism of Jesus Christ.

## Three Anglican Traditions

Near the beginning of your first chapter you mention the three traditional streams of Anglicanism – liberal, Catholic and Evangelical – and claim to belong to all three simultaneously. I could advance the same claim. It all depends on definitions.

If 'liberal' means respect for the scientific enterprise, the development of a critical judgement, an emphasis on the importance of reason and conscience, freedom to make up our minds in the light of Scripture, and belief in the mercy of God, whose light shines on all humankind, then emphatically I too could be called a liberal. Like yourself, I do not believe that the Bible provides 'a complete system of theology' or 'a comprehensive guide' to ethics. Systematic theology is certainly a legitimate and even necessary academic discipline, but God did not choose to reveal himself in systematic form, and all systems are exposed to the same temptation, namely to trim God's revelation to fit our system instead of adapting our system to accommodate his revelation. 'Beware of the systematizers of religion!' wrote Charles Simeon of Cambridge, one of my heroes. I agree with him. The same caution should apply to the systematizers of ethics. The Bible contains ample ethical instruction (in principle, precept and pattern), but it could not be called 'a comprehensive guide', not least because there are numerous complex modern issues to which it does not directly address itself.

But is yours a complete account of 'liberalism'? The liberalism which I feel obliged to reject lies under the surface of your definition. I too am grateful to critical scholars who have helped me to understand the Bible, but not to those who have encouraged me to reject its teaching. I too insist on our God-given freedom to make up our own minds, but only 'in the light of the vision or principle taught by the Bible', as you say. For freedom to disagree with the Bible is an illusory freedom; in reality it is bondage to falsehood. I too rejoice in God's mercy, and in his eternal *Logos* who is both the life and the light of human beings and 'the true light', coming into the world and giving light to everybody (John 1:4,9). But the John who expressed these sublime truths was himself not a universalist; he later wrote both that the light causes shadows as well as illumination, because sinners prefer darkness to light (3:19–21), and that judging and life-giving are alike characteristic activities of the Son of God (5:21–23).

If 'Catholic' merely describes those who value the Christian tradition as a precious heritage, who have a high view of the Church and its two gospel sacraments, and who find that the externals of architecture and liturgy, as well as the example of the saints, speak helpfully to them, then again I take my place beside you as a Catholic. But would Catholics (whether Anglican or Roman) accept your definition as adequate? Confining myself now to the Anglican Church, the Catholicism which I cannot myself accept, and which is still held by many, teaches (for example) that the historic episcopate is indispensable to a true Church; that Scripture is neither supreme in its authority nor sufficient for salvation, since it needs to be supplemented by tradition; that a baptism is a 'christening' since it makes people Christian irrespective of their repentance and faith; that the 'inner reality' of the bread and wine is changed into Christ's body and blood, and that therefore Christ is in some sense contained and localised in the consecrated elements; and that in the Eucharist we share in the sacrifice of Christ, meaning not that we share in its benefits and offer ourselves to him in humble gratitude (our sacrifice being a response to his), but that we share in the actual offering of it (our sacrifice blending with his). Such things cannot be proved from Scripture; Evangelicals believe that Scripture rather excludes them.

So when the definitions of 'liberal' and 'Catholic' are made a little more precise, I cannot call myself either. Can you, then, David, be called an Evangelical? Well, if an Evangelical is 'one who believes the gospel revealed in the Bible', who believes that God has acted and spoken 'supremely and uniquely in Jesus Christ', that because of endemic evil human beings need a Saviour, that Jesus Christ is that Saviour, who lived and died for us, and gives us his Spirit, and that we need to accept him as our Lord and Saviour – then you too are an Evangelical. I am very thankful that you can affirm what you do. I certainly agree that no conscious, crisis conversion experience is necessary. As Jim Packer has put it, 'the only proof of past conversion is present convertedness' (*Keep in Step with the Spirit*, 1984, p. 70).

But has your definition done justice to the historic under-standing of Evangelical belief since the Reformation? I do not want to exclude you. Nor is it my intention deliberately to define 'Evangelical' in such a way as to do so. But words are slippery things and need to be firmly grasped. I want to answer your question about Evangelical essentials with integrity, according to both the history of the word and our contemporary Evangelical self-understanding. Although I shall respond to you more fully chapter by chapter, as you press your questions upon me, and although I shall want to be as flexible as possible in terms of the formulation of Evangelical doctrines, I think I must make a preliminary statement now. Evangelicals regard it as essential to believe not just 'the gospel revealed in the Bible', but the full revelation of the Bible; not just that 'Christ died for us' but that he died 'for our sins', in some sense 'bearing' them objectively in our place, so that in holy love God can forgive penitent believers; not just that we receive the Spirit, but that he does a supernatural work in us, variously portrayed in the New Testament as 'regeneration', 'resurrection' and 're-creation'.

Here are three aspects of the divine initiative – God revealing himself in Christ and in the total biblical witness to Christ, God redeeming the world through Christ, who became sin and a curse for us, and God radically transform-ing sinners by the inward operation of his Spirit. Thus stated, the Evangelical faith is historic, mainline, trinitarian Christianity, not an eccentric deviation from it. For we do not see ourselves as offering a new Christianity, but as recalling the Church to original Christianity. You ask at the end of your chapter what Evangelicals are prepared to give up. Would it not be self-contradictory to sacrifice the evangel for the sake of evangelism? But are not such truths as these, you ask, a handicap to contemporary communica-tion? Not in our experience. On the contrary, they com-municate powerfully to men and women who are conscious of their alienation. Besides, the truth of the finality of God's revelation and redemption in Christ, and so of the Bible and the cross, does not (we believe) belong to 'a dead or dying culture' but to the everlasting gospel which, though we struggle to communicate it in modern idiom, we have no liberty to compromise. It may be possible to be saved with only a limited grasp of the truth (who can claim more?). In this sense it can be argued that some truth is not 'essential'. To concede this, however, does not imply that it is 'optional'. Whatever is truth from God demands our assent.

I fear this will bring you an initial disappointment, but let's continue our dialogue.

Yours ever,
John

# 2 The Authority of the Scriptures

## The Bible in the Modern World

What is the authority of the Bible for Christians living at the end of the twentieth century? The question fully deserves the importance given to it in innumerable sermons, talks, articles and books, for some of the answers have greatly damaged Christianity. There are some 'liberal' or 'modernist' Christians who appear to have decided that apart from some favourite passages the Bible has no authority for them. In practice they may neglect humble Bible study, even if they are professional preachers or theologians. They may attempt to construct a version of Christianity, or a post-Christian philosophy, which has little or no connection with the Bible's message about a real, living, active, creative, loving and saving God. And there are some 'conservative' or 'fundamentalist' Christians who go to the opposite extreme. They appear to believe that God dictated all the words, more than two million in number, in the original manuscripts (now lost) of the sixty-six books accepted by Protestants as the Holy Bible. Like Harold Lindsell in his alarming book of 1976, they wage a *Battle for the Bible* against those who in their judgement are not 'Bible believers'. Their attitude is in keeping with the belief of Philo of Alexandria in the first century AD, and of many of the 'fathers' of the ancient Church, that God used the authors of the Scriptures as a musician uses his instrument, but it does not seem to be in touch with modern knowledge about how the Bible was actually written. However, even these two extreme positions – both of which would be rejected by most Christians nowadays – can be helpful if they remind us that the most important question about the Bible is whether it speaks the truth.

We can also learn from the courage with which the 'liberals' and 'conservatives' whom we may regard as extremists have refused to answer that question untruthfully, whatever unpopularity they may incur. Many modernists have apparently given up wrestling with the Bible because they have despaired of ever being able to find truth in it. So much of it seems to belong to fairyland. Here, it seems, are legends which contradict what can be known scientifically and historically. Such fables are, it seems, accompanied by arguments appealing to authorities which are not truly authoritative. To leave the Bible behind is, they think, to leave behind tall stories and bad logic – and their consciences compel them to move forward into cleaner air. And many fundamentalists have apparently given up wrestling with modern knowledge because they have despaired of ever finding the true God in it. In the Bible they do find him – but that truth is, it seems, destroyed once any 'biblical criticism' is accepted. To leave modern knowledge behind is, they think, to submit to God's own truth. They, too, have consciences – and they, too, are prepared to sacrifice much for the sake of the truth as they see it. We can profitably learn from both these movements of 'extremists' how fundamental is the inquiry on which we have embarked. The truth is at stake.

But what is 'truth'? I am one of those who want from the Bible nothing but the truth, but who mean by 'the truth' at least two things. We mean something of what the 'liberals' have meant. We want to know, so far as we can, what actually took place, who really said what, who wrote what, how the tradition developed – for that is the scientific method and the light of science is one of the weapons which humanity has against the darkness of ignorance and error. But we also mean by 'the truth' something of what the 'Bible believers' have meant. We want to know what these books mean for today, teaching truth on the topics which basically concern them and us – man, God, evil, salvation, justice, death, life. To study the books of the Bible 'like any other book' – to study them critically as a varied collection of ancient literature – is essential to intellectual integrity nowadays. But not to know that these ancient books are more relevant than the newspaper is to miss their message. In 1970 an American scholar, James D. Smart, wrote a book called *The Strange Silence of the Bible in the Church*. He drew attention to the fact that while in this century there had been a spectacular expansion of literary and historical 'biblical science' in the universities and in the colleges training pastors and teachers, in the mainline Protestant churches there had been an equally spectacular decline of interest in the Bible, in pew and pulpit alike. Since then the situation has not altered enough, although the Roman Catholic Church has liberated biblical scholars and rediscovered the Bible with some excitement (Professor Smart's farewell survey of *The Past, Present and Future of Biblical Theology* said as much in 1979). The explanation is that in many colleges literary and historical studies have been thought to be all that is intellectually respectable, while in many churches it has been thought that to be passionately concerned about 'what the Bible says' is to be something dreadful – a 'fundamentalist'. But now many of us want to know the Bible's truth, which is historical *and* existential. We want to read the Bible both critically *and* humbly. For when we read the books of the Bible 'like any other book', these books read us.

What, then, is the Bible? Obviously it is not one book whose only author is God. The books (in Greek *ta biblia*) need to be interpreted by using the mind with all the aids that are accessible, including the aid of prayer for guidance by God. And that takes time. The exponent of the Bible who deserves attention is 'a workman who does not need to be ashamed and who correctly handles the word of truth' (2 Timothy 2:15). But the message of God does come through, and the attempt to hear and obey the Bible's message is one of the things that has made Christianity Christian. For all

Christians the Bible, in some sense, is or becomes or conveys 'the word of God'. Its history is, in some sense, 'salvation history'. Its great images are signs pointing to our salvation, from the Garden of Eden to the final City of God. That seems – to understate its value in our salvation – sufficient. The Bible can still be treasured as unique, supreme and more precious than any jewel if we agree with Professor Barr in *The Bible in the Modern World* (1973, p. 119): 'The status of the Bible is one of sufficiency rather than of perfection'. And so I hope that the days are past, or are rapidly passing, when it was thought necessary to take an extremely and exclusively 'liberal' or an extremely and exclusively 'conservative' position about the Bible. The Bible as it actually exists is truer than either position.

The war between 'Genesis and Geology' is, I reckon, over – or it ought to be over. Christians who accept science surely have no need to pretend that only science can give us reliable knowledge about our world. There is no need to claim that the study (or the contemplation) of 'nature' (or of evolution or of human history) can by itself teach us that our world is made and controlled by the God who is love. What has been called 'natural religion' turns out to say very little when tested. We can and we should turn to the Bible for a revelation, the self-revelation of God, after which the mysteries surrounding our short and feeble lives amid an ambiguous 'nature' become a little clearer. And there is no need for Christians who accept the Bible to pretend that the first chapter of Genesis (for example) is an accurate account of the origins of the universe, as if it covered the same field as science – only more authoritatively. That chapter is one of the most magnificent and most instructive pictures ever painted of man's place in the created universe. It sings aloud that 'nature' is good because of God. Triumphantly it takes Babylonian and other myths and it says about everything: 'In the beginning God created . . .' Thus the sun and moon, which people have often worshipped, are seen as mere lights in the sky which conveniently 'separate the day from the night' and 'mark seasons and days and years'. But it is not necessary to sweat over the ingenious attempts of the fundamentalist 'creationists' to reconcile the six working 'days' of that chapter with the thousands of millions of years known to science. Nor does it need to be explained tortuously how day and night could be created before sun and moon, plants and trees before sunshine and insects, birds before reptiles, and so forth.

Some readers may doubt whether I can take the Bible seriously enough since I do not take an extremely and exclusively liberal or conservative attitude to its truth. It may help if I say that I have studied the Bible for about fifty years and based sermons on it for about thirty. Although I have never been a professional biblical scholar I have had many friends in that profession; one of them, Professor C. F. D. Moule, has been so extraordinarily kind and patient as to comment on my bits of this book in draft, although he must not be blamed for my amateurish opinions. While I was Editor of the SCM Press in London in the 1960s I published many biblical studies by leading scholars. Later on I wrote my own shorter books, trying to share my enthusiasm – *A Key to the Old Testament, Jesus for Modern Man* and *The Last Things Now.*

I greatly admire John Stott's dedication and skill as an expositor of the Bible. Although he has been primarily a preacher and conference speaker, his teaching is now on record in many books. When I read his *The Bible: Book for Today* (B), I am in emphatic and grateful agreement with him for most of the time. I accept his points that 'the major function of Scripture is to bear witness to Christ' and that 'we do not worship the Bible'. But I also applaud his stress on the necessity of revelation ('unless God takes the initiative to disclose what is in his mind, we shall never be able to find out'). I agree with his insistence that God is revealed through words as well as deeds but that the word of God is spoken through the words of men ('divine inspiration was not a mechanical process reducing the human authors of the Bible to machines, whether dictating-machines or tape-recorders'). I share his recognition 'that not every word in the Bible is literally true, and that not everything contained in the Bible is affirmed by the Bible'. 'The biblical authors', he rightly says, 'used many different literary genres, each of which must be interpreted according to its own rules – history as history, poetry as poetry, parable as parable, etc.'

A typical example of his balance is to be found on pages 49–50 of *The Bible: Book for Today*. When interpreting the Bible, we have, he says, to seek 'both the *original* sense according to the biblical author's intention and the *natural* sense, which may be literal or figurative'. Yet 'we must come to the biblical text with a recognition of our cultural prejudices and with a willingness to have them challenged and changed'. If the Church comes to the Bible in that humility, it will find that the Bible sustains it, directs it, reforms it, unites it and revives it. 'I do not hesitate to say that the Bible is indispensable to every Christian's health and growth' – although in fact he does charitably hesitate to say that about people unable to read the Bible for themselves.

I welcome much in the *Willowbank Report* which Dr Stott drafted after an international conference on 'Gospel and Culture' in 1978. This recognises that 'the biblical writers made critical use of whatever cultural material was available to them for the expression of their message'. They referred several times to a creature of Babylonian mythology, a sea monster named Leviathan, for example. When they used the imagery of a 'three-tiered' universe (heaven above earth, earth above *Sheol*) 'they did not thereby affirm a pre-Copernican cosmology'. 'Similarly, New Testament language and thought-forms are steeped in both Jewish and Hellenistic cultures.' But 'out of the context in which his word was originally given, we hear God speaking to us in our contemporary context, and it is a transforming experience.' That seems to me a neat summary of points made also in Tony Thiselton's persuasive essay on 'Understanding God's Word Today' in the first volume of *Obeying Christ in a Changing World*, which Dr Stott edited in 1977. That essay, later expanded into a book on *The Two Horizons*

(1980), did something to popularise the word 'hermeneutics' for the art of interpreting texts and to enrol Evangelicals as students of it. Hermeneutics can never be entirely free of problems and controversies, for it was well defined by one of its most eminent and controversial recent practitioners (Rudolf Bultmann) as 'the technique of understanding expressions of life set in written form'. But anyone who seriously tries to interpret the Bible is doing hermeneutics.

I also welcome the 1979 lecture in which Dr Stott discussed *The Authority and Relevance of the Bible in the Modern World*. To say 'the Bible is the word of God is true', he declared, 'but it is only a half-truth, even a dangerous half-truth. For the Bible is also the word and witness of men . . . Normally he seems to have revealed his truth to them and through them in such a way that they were not conscious of divine inspiration, so fully were their own minds involved in this process'. The correct principles of interpretation are given as these: 'the true meaning of Scripture is the natural and obvious meaning'; 'a text means what its author meant' (a definition by E. D. Hirsch which John Stott quotes in several of his books); 'we shall seek to interpret the text in its context, and each Scripture in the light of all. God's message given in one culture must be allowed to impinge on us who live in another culture', and the judicious way is 'to preserve the inner substance of what God is teaching or commanding, while claiming the liberty to reclothe it in modern dress'. Yet 'if we come to Scripture with our minds made up, expecting to hear from it only an echo of our own thoughts and never the thunderclap of God's, then indeed he will not speak to us and we shall only be confirmed in our own prejudices'. Thus although Dr Stott rightly concentrates on the translation of the Bible's message so that it challenges a hearer in another culture, he says some important things about the Bible in its original setting. He urges us to attend to what the human author of a biblical passage meant originally. He rejects the idea that God inspired not the original, natural meaning but the 'fuller' or 'spiritual' meaning discerned by Christians. Without referring in detail to recent controversies between biblical scholars, he tackles a task which is essential in the construction of any 'biblical' theology: he builds a bridge between the Testaments. And because he insists on the original, natural meaning of the words in both Testaments, his bridge rests on foundations which are firmer than the rubble beneath some other bridges.

This account of the authority of the Scriptures has I think, many merits. It rightly rebukes the 'liberal' extremists who have virtually abandoned the Bible. But it also corrects the extreme conservatism which has still marked many Evangelical scholars (not merely the uneducated) in our own time. A convenient collection of illustrations of this conservatism was made by James Barr in his *Fundamentalism* (1977, revised 1981). Although Professor Barr tended to suggest – and to lament bitterly – that Evangelicals would always remain fundamentalists at heart, in fact Dr Stott has here laid down principles of hermeneutics, some of which would be passionately rejected by (for example) those American fundamentalists who support institutions such as Bob Jones University, the Moody Bible Institute and Dallas Theological Seminary; who applaud evangelists such as Jerry Falwell and Harold Lindsell, and suspect Billy Graham as a liberal; and who ignore the magazine *Christianity Today* in the conviction that it has sold out to the liberals. Some of Dr Stott's teachings would also have dismayed many previous Evangelical spokesmen. Some would have been rejected by those two great professors at Princeton in the USA, Charles Hodge and Benjamin Warfield, who were for long regarded as the defenders of the faith of modern (or anti-modern) Evangelicalism. Professor James Dunn is being more unkind than untrue when he describes Warfield's position as 'exegetically improbable, hermeneutically defective, theologically dangerous, and educationally disastrous' (*The Living Word*, 1987, p. 107) and Dr Stott's own much more cautious teaching healthily reflects the facts that Hodge died in 1878 and Warfield in 1921.

But I still ask whether other parts of Dr Stott's account of the authority of the Scriptures are as fully satisfactory as the teaching I have just quoted. I read this as his explanation of what the phrase 'verbal inspiration' means: 'what the Holy Spirit has spoken and still speaks through the human authors understood according to the plain, natural meaning of the words used, is true and without error'. The Holy Spirit, he maintains, spoke through persons 'in such a way that his words were theirs, and their words were his, simultaneously' (B, pp. 44, 55). 'The principle', he has written, 'should be clear: what Scripture affirms God affirms and what God affirms is true' (UB, p. 48). I ask: do such expressions take enough account of the human or cultural element in the Scriptures? And I ask this question expecting a sympathetic reply. For one of the things I admire about John Stott is his courage in criticising the Evangelical tradition from within. 'We have the highest doctrine of Scripture of anybody in the Church', he wrote when introducing *Obeying Christ in a Changing World*. 'We must therefore acknowledge with deep shame that our treatment of Scripture seldom coincides with our view of it. We are much better at asserting its authority than at wrestling with its interpretation. We are sometimes slovenly, sometimes simplistic, sometimes highly selective and sometimes downright dishonest' (OC, vol. 1, p. 21).

Dr Stott has himself explained that we need not take as the word of God passages in the Bible which are said within the Bible not to be spoken according to God's will. He mentions the speeches of Job's comforters but presumably would include much of what Job himself says. He also teaches that we need not take as history what is plainly poetry; for example, despite Revelation 7:14 we should not think that robes washed in blood can come out white (UB, p. 170). But a careful reading of Dr Stott's teaching shows that he still has a great deal of ground in common with those who affirm without any such qualifications that the Bible is 'infallible' or 'inerrant', leaving the impression on unsophisticated minds that it is believed to be flawless.

The plain, natural meaning of 'infallible' is 'not liable to be deceived or mistaken' and the plain, natural meaning of 'inerrant' is 'that does not err' (I quote the *Oxford English Dictionary*). Many Christians object to calling the Pope infallible and deny that popes in their teaching *ex cathedra* have been inerrant. Those who criticise the use of such words in connection with human beings nowadays include some vigorous Roman Catholics, as Hans Küng showed in his book *Infallible?* (in English, 1971). But these words have remained in the doctrinal standards or official declarations of many Evangelical societies. In his Preface to a collection of papers sponsored by the Evangelical Theological Society in the USA (*Evangelicals and Inerrancy*, 1984), Ronald Young-blood declared that the issue was: 'Given an inerrant and inspired Scripture, how shall we most accurately and faithfully interpret it in all its parts?' The translators of the New International Version of the Bible, in their Preface revised in 1983, were 'united in their commitment to the authority and infallibility of the Bible as God's Word in written form'. The Lausanne Covenant of 1974 affirmed 'the divine inspiration, truthfulness and authority of both Old and New Testament Scriptures in their entirety as the only written Word of God, without error in all that it affirms, and the only infallible rule of faith and practice'. Commenting on the Covenant, Dr Stott has written: 'It is important in all our Bible study to consider the intention of the author, and what is being asserted. It is this, whatever the subject of the assertion may be, which is true and inerrant'. Another commentary on the words from Lausanne came in *The Willowbank Report*, after Dr Stott's chairmanship of an international consultation in 1978. The report draws back from admitting that anything in the Bible may be out of date or irrelevant:

> The essential meaning of the biblical message must at all costs be retained. Though some of the original forms in which this meaning was expressed may be changed for the sake of cross-cultural communication, we believe that they too have a certain

normative quality. For God himself chose them as wholly appropriate vehicles of his revelation. So each fresh formulation and explanation in every generation and culture must be checked for faithfulness by referring back to the original. (WR, p. 9)

The *Evangelical Dictionary of Theology* edited by Walter A. Elwell (published in the USA in 1984 and in the UK in 1985), which I have often consulted, defines and defends 'inerrancy' as 'the view that when all the facts become known, they will demonstrate that the Bible in its original autographs and correctly interpreted is entirely true and never false in all it affirms, whether that relates to doctrine or ethics or to the social, physical, or life sciences' (p. 142). And Dr Stott has described as 'extremely judicious' (ARBMW, p. 6) the Chicago Statement on Biblical Inerrancy made after a conference in 1978. This included (Article XIII) the denial 'that generic categories which negate historicity may rightly be imposed on biblical narratives which present themselves as factual'.

The statement was summarised in five propositions:

1. God, who is himself Truth and speaks truth only, has inspired Holy Scripture in order thereby to reveal himself to lost mankind through Jesus Christ as Creator and Lord, Redeemer and Judge. Holy Scripture is God's witness to himself.
2. Holy Scripture, being God's own Word, written by men prepared and superintended by his Spirit, is of infallible divine authority in all matters upon which it teaches: it is to be believed, as God's instruction, in all that it affirms; it is to be obeyed as God's command in all that it requires; embraced, as God's pledge, in all that it promises.
3. The Holy Spirit, Scripture's divine Author, both authenticates it to us by his inward witness and opens our minds to understand its meaning.
4. Being wholly and verbally God-given, Scripture is without error or fault in all its teaching, no less in what

it states about God's acts in creation, about the events of world history, and about its own literary origins under God, than in its witness to God's saving grace in individual lives.

5. The authority of Scripture is inescapably impaired if this total divine inerrancy is in any way limited or disregarded, or made relative to a view of truth contrary to the Bible's own; and such lapses bring serious loss both to the individual and the Church.

I want to ask whether Dr Stott has remained too sympathetic with the spirit behind these propositions. For that spirit sometimes makes him feel qualified to damage good expositions of the Bible with claims which sound like fundamentalism.

I give only two examples. His exposition of the Sermon on the Mount (CCC) began by protesting against the tendency of most modern scholars. As W. D. Davies says, 'the impact of recent criticism in all its forms' has been 'to cast doubt on the propriety of seeking to understand this section . . . as an interrelated totality derived from the actual teaching of Jesus'. Dr Stott's own view is that the Sermon on the Mount does come totally from Jesus although it is a summary of teaching given over a period. He acknowledges that Luke 'condensed' this material differently from Matthew. Yet he writes: 'I find it hard to accept any view of the Sermon which attributes its contents rather to the early Church than to Jesus, or even regards it as an amalgam of sayings drawn from various occasions' (CCC, pp. 23–4). This approach seems to damage his exposition. It suggests that almost two thousand years before the invention of tape-recorders there must have been an absolutely accurate record of the teaching of Jesus available to Matthew and Luke; that the obvious differences between the gospels (for example, the different wording of the Beatitudes) are no more than different condensations; and that it matters vitally that the material 'condensed' by Matthew (5:1–7:29) and Luke (6:17–49) should not have been changed by them in any detail. I find all these claims incredible. And I ask why, if Matthew or his source was able to recall with total accuracy what Jesus said and did, he incorporated nine tenths of Mark's gospel in his own – but with alterations often different from the alterations which Luke made. I shall return to the Sermon on the Mount later, because even when literary criticism supplies the binoculars through which we view it this mountain remains sublime. The only point I am trying to make here is that Dr Stott is unrealistic in minimising the editorial element in Matthew's gospel.

For the sake of brevity I refer only to one other example of Dr Stott's lingering inclination towards fundamentalism – his summary of the Old Testament in his *Understanding the Bible*, published for the Scripture Union and 'fully revised' in 1984. Although he accepts that 'scientific discovery appears to contradict a six-day creation', and although he suggests 'tentatively' that 'some kind of purposive evolutionary development may have been the mode which God employed in creating', he believes in 'the historicity of Adam and Eve, as the original couple from whom the human race is descended' (UB, pp. 48–9) because Paul said so (UB, p. 178). Although 'today I am not so sure that we were ever meant to take literally the statement about the finger of God writing the law' (UB, p. 179), he believes that the regulations for the tabernacle in the wilderness which are generally regarded by scholars as belonging to the late, 'priestly' strand in the composition of the Pentateuch go back to the time of Moses (UB, p. 55). He believes that God commanded the Israelites to exterminate the Canaanites and that 'there is no need for us to be offended by this divine decree' (UB, p. 59). Although he quotes Isaiah 40–55 in the context of the restoration from Babylonian captivity, he too cautiously says that 'there is a continuing debate among biblical scholars whether these chapters were really written 150 or 200 years previously by Isaiah' (UB, p. 77). Perhaps none of these statements matters vitally. But I am bound to say that they all show a lamentable hesitation in accepting the fruits of scientific research into nature and into the Bible itself.

I do not think that a Christian has any duty to be so hesitant, for I cannot believe that all that the Bible's authors asserted was without mistake either in principle ('infallible') or in practice ('inerrant'). With due respect to the claims made in the *Evangelical Dictionary of Theology* and many similar places, I cannot discuss the alleged inerrancy of the original autographs of the Bible, now lost, in the light of facts not yet known – because I am one of those who have to base any discussion on the Bible which we *now* hold in our hands and on the facts to which we *now* have access. And on this basis 'infallibility' seems to be an obvious error and 'to impute inerrancy to the Bible is simply to mistake the sort of book it is', as James Barr wrote bluntly in *Escaping from Fundamentalism* (1984, p. 129). But we need not be merely negative and destructive.

Dr Stott has allowed himself to lament 'the extreme gravity of liberal theology. By undermining public confidence in the reliability of the Bible, it makes Christian discipleship all but impossible' (B, pp. 75–6). Of course I recognise – and regret – that some biblical scholarship in the hands of 'liberals' has helped to destroy Christian faith. There was no way, it seems, of avoiding such casualties if arguments based on evidence were to be allowed to lead where reason and conscience thought they should go; and there was no honest way of concealing the arguments of scholars from the public. But much biblical scholarship, for which Christians are indebted to liberals ˙as well as to conservatives, has helped modern people to do precisely those things which Dr Stott goes on to say are desirable. Christians who accept all sound scholarship (in so far as they are aware of it) can be helped to worship God, to believe and trust in him, and to obey him. And they can do this because the heart of the Bible's message, given by the Bible as it truly exists, seems compatible with the rest of truth. At the end of a spirited defence of the spiritual and intellectual basis of modern biblical research, James Barr has quoted a younger scholar. 'Theological truths,' Sean McEvenue wrote,

> are not reached by deduction or dialectic or any other form of reasoning restricted to the Canon or a deposit of faith. They are determined in judgements which have reflected on what scripture says and also on whatever other clearly relevant knowledge the theologian may process. There is no simple point of departure and no single final norm. Theological truths are discovered by open minds passionately hungry for contemporary, true understanding of God. (James Barr, *Holy Scripture: Canon, Authority, Criticism*, 1983, p. 126)

## Jesus and the Scriptures

The most important argument offered in favour of Dr Stott's position is the suggestion that it was the position of Jesus. 'We claim that he was inerrant,' he has written, 'that all his teaching was true, including his endorsement of the authority of Scripture' (UB, p. 153). And 'the major reason why we desire to submit to the authority of the Bible is that Jesus Christ authenticated it as possessing the authority of God' (B, p. 27). Warming to this theme in his 1981 essay on *Freedom, Authority and Scripture* written at the request of the International Council on Biblical Inerrancy, Jim Packer has declared:

> the New Testament view of the Old is consistent and clear. Authority was seen . . . as divine, the absolute, oracular authority of God telling truth about his work and will, and about the worship and obedience that we owe him. Not all that was said whether by the Old Testament or by the apostles was equally important, but all was part of the rule of faith and life since it came from God. (p. 41)

The surviving evidence shows what we should expect – that Jesus knew and loved the Hebrew Scriptures. He is said to have quoted them as the 'word of God' spoken 'by the Holy Spirit' (Mark 7:13; 12:36). It is reported that he

accepted the opinions commonly held in his time about
their authorship; thus his teaching in the gospels includes
quotations from 'Moses', 'David' and 'Isaiah' which few
modern scholars would attribute to those historical persons. He assumed that what appeared in the Scriptures as
history was historical; thus his teaching includes references
to the stories of Abel, Noah, Abraham and Lot and treats
the books of Jonah and Daniel as history. Above all it seems
that Jesus expressed his understanding of his own mission
by combining passages in the Scriptures which together
taught that in the 'day of the Lord', through the vindicated
suffering of his servant, God would create a new people for
himself. None of that is in the least unlikely, for Jesus was a
devout Jew and the knowledge of the Scriptures which he
gained from his parents and through the synagogue of
Nazareth was his only formal education. The gospels agree
that as an adult he kept up the custom of worship in a
synagogue every Sabbath. The complaints made about his
behaviour as being unconventional for a religious teacher –
he and his disciples were willing to heal on the Sabbath, did
not fast, did not wash their hands before meals, and ate
meals with 'sinners' – did not refer to acts which were
technically illegal under the written 'law of Moses'. It is
significant that his brother James, who became a Christian,
is said to have observed that law piously throughout his
life.

But Dr Stott goes too far, I reckon, in his description of the
dependence of Jesus on the Hebrew Scriptures. If, as he
claims, there is no example in the gospels of Jesus disagreeing with the doctrinal or ethical teaching in the Old
Testament (B, p. 29), it is indeed difficult to see why there
is so much evidence that Jesus was in dispute with the
Jewish religious authorities or why the movement which he
founded split from Judaism so thoroughly and so completely. Dr Stott claims that 'he adopted towards the
Scriptures of the Old Testament an attitude of reverent
submission . . . He accepted the statements of Scripture
without question, believing them to be true . . . The word

*gegraptai* ("it stands written") was enough to settle any issue for him' (CtC, pp. 93–4). But we have to account for the frequent references in the gospels to both the followers and the enemies of Jesus as agreeing that his teaching and behaviour were controversially new. In the fourth gospel Jesus is presented as a conservative, as in his saying that 'the Scripture cannot be broken' (John 10:35) – but the tradition that he was a radical reaches a climax in what can be interpreted as a dismissal of the entire religious history of Israel: 'All who ever came before me were thieves and robbers, but the sheep did not listen to them' (John 10:8). According to the whole of the New Testament the criticism of the novelty of the life of Jesus culminated in the part played by some of the Jewish leadership in bringing about his execution. As A. E. Harvey has observed in a summary which wisely does not exaggerate the contrast between Jesus and Judaism,

> it is hardly conceivable that the whole picture of an ongoing controversy between Jesus and the sages of his time is fictional. There must surely have been enough common ground between them for their differences to have come so sharply into focus and to have left such a mark on the gospel tradition. (*Jesus and the Constraints of History*, 1982, pp. 51–2)

I have the impression that Dr Stott is, like myself, a man with a sizeable private library who often consults books for information and guidance and who takes a pride in quoting them accurately. His knowledge of the Bible is vast and precise. And many Christians study their own Bibles daily. But one preliminary point which we need to keep in mind throughout this discussion is that Jesus did not live in a society full of books. The bookish monks of Qumran and scholars such as Philo of Alexandria were exceptional in having ready access to libraries. No doubt the 'scribes' who were legal experts had copies of the Scriptures or of considerable portions of them, but it seems highly unlikely that Jesus owned a complete copy of the Hebrew Scriptures, which was expensive and bulky. It is said that on the cross he quoted Psalm 22:1 in the Aramaic translation, not in Hebrew. It is even improbable that Paul carried a Bible around with him – and he was content to quote Scripture in Greek. Usually people quoted from memory or from single books or from edited collections of proof texts. Their dependence on the exact meaning of the Scriptures was inevitably less than would be expected of Jews or Christians who are able to check biblical references and to compare biblical translations. Another, connected, point has been well stated recently by Bruce Chilton (*A Galilean Rabbi and His Bible*, 1984, pp. 187–8). The chosen role of Jesus was

> as a popular teacher rather than a professional academic. He used Scripture as a starting point in his preaching, and therefore as a vehicle of his vision of God, but understanding Scripture was not for him the goal of preaching. His task as he understood it was not essentially interpretative . . . From the beginning, we must acknowledge that no account of the use of the Bible can be held to be consistent with the preaching of Jesus which stops with the mere question of what a text means.

We have to banish from our minds any picture of Jesus of Nazareth as a theologian in a book-lined study. And we have to open our minds fully to the fact that the early Christians used the Hebrew Scriptures with freedom, as did their Teacher and Lord.

It is instructive to examine the references to these Scriptures in Matthew's gospel. This is usually agreed to be the most Jewish of the four canonical gospels, repeatedly claiming that 'all this took place to fulfil what the Lord had said through the prophet', although the Scriptures are quoted mainly from the main Greek translation, the Septuagint. This gospel begins with a 'record of the genealogy of Jesus Christ' back to Abraham, largely based on the Scriptures but quite often deviating from them as well as from the genealogy given by Luke. It quotes the Septuagint version of Isaiah 7:14, 'the virgin will be with child', not the Hebrew original, which says merely that a 'young woman' will give birth; and it uses it as a prediction of the virginal conception of Jesus, although in the book of Isaiah it was a prophecy that better times were coming for Israel within that child's childhood. It alters a quotation from Micah 5:2 so that it now refers to the 'rulers' not the 'clans' of Judah, presumably in order to increase the significance of Bethlehem. (Of the twenty-two words in this passage in the Septuagint, only eight are reproduced by Matthew.) It says that 'out of Egypt I called my son' (Hosea 11:1) predicts the return of the child Jesus from exile, whereas the original referred to the exodus from Egypt in history. It turns the poetic statement by Jeremiah that the lamentation in the village of Ramah sounded like the weeping of the bereaved Rachel into a prediction of a massacre in Bethlehem (2:18). It ignores Jeremiah's message that 'Rachel' was to stop weeping. It quotes 'He will be called *Nazarios*' as a prophetic utterance although it does not appear in the Scriptures (2:23). The scholars have puzzled over what Matthew meant. Possibly he linked the name of Nazareth, a village of no significance for the Scriptures, with *Naser* or 'Branch' of the House of David (i.e. the Messiah) or *Nazir* or 'consecrated man'. A little later comes the quotation of a prophet's understanding of God's call to his people (Isaiah 40:3), used as a prediction of the coming of John the Baptist (3:3).

As Matthew recounts the baptism and subsequent temptations of Jesus, he shows that Jesus regarded words of Scripture as expressions of God's will for him. But in the story of the temptations real decisions are made, so that it is strange that Dr Stott claims that 'Jesus had no need to debate or argue with the devil' (CMMW, p. 78). The devil can quote Psalm 91 as promising a miraculous deliverance from danger (4:6). Then three straightforward scriptural quotations are followed by an apparently decisive endorsement of the 248 positive commandments and 365 prohibitions in the 'Law of Moses'. 'Until heaven and earth disappear, not the smallest letter, not the least stroke of a pen, will by any means disappear from the Law until everything is accomplished' (5:18). This Dr Stott interprets to mean that 'the law is as enduring as the universe', since 'what Jesus is contradicting is not the law itself but certain perversions of the law of which the scribes and Pharisees were guilty'. His opinion of the Pharisees is that 'they thought an external conformity to the law would be righteousness enough', but that so far from strictly adhering to the law they added interpretations which were in fact distortions; for example, they added 'and hate your enemy' to the command 'Love your neighbour' (Leviticus 19:18). The idea that Jesus was 'setting himself against Moses' is 'untenable' (CMMW, pp. 73–7). This idea is, however, held tenaciously by many scholars and there is much in the gospels that supports them.

The Sermon on the Mount's own plain, natural meaning is that what 'was said to the people long ago' (not only by recent scribes and Pharisees) is sometimes being replaced by what 'I tell you'. The 'Law of Moses' is not being merely reproduced without any addition or distortion when anger is said to be 'subject to judgement' no less than murder, and lustful looks no less than adultery; when divorce and the taking of oaths are condemned despite the clear provisions for them in the Scriptures; and when the disciples are told to reply to an evil person not by demanding 'eye for eye and tooth for tooth' according to the law but by offering the other cheek to strike and by an invitation to take the cloak as well as the tunic. There seems no good reason to doubt the tradition that Jesus rejected the Pharisees' belief that many regulations in addition to these found in the Scriptures (the 'oral law') went back to Moses and so belonged to the 'Law of Moses'. That was why he could be asked: 'Why do your disciples reject the tradition of the elders?' Instead of accepting this as criticism, he summoned his hearers to consider the written 'word of God' and its deep meaning (15:1–9). But had he merely been a conservative strictly adhering to the text of the Scriptures, he would have been close to the doctrinal position of the Sadducees, 'who say there is no resurrection' (Matthew 22:23) 'and that there are neither angels nor spirits' (Acts 23:8) because, they claimed, such things were not written in the Scriptures. In fact the gospels represent Jesus as being in dispute with the Sadducees no less than with the Pharisees, even before he signed his own death warrant by cleansing the Sadducees' headquarters, the temple. He was attacked both by those who accepted 'the tradition of the elders' and by those who accepted only the Scriptures. He was attacked, it seems, because he so often claimed direct access to God. Implicitly or explicitly he spoke or acted as the Father's unique representative. And he challenged his hearers to respond with a quite extraordinary urgency – in one case, not even delaying in order to bury a human father decently (Luke 9:57–60).

In Matthew 23 'the teachers of the law and the Pharisees' who 'sit in Moses' seat' are condemned for two basic reasons. They are hypocrites who do everything for show while really being full of 'greed and self-indulgence'. And they are bad pastors, for 'they tie up heavy loads and put them on men's shoulders'. In contrast with these hypocritical prigs, Jesus was the honest friend of sinners and could be criticised as a glutton and a drunkard (11:19). Most scholars agree that this is not a complete account either of the teachers of the Jewish religious law in the time of Jesus or of the attitude of Jesus to them. Other passages in the gospels present Jesus as agreeing with scribes and Pharisees that the essential teaching of the law is the love of God and of neighbour. Luke says that Jesus dined with Pharisees (7:36–50; 14:1) and that some of them warned him of a plot to kill him (13:31). In the Acts of the Apostles 'a Pharisee named Gamaliel' saves the apostles from death (5:33–40) and other Pharisees rescue Paul when he has called out: 'My brothers, I am a Pharisee, the son of a Pharisee' (23:6–10). The first Christian council included 'believers who belonged to the party of the Pharisees' (15:5).

It is therefore believed by most scholars that these denunciations in Matthew 23 do not entirely reproduce the teaching of Jesus. They have been influenced by the final and bitter breach between Jews and Christians in the period immediately before the writing of the gospel. But whatever exactly Jesus may have said in condemnation of the hypocrisy and harshness of some experts in the Jewish religious law, his basic confrontation with that law cannot have been solely a rejection of additions to it. Nor can it have been solely a rejection of the idea that 'an external conformity to it would be righteousness enough' – an idea frequently condemned in the Hebrew Scriptures themselves as well as in the rabbinic literature. The tension between Jesus and the legal experts must have gone deeper than Dr Stott allows. There have been many studies of that tension by Jewish and Christian scholars, for example the books on *Jesus and Judaism* (1985) and *Paul and Palestinian Judaism* (1977) by E. P. Sanders, and much of the scholarly debate has had its storm centre in disagreements about *The Interpretation of Matthew* (well introduced by Graham Stanton's collection of essays under that title in 1983). But the wisest summary known to me was contributed by Michael Ramsey to *Peake's Commentary on the Bible* (1962 edn, p. 3):

> As to the law, Jesus Christ came to fulfil it. This he did by teaching and practising a more radical obedience to the divine demand which the law had set forth . . . It involves (a) the right dispositions of the heart in matters where the law had enjoined right actions, (b) positive actions of righteousness in matters where the law had condemned actions of unrighteousness.

That basic tension between Jesus and the legal experts comes out in Matthew 12:1–13. In the 'Law of Moses' complete rest on the Sabbath (Saturday) was one of the ten commandments and the infringement of this law was punishable by death (Exodus 31:14). The commandment was understood in the Scriptures to prohibit activities such as gathering wood (Numbers 15:32–36) or lighting a fire (Exodus 35:3). The official Jewish commentary (the *Mishnah*) deduced thirty-nine specific prohibitions from Scripture. Saving life was not prohibited, but acts of healing which involved activity for healer and patient and which could be postponed for a day without harm were held to be contrary to the spirit of Scripture. Matthew's gospel repeats from Mark's the story that Jesus defended his disciples who picked and ate some ears of corn on the Sabbath and on the same day himself healed a man with a shrivelled hand. This defiance of the law of the Sabbath as it was commonly understood evidently troubled Matthew, for he does not repeat from Mark (2:27) the very radical saying that 'the Sabbath was made for man, not man for the Sabbath'. But Matthew does enable us to glimpse the reality that the message of Jesus was no mere repetition of the teaching of the Hebrew Scriptures.

Later, Matthew repeatedly shows that biblical quotations spring naturally to the mind of a devout Jew but that the Hebrew text as later accepted by Jews and Christians need not be quoted accurately – and that the original meaning can be altered. Thus in Matthew 13 passages which did not have this meaning originally are cited in support of the strange theory that Jesus taught in parables in order to conceal his message from his hearers. The claim that the Creator said something which was in fact a comment by the human author of Genesis (19:5) seems to be a slip. The claim that two animals, 'the donkey and the colt', were used in the entry into Jerusalem (21:7) seems to result from misunderstanding a Hebrew poetic convention, 'parallelism' or the repetition of an idea. Zechariah 9:9 refers to only one animal, 'a donkey, a colt the foal of a donkey'. A reference to 'praise' coming from the mouths of children (21:16) is made by quoting Psalm 8:2 in the Septuagint translation into Greek, whereas the New English Bible's translation of the obscure Hebrew is 'thou hast rebuked the mighty'. The reference to the king in Jerusalem as 'my lord' at the beginning of Psalm 110 is used to show that King David called the future Messiah 'my lord', whereas it is far more probable that the reference shows that David, who would not have called any man 'lord' (apart from Saul for a period), did not compose Psalm 110 (22:44). Dr Stott teaches that the denial of Davidic authorship is 'inadmissible', but does admit that 'such a direct address to the future Messiah would indeed be unique in the Psalter' (CSP, p. 131). The reference to the Zechariah who was reckoned as the last martyr in the Scriptures as 'the son of Berakiah' (23:35) seems to be a confusion between the martyred son of Jehoiada (2 Chronicles 24:20–22) and the earlier Zechariah whose father was indeed Berakiah. Another loose quotation from Zechariah (11:12–13) is wrongly ascribed to Jeremiah and, taken completely out of its context, it is said to be a prediction about Judas Iscariot (27:9).

Most scholars do not hesitate to say that these are examples of a 'free' use of the Hebrew Scriptures, like the little mistake ('Isaiah' for Malachi) which begins Mark's gospel or Mark's wrong reference to 'the days of Abiathar the high priest' (2:26, the correct name being given in 1 Samuel 21:1–6). In the time when Jesus lived and the New Testament was written everyone seems to have treated the Scriptures in this 'free' way – as is documented in, for example, John Barton's *The Oracles of God* (1986). And Christians who highly value the treatment of the Hebrew Scriptures by Jesus and his followers have no need to pretend that none of these references contained any error. Even if it could be shown that the historical Jesus made all these mistakes himself, it would not matter crucially. The truth of his gospel did not depend on his inerrancy as a biblical scholar. 'He taught as one who had authority, and not as their teachers of the law' (Matthew 7:29). His teaching sowed the seeds of abundant and eternal life – although despite Matthew 13:32 the mustard seed is *not* 'the smallest of all your seeds'. He was the Saviour, not a botanist.

I ought also to consider briefly the passage in Mark's gospel where Jesus abrogates the Old Testament's legislation by declaring all foods 'clean' (7:14–23). If this is an authentic piece of his teaching, it constitutes his most dramatic contradiction of the Hebrew Scriptures. But I am one of these students of the New Testament who prefer the extensive evidence of Paul's letters and of the Acts of the Apostles that there were many controversies between the early Christians about what food they might eat. These disputes would have been settled far more quickly, had the apostles been able to remember and cite the clear teaching of the Lord on this very point. It therefore seems probable that in this passage Mark is stating a tradition developed within the Church.

Dr Stott, having wrongly claimed that the New Testament always treats the Old Testament in its original Hebrew as the inerrant word of God with the authority of God, also claims that 'Jesus made provision for the writing of the New Testament' (CtC, p. 95; B, p. 29) with a similar character. But if the reference is to the historical Jesus (I have no doubt that in the Spirit the authors of the New Testament were inspired to write), that is not a claim which can be based on the instructions to the apostles given in the gospels. There Jesus is not said to have repeated the command to write which was given by, for example, Jeremiah in the Old Testament; and one probable explanation is that he hoped that the time would be short before the kingdom of God came fully. Indeed, he is not said to have had any interest in any book outside the Hebrew Scriptures. The only instance of writing in the gospels comes when he writes on the sand when discouraging the imposition of the 'Law of Moses' on the woman taken in adultery at John 8:6,8 – and we are not told what he wrote. Nor is the New Testament a miraculously perfect record of what Jesus said and did. On the contrary, the four gospels leave many historical questions about Jesus unanswered and unanswerable. John's gospel, which is the one which tells us of promises that the Spirit would make the disciples remember what Jesus had said to them (14:26; 17:7), is also the one which pays no explicit attention to the gospels of Mark, Matthew and Luke.

On such problems I can do no more than to refer to the magisterial summary of critical scholarship in W. G. Kümmel's trilogy, *Introduction to the New Testament*, *The New*

*Testament: The History of the Investigation of its Problems* and *The Theology of the New Testament*, available in English since the 1970s.

Although the writers of the letters in the New Testament make strong claims to authority, it is surely an oversimplification to say that (for example) 'what is Pauline is apostolic and therefore authoritative' (CoC, p. 183). C. H. Dodd may have put the matter indelicately when he wrote, to Dr Stott's indignation (OOW, p. 15), that 'sometimes I think Paul is wrong and I have ventured to say so'. But it seems right to remember that Paul did not hesitate to contradict his fellow-apostles, 'those who seemed to be important . . . those reputed to be pillars'. 'When Peter came to Antioch, I opposed him to his face, because he was clearly in the wrong' (Galatians 2:6–11). And the Paul who claimed to speak 'not in words taught us by human wisdom but in words taught by the Spirit, expressing spiritual truths in spiritual words', also wrote that 'my conscience is clear, but that does not make me innocent', and that 'no-one can lay any foundation other than the one already laid, which is Jesus Christ' (1 Corinthians 2:13; 4:4; 3:11). Dr Stott himself sometimes reckons with the human and cultural, and therefore changeable, element in Paul's teaching, as when he considers the instructions that no woman should pray with her head unveiled or speak in the congregation. About these instructions Paul says: 'what I am writing to you is the Lord's command' (1 Corinthians 14:37). But Dr Stott says that the 'inner reality of the apostolic instruction' is that male and female are equal but 'complementary rather than identical', so that 'veils and silence seem to me cultural symbols which belong to the past' (ARBMW, p. 9; WR, p. 9). The position to which I adhere is that the 'apostolic gospel' – the good news about Christ in which the apostles agreed – certainly has authority. But it should not be identified with all the teaching attributed to the apostles. What is permanently authoritative is, surely, the 'inner reality'.

The two texts in the New Testament to which many

'conservative' theologians, including Dr Stott, appeal do not support any claim that the New Testament or the Old is infallible or inerrant. A Christian is reminded (according to the New International Version) that 'from infancy you have known the holy Scriptures, which are able to make you wise for salvation through faith in Christ Jesus. All Scripture is God-breathed [in Greek *theopneustos*] and is useful for teaching, rebuking, correcting and training in righteousness, so that the man of God may be thoroughly equipped for every good work' (2 Timothy 3:15–17). Since the Greek sentence has no main verb, some of the meaning is not clear. Thus the New English Bible's translation teaches us merely that 'every inspired scripture is useful . . .' But plainly this text declares that the Hebrew Scriptures as known to Timothy were inspired by God in order to be used in the making the 'man of God' a wise teacher. It is a statement with which no devout Jew or Christian would disagree. Elsewhere Christians are told (according to the New International Version) that 'you must understand that no prophecy of Scripture came about by the prophet's own interpretation. For prophecy never had its origin in the will of man, but men spoke from God as they were carried along by the Holy Spirit' (2 Peter 1:20–21). The meaning here, too, is to some extent uncertain. The New English Bible's translation of the Greek teaches a far more modest lesson: 'no one can interpret any prophecy of Scripture by himself'. But it may well be that what is said here is that the true prophets of Israel were inspired by the Holy Spirit, although 'there were also false prophets among the people' (2:1). That claim also is non-controversial among devout Jews and Christians. And neither passage, however translated, claims that 'the original Hebrew or Greek text as it came from the authors' hands' (UB, p. 142) was infallible or inerrant. If Evangelicals claim that, they are going far beyond what these texts affirm.

On the contrary, the New Testament provides abundant evidence, outside the gospels as well as in them, that the Christians often gave new meanings to the Hebrew text of

the Scriptures or quoted versions of the text which differed
from the text preferred in later versions of the Bible. In this
they were like many devoutly orthodox Jewish students of
the Scriptures. What was of absorbing interest was not the
original, natural meaning of Scripture but the meaning of a
passage as 'typology' or 'allegory' – referring mysteriously
to some person, event or idea belonging to the reader's own
time. Thus the promise of Moses that God would 'raise up
for you a prophet like me from among your own brothers'
was taken to refer not to Joshua (as it did originally) but to
someone alive or expected in the commentator's own time.
The 'Teacher of Righteousness' who according to the Dead
Sea scrolls was the hero of the Qumran monastery, or some
other contemporary, might be 'the Prophet who is to come
into the world' (John 6:14). Philo of Alexandria, who held
such a high view of the inspiration of the Scriptures that he
can sometimes sound like an extreme fundamentalist, did
not hesitate to find in the sacred books 'allegories' whose
most important meaning was philosophical and could be
stated in terms familiar to the educated Jews who had
settled in Egypt under much Greek influence. For Philo as
for the Qumran monks, the tune played by God's biblical
orchestra was a tune which they could sing as their own
song.

The Christians thus had many predecessors when they
interpreted the Hebrew Scriptures freely. They combined
many texts to form a portrait of 'the Messiah', a royal figure
bringing salvation and a new age. Some of these passages
referred originally to the future success of a prince of the
house of David. Others looked forward in other ways to
good times coming. Surviving Jewish literature shows that
some of the Christians' contemporaries were making a
similar synthesis of 'messianic' hopes in the Scriptures in
order to draw a single portrait of the Messiah. (But two
Messiahs, one priestly and the other lay, were expected by
the Qumran community.) So the Christians' general
method of using the Scriptures was not, it seems, disputed
although their identification of a crucified carpenter of

Nazareth as the Messiah was rejected. Paul, pursuing this familiar method of interpretation, told the Galatians that 'the Scripture foresaw that God would justify the Gentiles through faith and announced the gospel in advance to Abraham'. He argued that in God's promise to Abraham 'your seed' must mean 'one person, who is Christ' (3:8,16). He interpreted another story about Abraham 'figuratively', so that 'Hagar stands for Mount Sinai in Arabia and corresponds with the present city of Jerusalem' (4:24–25). His first letter to the Corinthians claimed that a law about not muzzling an ox was meant to command the payment of the apostles (9:7–12) and that a rock which was believed to have accompanied the people of Israel through the wilderness 'was Christ' (10:4). And he twice quoted 'the righteous will live by his faith' (Habakkuk 2:4) as the supremely illuminating text in the Scriptures (to the Galatians at 3:11 and to the Romans at 1:17) – although this was originally an unexplained aside, translated in the New English Bible as 'the righteous will live by being faithful'.

In the Acts of the Apostles Psalm 16, which is a prayer about a recovery from illness, is quoted as a prediction of the Messiah's resurrection from death (2:25–28). Amos 9:12, which in the Hebrew is a promise of territorial expansion by Israel ('that they may possess the remnant of Edom'), is quoted in its Septuagint translation ('that the remnant of men may seek the Lord') as a prediction of the admission of the Gentiles into the Church (Acts 15:17). Near the beginning of the letter to Hebrews one text (Deuteronomy 32:43) is quoted from the Septuagint ('and let all God's angels worship him') to show the superiority of Jesus over the angels and a psalmist's prayer to the eternal God is said to have been addressed to Jesus as the Son. In Hebrews 7 the comparison of Christ with Melchizedek depends on a forced reading of the few references to that ancient king in Genesis. It was certainly not the meaning of the original author that the obscure Melchizedek was king of righteousness and peace, 'without father or mother, without genealogy, without beginning of days or end of life, like the Son of God he remains a priest for ever' (7:3). In the letter to the Ephesians (4:8) Psalm 68:18, which in the Hebrew is a prayer to God,

> When you ascended on high,
> you led captives in your train;
> you received gifts from men,
> even from the rebellious . . . ,

is used to introduce a list of the various ministries given to the Church by the ascended Christ. This is done by quoting the psalm to read 'gave gifts to men'. The conclusion seems irresistible that the early Christians either quoted the version of Scripture which most suited their purpose, or altered it in text or meaning, in a way that often does not suggest that they believed the original and natural meaning of the Hebrew text later received as authoritative to be the infallible and inerrant word of God. Their consistent style of hermeneutics might be called non-Evangelical.

Partly because they combined great reverence for 'the Law of Moses, the Prophets and the Psalms' (Luke 24:44) with considerable freedom in quoting and using them, these early Christians seem to have found it natural to treat the teaching of Jesus in the same way. The letters of John name Jesus and Cain but otherwise do not contain a single reference to Scripture. Paul's letters repeatedly show how he combined a passionate devotion to Jesus with a disinclination to quote the exact words of his teaching. He directly quotes only three sayings of Jesus (1 Thessalonians 4:15; 1 Corinthians 7:10; 9:14) in addition to the Last Supper material. His letter to the Galatians shows that after his conversion as a Christian he did not regard it as a duty to find out precisely what Jesus had said. As Dr Stott comments, 'Paul's first visit to Jerusalem was only after three years, it lasted only two weeks, and he saw only two apostles. It was, therefore, ludicrous to suggest that he obtained his gospel from the Jerusalem apostles' (OOW, p. 35). If a record of the teaching of Jesus was preserved in the original Aramaic, it was later lost. It seems almost certain that at least one collection of sayings was compiled in Greek and certainly gospels were written in that language, the first (or the first to survive) being Mark's. But when Matthew and Luke used Mark they edited his gospel extensively and they treated any collection of sayings in the same way. It is uncertain whether John used any previous gospel; if he did, he used it very freely.

In this freedom the writers of the New Testament resembled many of the authors of the Old. When the law code which came to be called Deuteronomy was made public in 622–621 BC, the Jews started to become what Muslims call them – a 'people of the book'. The process was intensified during their exile and as a result of Ezra's mission (probably at the end of the fourth century BC). In the book called *Ecclesiasticus*, a teacher of 'wisdom', Jesus the son of Sirach, meditates on the Hebrew Bible approximately as we have it, about 180 BC. But the earlier material which came to be collected and edited in 'the Scriptures' does not leave the impression that its authors took much trouble to harmonise one law with another, one narrative with another, one prophecy with another, or one psalm or proverb with another. They based their own writing not on what was already written but on their own experience or on the tradition of their group. The fact that the authors of Ecclesiastes and the book of Job look at life with their own eyes, and do not rely on Scripture, is not entirely out of keeping with the general character of the Hebrew Bible. They felt 'carried along by the Holy Spirit', as is said in 2 Peter 1:21. They would share Paul's own impatience with what is merely written: 'the letter kills, but the spirit gives life' (2 Corinthians 3:6). In his *The Interpretation of Scripture* (1961, p. 188), James D. Smart summed up the truth of the matter: 'Paul's relation to the letter of Jesus' teaching is similar to Jesus' relation to the Old Testament and the relation of the Old Testament prophets to each other.'

It was a consequence of this widespread attitude that there was for long no great anxiety to know exactly what 'the Scriptures' were. The exact text of the Hebrew Scriptures was often uncertain, particularly until the vowels were added to the consonants in the period AD 600–900. That is one reason why the Greek translation often used by the early Christians differed in places from the Hebrew texts known to us – although it may have agreed with Hebrew texts now lost. The 'canon' or list of books constituting the Hebrew Scriptures was not finally agreed by the rabbis in Palestine before the middle of the first century AD. Probably that canon was not treated as authoritative when Timothy was a child being taught 'the Scriptures' for the letter of Jude in the New Testament shows the continuing uncertainty by quoting (in verse 14) a book attributed to Enoch which was excluded from the rabbinic canon. We know that in the Western Church a larger canon, including some books which came to be called the Apocrypha, was generally accepted despite some protests. The acceptance of these extra books was made formal at the Council of Florence in 1441, and confirmed by the Council of Trent more than a century later, although it was rejected by the Protestant Reformers including Luther in favour of the rabbinic canon. The longer canon may have originated among the Jews of Alexandria although that is far from certain.

2 Peter 3:16 refers to the letters of Paul among 'other Scriptures' and 'Scripture says' in 1 Timothy 5:18 may refer not only to Deuteronomy 25:4 but also to a quotation from Luke's gospel. Evidently towards the end of the first century AD the Church's formation of its own canon of Scripture (the New Testament) was beginning. But that process was not complete until the fourth century. The list of twenty-seven books was never settled by a formal council and the first official publication of it to have survived was the Easter Letter of Athanasius in 367. Until about that date, it was not certain exactly what the New Testament was.

The reference to Paul's letters as 'Scripture' in 2 Peter is among the factors which persuade most scholars that this document dates from a late period, perhaps a hundred

years after the deaths of Peter and Paul. (2 Peter incorporates most of the letter of Jude and is not quoted in any other
surviving document earlier than the third century. Disagreement about its authenticity helped to delay the
finalisation of the canon of the New Testament.) The sense
that 2 Timothy is also written to a situation where the
Church already has a long tradition is one of the reasons
why most scholars think that the whole of it is not authentically Pauline. But whether or not these teachings are genuinely apostolic, they do not support the idea that a carefully
agreed list of books constituting the Old Testament was
regarded as infallible or inerrant in detail and was being
matched by a New Testament of the same character.

I do not think that I need spend much of my precious
space on explaining why most modern scholars think that
the Bible includes errors. Innumerable passages are
asserted by their authors, either implicitly or explicitly, to
be law, history, etc., and are therefore according to Dr Stott
to be accepted as 'inerrant' as law, history, etc. – yet are
contradicted either by other passages in the Christian Bible
or by the proofs or probabilities of modern historical knowledge. It seems to me a wholly inadequate response to this
laboriously accumulated body of knowledge, one of the
most splendid achievements of the human mind inspired
by the Spirit of truth, to say, as Dr Stott says, that if 'the
seeming discrepancy remains, whether between science
and the Bible, or between two parts of the Bible, or between
our theological understanding of the Bible and our historical critical methods of studying it', the wise Christian 'sus-
pends judgement and goes on looking for harmony rather
than giving up in despair' (ARBMW, p. 8).

Here I confine myself to repeating briefly some standard
critical comments on John's gospel, choosing that document because it is of central importance. As Dr Stott notes,
'every reader of John's gospel is immediately struck by the
differences between it and the synoptic gospels in subject
matter, theological emphasis, literary style and vocabulary'
(UB, p. 89). It is no accident that I do not quote it as

providing the actual words of Jesus, although Dr Stott frequently does. I do not doubt that the fourth gospel contains some historical material; for example, it supplies the most probable date for the crucifixion (7 April 30). But I am equally sure (having learned it from many better scholars) that this gospel is in the main a meditation on the meaning of Jesus by a Christian saint with a group and a tradition behind him. It often seems impossible to separate the history from the meditation, the Jesus of history from the Christ of faith. Some of the most striking sayings of 'Jesus' come in the narrative when he is alone with Pilate, out of the hearing of any disciple. In the course of a long prayer by 'Jesus' – the great 'high priestly' prayer at the Last Supper – we read the words: 'Now this is eternal life: that they may know you, the only true God, and Jesus Christ, whom you have sent' (17:3). The best comparison seems to be with Plato's reconstruction of the teaching of his master, Socrates. Plato's *Dialogues* give not the words but the spirit.

It is spiritually important to see that John's gospel is only partly historical. Many readers of John Stott's *Basic Christianity* must have been puzzled by the contrast between the claims that 'Jesus was sinless because he was selfless' (BC1, p. 45) and that 'the most striking feature of the teaching of Jesus is that he was constantly talking about himself' (BC1, p. 23). But the second claim is based upon John's gospel alone. Dr Stott immediately quotes some of the seven great 'I am' sayings in that gospel – very striking sayings which, however, are not included in any other gospels. In John's gospel Jesus uses 'I' in self-reference 118 times and refers to God as 'the Father' or 'my Father' 173 times. The kingdom of God is mentioned only five times. It is the message of the whole gospel that Jesus is the Son of the Father. That certainly agrees with the message of Mark that he is the Son of God. But in Mark's gospel Jesus talks mainly not about himself (there are only nine 'I' references) or about his Father (the word is used only four times), but about the kingdom of God (the phrase is used eighteen times). In Matthew's gospel there are seventeen 'I' references and forty-seven references to the 'kingdom of heaven'; in Luke's, ten 'I' references and thirty-seven references to the 'kingdom of God'. The teaching about who 'I am' in John's gospel is, it seems clear, the expression of Christian devotion to Christ as the Son of the Father. The historical Jesus proclaimed the kingdom of God, not himself – except as God's agent in the arrival of that kingdom. According to Mark, when Peter had privately greeted him as Messiah 'Jesus warned them not to tell anyone about him' (8:30). Unless Mark 9:41 really was spoken by Jesus, it was only when on trial that Jesus accepted the title of Messiah (14:62). Although the evidence is fragmentary and does not enable us to understand at all fully the self-consciousness of Jesus, it seems clear not only that he did not encourage use of this title (which was dangerously political) but also that he did not welcome all other compliments. Mark (10:17–18) has a story, toned down by Matthew and Luke, that he rebuked a young man who called him 'good teacher' with the words: 'Why do you call me good? No-one is good – except God alone.' But in John's gospel Andrew tells his brother Peter that Jesus is the Messiah before Peter has met him (1:41) and Jesus himself tells the Samaritan woman (4:25–26). And that is only the beginning of the claims of Jesus, which are coupled with warnings that 'if you do not believe that I am the one I claim to be, you will indeed die in your sins' (8:24). A few days before his death, according to three of the gospels, Jesus exercised a messianic (or almost messianic) authority by cleansing the temple, driving out the moneychangers – an intensely dramatic challenge to the Jewish authorities which sealed his fate. Because John puts the cleansing near the beginning (2:13–25), Dr Stott feels compelled to claim that Jesus cleansed the temple amid general consternation *twice* (UB, p. 100)! This seems to be an example of the difficulties which beset any attempt to harmonise all the gospels.

Many readers who are assured that Jesus utterly disregarded self in order to serve 'the will of God and the welfare of mankind' (BC1, p. 44) must have been puzzled to notice

that in John's gospel and letters the 'love' which is commanded seems to be the love which the disciples are to have
for each other ('the brethren') while mankind as a whole
(the world) lies in darkness. In particular readers conscious
of the terrible history of antisemitism must have been
puzzled to read what Jesus says to a group called 'the Jews'
– for example, 'you belong to your father, the devil' (8:44).
In John's gospel there is outright hostility between 'the
Jews' who are thus condemned and Jesus and his disciples.
Already by 9:22 'the Jews had decided that anyone who
acknowledged that Jesus was the Christ would be put out of
the synagogue'. But it seems clear from the other gospels
that the historical Jesus, who was a Jew, preached and
practised love for all including other Jews, even if sometimes it had to be a stern love. And it seems clear from
Paul's letters and the Acts of the Apostles (as well as from
other evidence) that the total separation of Church and
synagogue was a slow process. In Acts, the apostles and
other Christians regularly worship in the temple in
Jerusalem.

Very gladly and very gratefully I count myself among
the many millions who have been given light by John's
gospel. But its whole character counts against the theory
that the Scriptures contain no contradictions because they
contain no errors. 'The Scripture cannot be broken' (10:35)
is often quoted from this gospel by conservative writers.
But it is significant that the context of this text is a citation of
Psalm 82 (curiously described as 'your law'): 'I have said
you are gods'. In John's gospel it is used to show that
men can rightly be called gods. But that was probably not
the original meaning of the psalm, which seems to be ironic
in this verse. The New International Version, for example,
translates the Hebrew to mean that rulers who 'defend the
unjust' may be called 'gods' but 'will die like mere men; you
will fall like every other ruler' (verses 2, 6–7). It seems clear
that John did not think it necessary to base his gospel on a
Scripture which was inerrant in its original meaning.
For him as for countless Christians after him, it was the

Christian meaning of the Scriptures that could not be broken.

## After Fundamentalism

That, I have learned, is the character of the Bible. It is not truly expounded when fundamentalists feel obliged to claim that it contains no contradictions. In a presentation of *The Scripture Principle* (1985) which is on the whole scholarly, Professor Clark Pinnock declares that 'if contradiction exists our doctrine of Scripture is overthrown' (p. 147). He considers that this is the necessary consequence of a belief in the Bible's inerrancy, for 'inerrancy simply means that the Bible can be trusted in what it teaches and affirms'. Another result is that it is necessary to hold that even a piece of fiction is somehow inerrant, for 'the inerrant truth of a parable is of course parabolic and the inerrant truth of a fable is fabulous' (p. 78). But on the same page he commends a much more carefully qualified statement by Millard Erickson: 'The Bible, when correctly interpreted in the light of the level to which culture and the means of communication had developed at the time it was written, and in view of the purposes for which it was given, is fully truthful in all that it affirms'. And Jim Packer, in his *Under God's Word* (1982, p. 53), ends up with a similar set of qualifications. He says that the two words 'infallibility' and 'inerrancy' express

> no advance commitment of any kind in the field of biblical interpretation, save that whatever Scripture, interpreted with linguistic correctness, in terms of each book's discernible literary character, against its own historical and cultural background, and in the light of its topical relation to other books, proves to be saying should be reverently received, as from God.

Qualifications such as these, which take account of the Bible's true character, empty words such as 'infallibility' and 'inerrancy' of their plain meaning. Yet these or similar qualifications are increasingly seen by conservative scholars to be necessary, despite many dire warnings by the ultraconservatives. Thus Clark Pinnock has modified the position which he adopted in an earlier book, *A Defense of Biblical Infallibility* (1967). The leading Calvinist theologian in the Netherlands, G. C. Berkouwer, is even more cautious than Erickson, Packer and Pinnock. Bernard Ramm, whose earlier work on the Bible and science was pilloried by Professor Barr, has since written a book aptly called *After Fundamentalism* (1983). And what might come after it, theologically, has been outlined in, for example, two brave books by William J. Abraham on *The Divine Inspiration of Holy Scripture* (1981) and *Divine Revelation and the Limits of Historical Criticism* (1982). He is an American Evangelical who shows a perceptive sensitivity to recent British theology, which he might have been expected to find repulsive. Professor I. Howard Marshall in his *Biblical Inspiration* (1983) says that 'it is arguable that the Bible does contain what may be regarded as errors and contradictions by modern standards but which are not in fact contrary to its own standards and purpose' (p. 71). He quotes the Chicago Statement:

When total precision of a particular kind was not expected nor aimed at, it is no error not to have achieved it. Scripture is inerrant, not in the sense of being absolutely precise by modern standards, but in the sense of making good its claims and achieving that measure of focused truth at which its authors aimed. (p. 60)

His conclusion is: '"Infallible" means that the Bible is entirely trustworthy for the purposes for which God has inspired it' (p. 53).

Here these theologians come close to the words of the Second Vatican Council's Dogmatic Constitution on the Divine Revelation (III.11) that since everything asserted by the inspired authors or sacred writers must be held to be asserted by the Holy Spirit, it follows that the books of Scripture must be acknowledged as teaching firmly, faithfully and without error that truth which God wanted put into the sacred writings for the sake of our salvation.

In previous sentences the council had come closer to fundamentalism, teaching that both Testaments 'in their entirety, with all their parts, are sacred and canonical because, having been written under the inspiration of the Holy Spirit . . . they have God as their author', their human authors having 'consigned to writing everything, and only those things, which God wanted'. But the bishops rejected the first draft *schema* which proposed that 'since divine inspiration extends to all things in the Bible, it follows directly and necessarily that the entire Sacred Scripture is absolutely immune from error'.

Do such admissions of the possibility of what is by modern standards error in the Bible destroy the Bible's authority? Many Evangelicals are fairly confident that even after such admissions the Bible can still be said to be authoritative, even 'infallible'. S. T. Davis documented this in *The Debate about the Bible: Inerrancy versus Infallibility* (1977) and P. J. Achtemeier in *The Inspiration of Scripture* (1980). But there has been much alarm. Commenting on the Second Vatican Council, a very conservative Evangelical scholar has written: 'Everyone from a Fundamentalist to a "Christian atheist" could assent to this formulation' (D. A. Carson in *Hermeneutics, Authority and Canon*, which he edited with J. D. Woodbridge in 1986, p. 9). I recognise that it may say very little to say that one believes in 'that truth which God wanted put into the sacred writings for the sake of our salvation'. So I shall end this chapter by stating briefly what I understand to be the saving truth which is affirmed by the Bible. And I shall also mention a few things which are in the Bible but not, I think, God-breathed.

God's purpose in inspiring the composition of the Bible

which Christians hold in their hands today was 'severely practical'. (So Dr Stott wisely teaches, UB, p. 23.) It was to tell us that we and the rest of the universe are wonderfully his creation – not to propose that science is corrected by either Genesis 1 or Genesis 2 (the myths in these two chapters, which come from different sources and dates, contradict each other in some details). It was to tell us that we are sinners – not to instruct us how the serpent who was already wicked could speak to Eve or how the murderous Cain, so primitive that he was Adam's firstborn son, found a woman to be a farmer's wife, or how a flood covered the earth (including the mountains) without leaving any world-wide traces. It was to assure us that, although we are sinners, we are loved and delivered by God – not to inform us that the children of Israel included no fewer than 603,550 adult males plus families during the journey to Canaan (Numbers 1:46). It was to command us to live as God's children – not to persuade us that he dictated the law of Moses 430 years after his promise to Abraham (Galatians 3:17) although the time spent by the people of Israel in Egypt before the exodus had also been 430 years (Exodus 12:40). It was to tell us how he used a unique people, Israel, 'people who live apart and do not consider themselves one of the nations' – not to inform us that Balaam prophesied this having held conversations with a donkey and an angel (Numbers 22:21–35). It was to teach us, through his self-revelation to the Israelites, that we must worship God alone – not to complain that the genocide of the Canaanites was incomplete. It was to show that the holy God demands holiness – not to tell us that the number of wicked Israelites killed off by the plague in Shittim was twenty-four thousand (Numbers 25:9) or twenty-three thousand (1 Corinthians 10:8). It was to reveal his holy love through Israel's great prophets – not to provide fully accurate predictions of coming events. It was to proclaim his demand for justice – not to give us a completely coherent account of the origins of the Israelite monarchy. It was to reveal himself in the whole bitter-sweet history of Israel – not to recount that history with complete accuracy (somehow reconciling the books of Samuel and the Kings with the later Chronicles). It was to show how when swallowed up into victorious empires amid the storms of history, when exiled and deprived of all political identity, the Jews reached a better understanding of God's holiness and mercy – not to tell us how a whale could swallow and regurgitate Dove (in Hebrew *Jonah*). It was to give us spiritual strength, whether the Philistine giant Goliath was killed by the boy David (1 Samuel 17) or by Elhanan (2 Samuel 21:19), who is elsewhere said to have killed Goliath's brother (1 Chronicles 20:5). It was to give us spiritual light – not to affirm that the sun once halted its journey across the sky for 'about a full day' (Joshua 10:13) or went backwards (Isaiah 38:8).

God's purpose was to proclaim that Jesus is 'a light for revelation to the Gentiles and for glory to your people Israel' – not to tell us whether Joseph's father was called Jacob (Matthew 1:16) or Eli (Luke 3:23). It was to say that the love of God was embodied in the carpenter of Nazareth – not to argue with the historians about the dates when Quirinius took a census in Judea (Luke 2:2) and when Judas and Theudas led their rebellions (Acts 5:36–37). It was to give us the message of Jesus which was like new wine – not to assert that it never contradicted the Hebrew Scriptures. It was to preserve enough of that message to make us feel its force – not to persuade us that different versions of the sayings of Jesus must have been spoken on different occasions, for example, one set of Beatitudes on a hill (Matthew 5:1), another on level ground (Luke 6:17). It was to tell us that Jesus heals – not to inform us whether the daughter of Jairus was dead (Matthew 9:18) or only dying (Mark 5:23) when Jesus was summoned, or whether blind Bartimeus was cured before (Luke 18:35) or after (Mark 10:46) entering Jericho, or whether the centurion who begged for the healing of his servant addressed Jesus personally (Matthew 8:5) or not (Luke 7:3). It was to tell us that Jesus died for us (whether he died on the day of the Passover feast, as in three of the gospels, or on the day before as related by John) and was raised from the dead (whatever may have been the details of his resurrection, which the gospels report differently). It was to send us out into the world with that good news – whether Jesus allowed his apostles to take a staff and wear sandals on their first missionary journey (Mark 6:8–9) or not (Matthew 10:10). It was to promise us the Holy Spirit – whatever may have been the nature of the charismatic event on the Day of Pentecost. It was to inspire the mission of Paul to the Gentiles – although the author of the Acts of the Apostles does not seem to have had available to him either the chronology, or the theology, which we can read in Paul's surviving letters. It was to proclaim that 'the life I live in the body, I live by faith in the Son of God, who loved me and gave himself for me' (Galatians 2:20) – whether the apostles insisted that Gentile converts must 'abstain . . . from the meat of strangled animals and from blood' (Acts 15:20) or 'added nothing' to Paul's message (Galatians 2:6). It was to speak with converting and sustaining power about ourselves and our salvation. 'For the word of God is living and active. Sharper than any double-edged sword, it penetrates even to dividing soul and spirit, joints and marrow; it judges the thoughts and attitudes of the heart' (Hebrews 4:12).

# John Stott's Response to Chapter 2

My dear David,

You have certainly done a magnificent demolition job! This little Evangelical peanut lies bruised, battered and broken beneath the Mighty Liberal Steamroller! But (to wrench a text out of its context in a way of which neither you nor I would approve) I am 'hard pressed . . . but not crushed; perplexed, but not in despair; . . . struck down, but not destroyed' (2 Corinthians 4:8–9). So I pick myself up from the ground, shake off the dust, adjust my dishevelled hair and clothing, take a few deep breaths, lift my heart to heaven, and rally to the defence of the Evangelical cause.

First, I am very glad that you can so firmly endorse what I have written about divine revelation and its indispensability. The old Deist attempt to replace revelation by reason was wrong-headed from the beginning. Reason has a vital role in the understanding and application of revelation, but it can never be a substitute for it. Without revelation reason gropes in the dark and flounders in the deep.

Can we not go a step further than this together and agree that what we need is more than a revelation in general; it is a *reliable* revelation? Indeed, we have strong Christian reasons for expecting God to have given us one. We both believe that God said and did something through Jesus Christ which was unique in itself and decisive for the salvation of the world. Is it not inconceivable, therefore, that God should first have spoken and acted in Christ and then have allowed his saving word and deed to be lost in the mists of antiquity? If God's good news was meant for everybody, which it was and is, then he must have made provision for its reliable preservation, so that all people in all places at all times could have beneficial access to it. This is an *a priori* deduction from our basic Christian beliefs about God, Christ and salvation.

But can this saving revelation be equated with the Bible? And is it legitimate to regard the Bible as a reliable, let alone 'inerrant', guide? It is entirely proper that you should have put these questions to me, although you buttress your case with such a mass of detail that I cannot hope within the compass of this response to attend to it all. So where shall I begin?

I could begin by reminding you that the doctrine of biblical inspiration and authority held by Evangelicals was for centuries the universal Church's doctrine, and still is the official position of the Roman Catholic Church and of some Protestant churches. If, then, we were to consult the total Christian Church, triumphant as well as militant, this doctrine would be seen to be the majority view. That is why Harry Blamires in his book *Where Do We Stand?* (1980) bids us beware of innovators. He quotes G. K. Chesterton's definition of tradition as 'an extension of the franchise', namely 'giving votes to that most obscure of all classes, our ancestors'. Mr Blamires continues: 'If you accept the "one man, one vote" principle for the Christian church, the pollsters will have to do most of their opinion sampling in heaven . . . If you extend the franchise fully . . . you can never put the traditionalists in a minority. They have a built-in majority from the past' (pp. 79–80). But that argument will not weigh with you, David, since it ignores the last two centuries of biblical criticism.

Alternatively, I could underline the elaborate internal cross-attestation of Scripture and take you to task for accepting the NEB interpretation of 2 Timothy 3:16, that the word *theopneustos* ('God-breathed') applies only to *some* Scriptures. It is true, of course, that the Greek sentence has no main verb, but (according to the best reading) it includes the word *kai* ('and'), indicating that two assertions are being made, not one, namely that 'all Scripture is God-breathed *and* useful . . .'

Instead of pursuing these approaches, however, I will go straight to what you call my 'most important argument'.

## The Example of Jesus Christ

Since you tell me that you are yourself not convinced by this reasoning, and since our readers will probably not have read my attempted expositions of it, I need to develop it a little. Submission to Scripture is for us Evangelicals a sign of our submission to Christ, a test of our loyalty to him. We find it extremely impressive that our incarnate Lord, whose own authority amazed his contemporaries, should have subordinated himself to the authority of the Old Testament Scriptures as he did, regarding them as his Father's written word. You urge us to banish from our mind pictures of Jesus either as 'a theologian in a book-lined study' or even as possessing his own complete copy of the Hebrew Bible. Quite so. But we may not conclude from this that he could not have known it intimately. For his local synagogue, where he both studied and worshipped, will almost certainly have had an accessible copy.

When I have pointed out that in Jesus' temptations in the Judean desert each issue was settled by an apt quotation from Deuteronomy 6 or Deuteronomy 8, and that he had 'no need to debate or argue with the devil', I was not intending to imply that he did not have to make 'real decisions'. He did. The temptations were insidious enough to call in question both his identity ('if you are the Son of God') and his vocation (whether to achieve his ends by compromise or by the cross). My point was to draw attention to the way in which his decisions were made, namely by reference to Scripture: *gegraptai gar* ('for it stands written') was for him the conclusive argument.

The same loyalty to Scripture was apparent as his public ministry unfolded. We do not know (for we are not told) by what process he came to understand who he was and what he had been sent into the world to do. But it seems probable that the revelation was given him through Scripture, since it was according to Scripture that he came to define his mission. In particular, by applying to himself both the designation 'son of man' (Daniel 7) and the prophecies relating to the suffering servant (Isaiah 53), he fused two Old Testament images which in Judaism represented respectively 'the highest conceivable declaration of exaltation' and 'the expression of deepest humiliation'. These are Oscar Cullmann's expressions, taken from his *The Christology of the New Testament* (1959). He continues: 'This is the unheard-of new act of Jesus, that he united these two apparently contradictory tasks in his self-consciousness, and that he expressed that union in his life and teaching' (p. 161). He would enter into his glory only through suffering and death. Hence his sense of compulsion, so often repeated, that he 'must' go to Jerusalem and be rejected and suffer and die. Why must he? Because of what stood written in Scripture. This was the reason he would not call for angels to rescue him from arrest in the garden: 'how then would the Scriptures be fulfilled that say it must happen in this way?' (Matthew 26:54).

Then there were his public controversies with the religious authorities. You allude to their opposition to him as if it were evidence that he disagreed with the Old Testament. But it was with their traditions that he disagreed, I must insist, not with the Scriptures, for in nearly every debate with them he appealed to Scripture to support his position against theirs. Indeed, it was the true interpretation of the Old Testament Scriptures which was at stake in his quarrel with both the Pharisees and the Sadducees, who, incidentally, were not the simple Bible believers that you suggest. He criticised the former for adding to Scripture (their traditions) and the latter for subtracting from it (the supernatural).

Thus Jesus' determination to resist the devil, to fulfil his costly messianic role and to oppose the authorities all stemmed from his prior determination to obey his Father's will as he discerned it in Scripture. The evidence has been thoroughly set out by Richard T. France in his *Jesus and the Old Testament* (1971) and by John W. Wenham in his *Christ and the Bible* (1973). Certainly Jesus went *beyond* the Old Testament, but he did not go *against* it. Even in the debate over divorce, which we will consider at greater length in chapter 5, what Jesus criticised was not Moses but the hardness of human hearts, and the direction in which he led his hearers was not away from the Pentateuch but back to the creation narrative. Again, in 'declaring all foods clean' (Mk 7:19), he was not saying that the law's dietary regulations had never been God's will, but that they were a temporary divine arrangement, which was now 'fulfilled in the purity of heart demanded in the Kingdom of God

In criticising this Evangelical position, you make two points which do not appear to be compatible with each other, since one assumes that Jesus did hold this high view of Scripture, while the other argues that he did not. First, you write that it was 'natural' and not in the least 'unlikely' that Jesus believed in the authority of Scripture, since he was 'a devout Jew' who accepted the views commonly held in his day. The implication seems to be that you think he was mistaken, which I find intolerably derogatory to him. Your other argument is that he did *not* hold this doctrine of Scripture, but dissented from it, for his views were 'controversially new', so that he was not a conservative but a radical. These are not alternatives, however, for surely he was both – conservative in his attitude to Scripture, and radical in his interpretations of it which challenged the accepted wisdom of his day. I am convinced that his radicalism was not directed towards the Old Testament itself. Do you seriously believe that his words 'all who ever came before me were thieves and robbers' (John 10:8) were a rejection of 'the entire religious history of Israel'? William Temple was clear that he was referring to 'false Messiahs'. As for the six antitheses of the Sermon on the Mount ('you have heard that it was said . . . but I say to you . . .'), it is certain that Matthew did not understand them as contradictions of the Old Testament, since they are immediately preceded by the strong statement that Jesus had not come to abolish the law and the prophets, but to fulfil them. In this way Jesus stated the principle first (Matthew 5: 17–20) and then gave a series of examples to illustrate it (5:21–56), which is exactly how the rabbis taught, as David Daube has shown in his *The New Testament and Rabbinic Judaism* (1956).

What Jesus was rejecting, then, was not the law itself but interpretations of it which were either too literal, or too superficial, or thoroughly perverted. In place of such distortions he substituted his own radical interpretation, which belonged to the ethic of the kingdom. It was the same in the controversies over Sabbath observance and his fraternisation with the outcasts of Jewish society. Jesus was not rejecting Old Testament teaching, but giving his own authoritative application of it, which was in conflict with the scribes and Pharisees. And his use of Hosea 6:6 ('I desire mercy, not sacrifice') in relation to both these controversies (Matthew 9:13; 12:7), is a good example of his creative application of a biblical principle.

It is, I believe, to a similar radical conservatism that the disciples of Jesus are called today. The disciple is not above his master. If submission to Scripture was right for him, as it was, it must be right for us also. *Not* a wooden conformity to its letter, however, but a profound penetration into its demanding implications for the life of the kingdom. For the supremacy of Scripture carries with it a radical calling into question of all human traditions and conventions, however ancient and sacred. That's why I personally do not like the label 'conservative Evangelical'. It conjures up the wrong image, an image of stubborn resistance to challenge and change. 'Evangelical' should be enough on its own; but if you insist on the addition of a qualification, then please make it a 'radical conservative Evangelical'. Thanks!

I have concentrated on Jesus' attitude to the Old Testament, and have room only for the briefest allusion to the New Testament. You are right to take me up on my assertion that Jesus 'made provision for the writing of the New Testament'. Understood as a statement of his deliberate intention, this claimed too much, for indeed there is no evidence that he envisaged New Testament documents or that he commissioned his apostles to write them. But he did commission them to teach in his name; he did call them to be with him so that they might bear witness to what they heard and saw; and he did promise them the illumination of the Spirit of truth, both to remind them of his teaching and to lead them into all the truth which they had not yet been able to receive. And these privileges uniquely equipped them to teach, whether by the spoken or by the written word. Moreover, his use of the vocabulary of 'sending' – he designated them 'apostles', 'sent them out to preach', (Mark 3:14) and told them 'I am sending you out like sheep among wolves' (Matthew 10:16) – must have been a deliberate parallel to the 'sending' of the prophets. The prophets and the apostles were 'sent' to exercise the same basic ministry: to see, record and interpret the mighty acts of God.

## Evangelicalism and Fundamentalism

For thirty-five years now I have felt it right to repudiate the label 'fundamentalist', and in my second book *Fundamentalism and Evangelism* (1956) I attempted to make some distinctions between Evangelicals and fundamentalists. In an exchange of letters with Professor James Barr in 1978, after the publication of his book *Fundamentalism*, I complained that he seemed to lump us all together. He denied this, but added that 'the overlap was very great'. Now you write, David, that I make claims which 'sound like fundamentalism', that I have a 'lingering inclination towards fundamentalism', and that you hope to wean me away from my 'near-fundamentalism'.

In desiring to dissociate myself from fundamentalists, I shall try neither to caricature them (for I do not know that they have ever delineated themselves over against Evangelicals), nor to repudiate them (for they are true – even if sometimes embarrassing – brothers and sisters in Christ). At first the word 'fundamentalist' (coined in 1920) had an entirely honourable connotation.[1] Although its antecedents may be traced back to the nineteenth century, it really owed its origin to the publication in the United States of a series of twelve paperback books entitled *The Fundamentals*, beginning in 1910. Their sixty-five topics included, in addition to aspects of biblical authority, such basic doctrines as the deity, virgin birth, atoning death, and bodily resurrection of Jesus. And their authors included such well-known scholars as Dyson Hague, James Orr, W. H. Griffith Thomas, B. B. Warfield, and Bishops Handley Moule and J. C. Ryle. At that time 'fundamentalism' was seen as a defence of the fundamentals of the faith, in opposition to 'modernism', which was seen as a denial of them. But gradually all words change their meaning, and today 'fundamentalism' is associated in many minds with certain extremes and extravagances which Evangelicals reject. Refraining from naming any names of people or institutions (they are in any case more numerous in America than in Europe), I list eight tendencies of the mind-set styled 'fundamentalism', although of course not all 'fundamentalists' exhibit all of them:

(1) A general suspicion of scholarship and science, which sometimes degenerates into a thoroughgoing anti-intellectualism;
(2) a mechanical view or 'dictation theory' of biblical inspiration, with a consequent denial of the human, cultural element in Scripture and therefore of the need for 'biblical criticism' and careful hermeneutics;
(3) a naive, almost superstitious, reverence for the Authorised (King James') Version of the Bible, warts and all, as if it

---

[1] For a well-documented history, see George M. Marsden, *Fundamentalism and American Culture*: The Shaping of Twentieth-century Evangelicalism 1870–1925 (Oxford University Press, 1980).

were quasi-inspired, which leads to a neglect of textual criticism;

(4) a literalistic interpretation of all Scripture ('the interpretation of every word of the Bible as literal truth' – *Collins English Dictionary*), leading to an insufficient recognition of the place of poetry, metaphor and symbol;

(5) a separatist ecclesiology, together with a blanket repudiation of the Ecumenical Movement and the World Council of Churches;

(6) a cultural imprisonment, whose evil consequences have included racial prejudice and prosperity teaching;

(7) a denial of the social implications of the gospel, except for philanthropy and some extreme right-wing political concerns; and

(8) an insistence on premillennial eschatology, with a rather dogmatic contemporary interpretation of prophecy, including an uncritical espousal of Zionism.

Of these tendencies, the second is the most germane to our discussion. You rightly reject as an extreme position the notion that God 'dictated all the words' of Scripture and treated the biblical writers 'as a musician uses his instrument'. Moslems believe that Allah dictated the Koran in Arabic to Muhammad, and Christian fundamentalists tend to believe that the Bible had a somewhat comparable origin, although its diversity of authorship makes the comparison inexact. Evangelicals, however, affirm the double authorship of the Bible, since the Bible's own account of itself is both that 'God spoke' to and through men, and that 'men spoke from God' (Hebrews 1:1; 2 Peter 1:21). I enlarged on the human element of Scripture in my 1979 Olivier Béguin lecture in Australia (ARBMW), pointing out that the process of divine inspiration was not incompatible with the researches of the biblical historians, the reflections of the wise men (e.g. Proverbs 24:30–34), the crafted poetry of the psalmists, or (in the New Testament letters) the pastoral concerns of the apostles. Nor did inspiration iron out the biblical writers' different literary styles or theological emphases. How, then, were the divine and human elements related to each other? Both Roman Catholic and Protestant theologians, ancient and modern, have suggested an analogy (however imperfect) between the two authorships of Scripture and the two natures of Christ. Just as we must emphasise neither the deity of Jesus at the expense of his humanity, nor his humanity at the expense of his deity, so we must equally affirm the human and divine origins of Scripture. On the one hand God spoke, deciding himself what he intended to say, yet not in such a way as to distort the personality of the human authors. On the other hand men spoke, using their faculties freely, yet not in such a way as to distort the message of the divine author. We have no basis for saying that because the origin of Scripture was human as well as divine, it must therefore contain error, any more than we have for saying that because Jesus was human as well as divine he must therefore have sinned. Further, we have no right to say that the conjunction of the divine and the human in the production of Scripture is impossible. As Dr J. I. Packer has said in his *Fundamentalism and the Word of God* (1958), such a denial

> assumes that God and man stand in such a relation to each other that they cannot both be free agents in the same action. If man acts freely (i.e. voluntarily and spontaneously), God does not, and *vice versa*. The two freedoms are mutually exclusive. But the affinities of this idea are with Deism, not Christian Theism. (p. 81)

Again, 'the cure for such fallacious reasoning is to grasp the biblical idea of God's *concursive operation* in, with and through the free working of man's own mind' (p. 82).[2]

The double authorship of Scripture has practical as well as theological implications. For the two authorships demand two distinct and appropriate approaches. Because the Bible is the word of God, we should read it like no other

---

[2] See also I. Howard Marshall in *Biblical Inspiration* (Hodder & Stoughton, 1982; Wm B. Eerdmans, 1983), pp. 40–7.

book, on our knees in great humility before him. But because the Bible is also the words of men, we should read it like every other book, applying our minds diligently to its study. As you rightly say, we should read it 'both critically and humbly', though I would prefer to reverse the adverbs! This, then, is the justification of biblical criticism, indeed the necessity of it. 'Criticism' in this context, as we know, means 'investigation' or 'analysis', and does not necessarily imply a destructive judgement. Textual criticism (establishing the original text), historical criticism (enquiring into the circumstances of the composition), source criticism (determining the literary sources), form criticism (studying the structures in which the tradition was preserved and why) and redaction criticism (understanding the theological concerns behind the editor's use of his sources) are all indispensable tools for comprehending and applying the Scriptures.

There are several reasons, however, why Evangelicals have been suspicious of biblical criticism as it has developed.

(1) Many of its exponents have been so preoccupied with the mechanics of a book's composition that they have overlooked, and even shown no interest in, its message.

(2) The earliest critics were products of the Enlightenment, imbued with secular or unbelieving presuppositions. Being rationalistic in their approach, they were consistently destructive in their conclusions. Reimarus of Hamburg in the middle of the eighteenth century, for instance, who could almost be called the 'father' of biblical criticism, was a thoroughgoing Deist, outspoken in his rejection of revelation and miracle, and of the deity, atonement and resurrection of Jesus. Contemporary liberal scholars are, of course, much more moderate than he. Yet many seem to us to be controlled by their sceptical presuppositions. Having decided against miracles, for example, they naturally conclude that all material containing miracle is secondary, i.e. legendary. Again, on the widely held (but unproved)

assumption that evolution applies as much to the development of ideas as of forms, they reject the biblical picture of an original, revealed monotheism, from which Israel declined, and reconstruct the history of religion as a slow and painful rise from animism through polytheism to monolatry and finally monotheism. They then declare every expression of monotheistic faith before the eighth- and seventh-century prophets an anachronism and therefore a later interpolation. A third example is the rejection of the possibility of predictive prophecy, so that whatever claims to be a forecast of the future is immediately dismissed as a *vaticinium ex eventu*, a description of what has happened in the guise of a prophecy of what will. But the *a priori* denial of miracle, revelation and prediction betrays a secular not a Christian mind. It is a safer and sounder principle – even if an oversimplification – that biblical criticism requires biblical presuppositions.

(3) Many of the early claims to 'assured results', which were made by some of the more negative biblical critics, have proved to be premature. Still today, the opinions of liberal commentators, especially when based on subjective criteria, are often in conflict with each other, and even cancel each other out.

(4) The fairly recent development of redaction criticism (the term was coined by Willi Marxsen only in 1954) has on the whole been welcomed by Evangelicals because it credits the biblical authors (especially of the gospels and the Acts of the Apostles) with being theologians in their own right. That is, instead of passing on the tradition they have received (from their sources) uncritically and unimaginatively, they reflected on its significance in relation to their readers, and selected, shaped and arranged their material in order to suit their theological purpose. It is a strange assumption, however, adopted by some leading redaction critics that, because an author has theological interests, his *tendenz* must inevitably have overridden his tradition, and his teaching must be unhistorical. But there is no *a priori* reason why a theologian should not also be a historian

and vice versa. On the contrary, since biblical history is salvation history, history and theology are inseparable.

This is not to denigrate the practice of biblical criticism, which I have already declared to be essential. It is rather to explain why the scepticism of some critics arouses the scepticism of many Evangelicals who read them. Even you, David, seem to me to repeat rather uncritically the critics' conventional conclusions, as if they were established fact. A more critical examination of their (and our) presuppositions would be a healthy exercise for us both.

## The Inerrancy Debate

I confess that I have never myself been greatly enamoured of the word 'inerrancy', mainly because I prefer a single positive ('true' or 'trustworthy') to a double negative ('inerrant', or for that matter 'infallible', which is its historic British equivalent). These words could even obscure what you rightly call 'the most important question about the Bible', which is 'whether it speaks the truth'.

Nevertheless, negatives are sometimes necessary in order to strengthen and clarify the corresponding positive. Thus, the apostle Peter's way of emphasising the eternal nature of our heavenly inheritance is to say that it 'can never perish, spoil or fade' (*aphthartos, amiantos* and *amarantos*, 1 Peter 1:4). Similarly, the fifth-century Chalcedonian definition safeguarded its affirmation that Jesus Christ was one person in two perfect natures by adding the four adverbs 'unconfusedly, unchangeably, indivisibly and inseparably'.

In your judgement, however, the presence of (alleged) errors in the Bible makes the assertion of inerrancy untenable. Evangelicals are, of course, as familiar with these problems as anyone else. They have been discussed at least since Jerome and Augustine. We don't read the Bible with our eyes shut or our minds inert! Broadly speaking, they fall into two categories of apparent discrepancy – on the one hand between Scripture and science, and on the other between different biblical books (e.g. Kings and Chronicles, the four gospels, the Acts and the epistles).

I take Scripture and science first. You and I are agreed that God has revealed himself both through the created universe and through Scripture; that nature and Scripture, or science (the study of nature) and theology (the study of Scripture), cannot ultimately be in conflict with one another, since all truth is God's truth; and that, although science and theology belong to some extent to different spheres, and ask different questions, we can confidently expect them to prove complementary and not contradictory to one another. We also agree that the Bible is prescientific in time and non-scientific in purpose. Many biblical references to the natural order – the heavens as 'the work of your fingers' (Psalm 8:3), the sun as 'like a bridegroom coming forth from his pavilion' (Psalm 19:5), God 'wrapping himself in light as with a garment' (Psalm 104:2) and 'opening his hand' to feed the animals (Psalm 104:28) etc. – are poetry not science. As for Genesis 1, I could echo all your eloquent allusions to its teaching. Although I affirm the right of six-day creationists to continue their investigation into origins and dates, so long as they see their task as marshalling *scientific* arguments to corroborate their belief, I reject their *exegetical* insistence that faithfulness to the biblical text absolutely requires belief in a young earth. They have misunderstood the *genre* of Genesis 1, which is evidently a highly stylised literary and theological, not scientific, statement.

Moving on to Genesis 2 and 3, I have long held and taught that they contain figurative or symbolic elements, so that we should not dogmatise about the snake and the trees. But I cannot agree with you that the Adam and Eve story is a myth, whose truth is purely symbolical, not historical. The important theological statement in the second half of Romans 5, by the parallels it draws between the first and second Adams, depends for its truth on an act of disobedience by Adam as historical as Jesus' act of obedience, and all who deny the historicity of the fall find themselves in grave theological difficulty regarding the good creation and the origins of evil. The fall really cannot be reconstructed in evolutionary terms. Moreover, the anatomical, physiological, genetic and psychological unity of the human race as one species points straight to our common origins. Writing as a physical anthropologist, Dr Ashley Montagu stated: 'All varieties of man belong to the same species and have the same remote ancestry. This is a conclusion to which all the relevant evidence of comparative anatomy, palaeontology, serology and genetics points' (*Man's Most Dangerous Myth: The Fallacy of Race*, 1974, p. 74). I understand that among scientists there is no disagreement about this.

Of course there are still problems, not least about the dating of Adam and Eve, Cain and Abel. The Genesis story seems to put them in the Neolithic Age, the cultural period marked by crop-cultivation, stock-rearing, and settled communities (cf. the 'city' of Genesis 4:17). The forging of tools of bronze and iron, and the making of musical instruments, are clearly placed several generations later (Genesis 4:21–22). In this case, the hominids which date from several hundreds of thousands of years earlier, though some are named *homo habilis* and *homo erectus*, were not fully human in the biblical sense, but pre-Adamic creatures. It all depends on how we define 'human'; all Christians agree that to be human is to bear the image of God, and that this consists at least of a moral, social and spiritual awareness. This kind of reconstruction is not incompatible with evolution, although, theologically speaking, it has to be stated in terms of creation. Adam's body may well have evolved from hominids. But alongside this continuity with the animal creation, he enjoyed a radical discontinuity, owing to his having been created in God's image.

This raises another problem. If the first true man Adam (according to Scripture 'made in the image of God') lived about 10,000 BC, and if the most developed pre-Adamic hominids (according to science *homo sapiens*) preceded him

by hundreds of thousands of years, were culturally advanced, had populated much of the earth and were now
Adam's contemporaries, what was the relationship between him and them? Some Christians argue (though with
insufficient evidence) that they remained sub-human and
later became extinct, either unaccountably like *australopithe-
cus* a million or two years previously or through a universal
flood. Others suggest that they came to share in Adam's
createdness and fallenness not by heredity but by solidarity. Derek Kidner puts it in this way in his Tyndale Commentary on *Genesis* (1967). After the special creation had
'established the first human pair' and had

> clinched the fact that there is no natural bridge from animal to
> man, God may have now conferred his image on Adam's
> collaterals, to bring them into the same realm of being. Adam's
> 'federal' headship of humanity extended, if that was the case,
> outwards to his contemporaries as well as onwards to his
> offspring, and his disobedience disinherited both alike. (p. 29)

If, as you chide me, I have been guilty of 'a lamentable
hesitation' in accepting the fruits of scientific research, it is
due in the main to a necessary caution (in view of the
mistakes of the past, not to mention the over-confident
liberalism of the present!). Incidentally, the best popular
yet scholarly Evangelical book I know, which handles the
exegetical questions posed by Genesis 1–3, is Henri
Blocher's exposition of these chapters entitled *In The Beginning* (1984); it judiciously combines faithfulness to Scripture with openness to science.

Turning to the synoptic gospels, I begin by saying that
most Evangelicals probably still accept the documentary
hypothesis that Matthew and Luke used two main sources,
namely Mark and Q, although some hold the priority of
Matthew. The material which is unique to Matthew and
Luke is generally attributed either to two further literary
sources (M and L) or simply to independent information to
which each had access. Evangelicals also welcome the

emphasis of redaction criticism that the evangelists selected and shaped (though did not invent) their material to suit their theological purpose, perhaps making more editorial changes than we have sometimes thought. The resulting discrepancies certainly pose problems, as do apparent 'slips' or 'mistakes' (like one of those you mention, namely the identity of 'Zechariah the son of Berakiah'). But what you seem reluctant to acknowledge is that possible – in many cases plausible – explanations have been proposed in the commentaries and other studies which competent Evangelical scholars have now written. Among these are Dick France's *Matthew* and Alan Cole's *Mark* in the Tyndale New Testament Commentary Series, D. A. Carson's commentary on *Matthew* in volume 8 of the Expositor's Bible Commentary, Ralph Martin's *Mark: Evangelist and Theologian*, Howard Marshall's *Luke: Historian and Theologian* and *The Gospel of Luke*, and Stephen Smalley's *John: Evangelist and Interpreter*, all published by Paternoster and Eerdmans, together with William Lane's *The Gospel of Mark* and Leon Morris's *John* in the New International Commentary on the New Testament series. Many problems of composition and interpretation are also debated in *New Testament Interpretation* (1977), edited by Howard Marshall. In addition, the 'Gospels Research Project' team, sponsored by Tyndale House, Cambridge, has now published six volumes of *Gospel Perspectives* (1980–1986), whose findings have been admirably summarised by Dr Craig Blomberg in *The Historical Reliability of the Gospels* (1987). In supplying this list of Evangelical works, I do not wish to give a false impression. I am not claiming that between them they provide adequate or even agreed answers to all the problems you raise, but rather that they are responsible explorations into the areas of debate, in the course of which many traditional problems have either fallen into place or received fresh light.

Among many points which Evangelicals would want to make, in regard to alleged discrepancies in the gospels, are the following, which all relate to the intention of the author and the unfairness of criticising him for not doing what he never set out to do. Thus, it is possible to condense speeches, paraphrase them, and translate them into a different cultural idiom, without thereby falsifying their meaning; to change the sequence of events, deliberately subordinating chronology to theology, without by this practice committing an error; to give round figures and make free quotations, according to the literary conventions of the pre-computer age, without being accused of making mistakes (imprecision is not a synonym for inaccuracy); and to quote the Old Testament in such a way as to draw attention to a principle, parallel or pattern, rather than to the detailed fulfilment of a specific prophecy, without being guilty of misquotation.

As for the differences between the synoptic gospels and the fourth gospel, these have of course been noticed and discussed from the beginning, and the fact that we cannot easily tell in the discourses when Jesus stops and John starts shows that John had deeply assimilated the teaching of his Lord. But it is possible to exaggerate the contrast between the claims of Jesus in John and their alleged absence in the synoptic gospels. For if the 'I am' statements may not have been such unambiguous assertions of deity as I suggest in *Basic Christianity* (e.g. 'I am the light of the world' and 'I am the bread of life' *could* have been understood in different ways), yet Jesus' claims recorded by the synoptists (to have inaugurated the kingdom, to have authority to forgive sins, to be accorded his disciples' first love and loyalty, and to be the central figure on the judgement day) are comparable in significance to the most direct claims to deity recorded by John.

Supposing, however, as is indeed the case, that some discrepancies remain which cannot with integrity be reconciled or harmonised, how should we handle this situation? That is what our domestic Evangelical debate over inerrancy is about. Two main possibilities have been proposed.

Some Evangelicals conclude that they must recognise in the Bible a few, largely trivial, factual mistakes. But they add that these belong to the spheres of history, literature and science, so that in the spheres of religion and ethics, and especially in teaching about God, Christ and salvation, the Bible remains inerrant, 'the only infallible rule of faith and practice' (Westminster Confession). This position is sometimes called 'limited inerrancy'. Now to concede a few factual errors will emphatically not cause the whole Evangelical edifice to collapse like a pack of cards. No, the firm foundations on which the Evangelical view of Scripture is built remain in place. In consequence, we have no liberty to deny the epithet 'Evangelical' to such people or to make total inerrancy an indispensable criterion of Evangelical orthodoxy. I agree with both Dr Carl Henry and Dr Kenneth Kantzer that, although limited inerrantists could be called 'inconsistent', they should not be called 'false' Evangelicals.[3]

Other Evangelicals do not feel the necessity to make this concession, however, but continue to affirm the Bible's inerrancy in every area in which it speaks. At the same time we are concerned to add two riders (more clarifications than qualifications), namely that Scripture is without error (1) as originally given, and (2) as correctly interpreted. These additions are not evasions, but commonsense explanations of what we mean by inerrancy. Our critics may retort that, since we don't possess the autographs and are not sure of the correct interpretation, our concept of an inerrant Bible is useless, even meaningless, because it does not exist. But the value of our clarifications is that they lay upon us the urgent importance both of textual criticism (to establish the most reliable text) and of the hermeneutical task (to establish its correct meaning). For Evangelicals emphatically do not claim inerrancy either for a faulty text or for every weird and wonderful interpretation which Bible students produce.

---

[3]See Carl F. H. Henry, *Confessions of a Theologian* (Word Books, 1986), p. 365, and Kenneth Kantzer's contribution to R. Webber, *Evangelical Roots* (Nelson, 1978), p. 91.

By the way, those who speak and write for the International Council on Biblical Inerrancy are scholars, not fools! They now have several significant books to their credit, beginning with two wide-ranging symposia: *The Foundation of Biblical Authority* (1978), edited by James M. Boice, and *Inerrancy* (1980), edited by Norman L. Geisler. More recently, two more valuable symposia have appeared, both edited by D. A. Carson and John D. Woodbridge. Although these essays are not sponsored by ICBI, their authors 'hold that what the Scriptures teach is infallibly true and that this belief is not only patient of reasoned defence but is extremely important for the well-being of the church'. Their titles are *Scripture and Truth* (1983) and *Hermeneutics, Authority and Canon* (1986).

It will by now be apparent that I belong to the second category of Evangelicals, for I still see no reason to abandon the concept of inerrancy, if it is properly understood, even though I like the positive word 'truth' even better. So let me tell you why I prefer inerrancy to limited inerrancy, and why I defend the suspended judgement on the unresolved problems which you describe as 'wholly inadequate', but which I maintain is thoroughly Christian!

(1) Our theological *a priori* that the Bible is God's word through human words carries with it the conviction that the God who has spoken has not in the process contradicted himself. That is why patient attempts at harmonisation seem to me more Christian than either a premature declaration of error or a resort to artificial manipulation.

(2) A number of old problems, which decades ago were confidently pronounced 'biblical errors', have subsequently proved not to have been. They have yielded to patient study and further light. I will give only one example. In Acts 17:6 and 8 Luke calls the city rulers or magistrates in Thessalonica 'politarchs', a word which occurs nowhere else in the New Testament and has not been found in any other Greek literature. So earlier critical scholars accused Luke of either ignorance or carelessness. But

since then a number of inscriptions have been found, dating from the second and third centuries AD, several in Thessalonica itself, which have vindicated Luke's use of the title. It is now known that the city council in Macedonian towns consisted of a group of politarchs, and that there were five or six of them in Thessalonica. This seems to me to illustrate the wisdom of referring to 'unresolved problems' rather than 'proven errors'.

(3) The distinction between spheres of inerrancy (theology and ethics versus history and science), though understandable, is nevertheless arbitrary. Neither Jesus nor his apostles made it. They seem to have regarded Scripture as 'without error in all that it affirms' (Lausanne Covenant para. 2), to whatever sphere each affirmation belongs. It would seem more consistent for us to do the same.

(4) This is how Christians learn to handle all their other theological problems. No single Christian doctrine is problem-free, and if we were to delay faith until we had solved all the problems, we would never believe anything. Take as an example the love of God, which Christians of all shades believe. Enormous problems stand in our way, like the origin and power of evil, the prevalence of injustice, the sufferings of the innocent and the occurrence of catastrophes. Faced with such problems, however, we do not hold our conviction of God's love in abeyance until we have solved them. Instead, we wrestle with them, and as we do so, some light is thrown on them. But in the end we persist in our belief that God is love, *in spite of the unresolved problems*, because Jesus himself taught and exemplified it. It should be the same with our confidence in God's word.

(5) The acceptance of inerrancy is more conducive to an attitude of reverent humility before God's word, than a belief in limited inerrancy, let alone errancy. True, as I have already mentioned, to admit that Scripture contains a few, minor mistakes of a factual kind does not logically undermine the Evangelical doctrine of the authority, supremacy and sufficiency of Scripture. Nevertheless, as experience

has shown, it puts people's feet on a slippery slope, and fosters more a critical than a humble spirit.

This leads me to my last comment.

## Evangelical or Liberal?

As I reflect on the correct answer to your question, What is essential for Evangelicals?, I find myself asking, What is essential for Liberals? In other words, what is the fundamental difference between us?

I think I would characterise Evangelicals as those who, because they identify Scripture as God's word, are deeply concerned to submit to its authority in their lives (whatever their precise formulation of the doctrine of Scripture may be). In other words, the hallmark of Evangelicals is not so much an impeccable set of words as a submissive spirit, namely their *a priori* resolve to believe and obey whatever Scripture may be shown to teach. They are committed to Scripture in advance, whatever it may later be found to say. They claim no liberty to lay down their own terms for belief and behaviour. They see this humble and obedient stance as an essential implication of Christ's lordship over them.

Such an open, unconditional commitment to Scripture would not be acceptable to liberals, would it, David? True, you write that 'these books read us', but are you willing for them to teach us too? Sometimes you seem anxious to demonstrate that your position is more biblical than mine. I wonder why? I mean, if you could prove this to me, I would want to change my mind and position at once. But if I could show you that my position is more biblical than yours, would you be willing to change? I guess your reply would be conditional, i.e. 'Yes, provided that my mind and heart would approve of the change.' What worries me is your biblical selectivity. In later chapters you reject traditional Christian teaching about the atonement, miracles, homosexual partnerships, and the awful reality of hell, not on the ground that you consider it unbiblical, but because on other grounds you find it unacceptable. Does this not mean that in the end you accord supremacy to your reason rather than to Scripture? We are back in the conflict between the Reformation and the Renaissance. As Luther said to Erasmus, 'The difference between you and me, Erasmus, is that you sit above Scripture and judge it, while I sit under Scripture and let it judge me!'

I also wonder why you seem so anxious to persuade me that inerrancy is untenable? Is it entirely your concern for intellectual integrity? But I am committed to this also. Your assault has reminded me a little of Dr B. T. D. Smith, who taught the synoptic gospels at Cambridge in the 1940s when I was a theological student. It was said that as a young man he had been an ardent Anglo-Catholic, but that now he had entirely lost his Christian faith. He seemed to take what Oscar Cullmann called (in *The Christology of the New Testament*, 1959) 'an almost sadistic pleasure' in finding discrepancies! I shall always remember the beginning of his lecture on Luke 3:1 ff. Rubbing his hands and licking his lips with evident glee, he said with his famous lisp: 'Thith pathage thimply brithleth with difficultieth!' Now, please, I'm not likening you to him! But I still ask, 'Why?' I wonder whether it has anything to do with a fear of what C. S. Lewis in *Surprised by Joy* (1955) styled 'the tyrannous noon of revelation' (p. 63)? Could it be that you think submission to biblical authority is incompatible with intellectual freedom?

Let me finish my response to your second chapter (a response which, though long, is foundational to the rest of our dialogue) by developing a little parable. It uses flight as a picture of freedom (memories of *Jonathan Livingstone Seagull!*) and seeks to characterise (not, I hope, caricature) the essential difference between the fundamentalist, the liberal and the Evangelical.

The fundamentalist seems to me to resemble a caged bird, which possesses the capacity for flight, but lacks the freedom to use it. For the fundamentalist mind is confined or caged by an overliteral interpretation of Scripture, and by the strict traditions and conventions into which this has led him. He is not at liberty to question these, or to explore alternative, equally faithful ways of applying Scripture to the modern world, for he cannot escape from his cage.

The liberal seems to me to resemble (no offence meant!) a gas-filled balloon, which takes off and rises into the air, buoyant, free, directed only by its own built-in navigational responses to wind and pressure, but entirely unrestrained from earth. For the liberal mind has no anchorage; it is accountable only to itself.

The Evangelical seems to me to resemble a kite, which can also take off, fly great distances and soar to great heights, while all the time being tethered to earth. For the Evangelical mind is held by revelation. Without doubt it often needs a longer string, for we are not renowned for creative thinking. Nevertheless, at least in the ideal, I see Evangelicals as finding true freedom under the authority of revealed truth, and combining a radical mind-set and lifestyle with a conservative commitment to Scripture.

I hope my little parable has not offended you!

Yours as ever,

John

# 3 The Cross of Christ

## Explaining Calvary

What does the cross mean? Probably every real Christian since the beginning of Christianity has sooner or later been stirred to the depths by Jesus when he is at his most human – when he is dying. 'May I never boast', exclaimed Paul on behalf of us all, 'except in the cross of our Lord Jesus Christ, through which the world has been crucified to me, and I to the world' (Galatians 6:14). And there have been as many personal responses as there have been Christians. A response at that depth cannot be the mere endorsement of an 'atonement theory' which means nothing for one's personal existence. Paul's response can be understood readily as arising out of his life 'in Christ' but even images or theories which seem very strange to others sprang out of someone's experience. Someone's life was crossed.

Few people today have much respect for the theory that the devil was tricked into accepting the death of Jesus as the ransom due to him for the liberation of sinners, while all along Jesus was stronger than death, being divine. Dr Stott thinks it 'intolerable, monstrous and profane' (CoC, pp. 113–14). But this theory, eloquently expounded by many teachers of the Church including Gregory of Nyssa in the fourth century and Pope Gregory the Great in the sixth, and outlined earlier by Irenaeus and Origen, had some substance in it. It could appeal to Scripture. Jesus, we are told, 'saw Satan fall like lightning from heaven' (Luke 10:18). The letter to the Colossians refers to 'the powers and authorities', apparently meaning supernatural beings (as in

Ephesians 6:12), and says that having disarmed them Christ 'made a public spectacle of them, triumphing over them by the cross' (2:15). The letter to the Hebrews declares that by his death Jesus destroyed 'him who holds the power of death – that is, the devil' (2:14). And the first letter of John affirms that 'the reason the Son of God appeared was to destroy the devil's work' (3:8). And the theory could appeal to experience. Christians then saw life as a vast, cosmic struggle of good against evil and knew that Christ had won a victory which meant that evil could not really hurt them. They had this experience in the setting of a society where evil was thought of as the work of the devil, where God was thought to be so just that he must deal justly with the devil himself, and where shrewd bargains were struck in business and shopping so that the idea of a bargain with the devil did not seem strange. In his *Christus Victor* (translated into English in 1931) Gustav Aulen re-created that whole world of thought. Europeans could understand it to some extent after their own experiences of 'demonic' evil in the two great wars. In Africa and elsewhere twentieth-century Christians have often experienced their faith primarily as liberation from the power of evil spirits. And if we revise this atonement theory to say that the devil was conquered, not tricked or paid, on Calvary – as Augustine, for example, did – surely we are saying something which is not obviously ridiculous. We are saying that the darkness of this world, with its rulers, whoever they may be, has been overcome so that we can live in the light.

Another theory was proposed some seven hundred years after Gregory of Nyssa by a great theologian and archbishop, Anselm of Canterbury. He developed the idea of a second-century lawyer turned theologian, Tertullian, that Christ's death provided a *satisfactio* (a Roman legal term). He was sure that God owed nothing to the devil except punishment. But he was also sure that sin meant 'not to render God his due' – and he lived in a feudal world where kings insisted on very harsh justice if what was due to them was not paid to them. In the Church of his time the appropriate act of penance and restitution was required if the law of God had been broken by sin. So he taught that the death of God the Son was the satisfaction or compensation due to God the Father whose honour had been insulted by the whole of human sin. This theory can be greatly improved by insisting that it was God's justice, not merely his honour conceived in feudal terms, that was satisfied (Thomas Aquinas taught that). And it is good to be reminded by the experts that none of the ancient or medieval theologians who were for a time greatly honoured by the Church taught one theory to the complete exclusion of all others. Quoting an odd-sounding sentence or two from their works can give an unfair impression of the richness and profundity of their thought. We may – indeed, I am sure that we should – reject some of their phrases. We should not dismiss these Christians entirely. They were pioneers in the theological task which must be ours.

What are we to put in the place of their discarded theories? Few sensitive Christians would nowadays think it adequate to say merely that Christ is our teacher and example. That was the main theory of the apologists who pioneered a more philosophical type of Christian theology in the second century, and it was revived eloquently as an alternative to Anselm's theory by Peter Abelard, who died in 1142. Abelard, whose love for Heloise is an immortal story, taught that 'our redemption is that greatest love kindled in us by Christ's passion', for 'kindled by so great a benefit of divine grace, love should not be afraid to endure anything for his sake'. And this 'exemplarist' theory appealed to many Christian teachers who were determined to make their message thoroughly rational and ethical in modern times, the classic statement in English being *The Idea of Atonement in Christian Theology* by Hastings Rashdall (1919). But Christian reflection has usually seen that this is unsatisfactory, particularly under the many shocks of twentieth-century tragedies. Human sin is so great that any at-one-ment between the Holy God and us sinners must be something achieved by God much more than by sinners. It must be (in the traditional word) 'objective', not merely subjective. That is likely to be our modern (or post-modern) conviction if we are Christians, arising out of many disillusionments, and it has opened many eyes to the unsentimental teaching of the New Testament. Thus a modern, liberal theologian such as Professor John Knox went so far as to permit himself to say that the conceptions of the cross as a victory won and a sacrifice offered 'belong to the very warp and woof of the New Testament' while 'there is no evidence whatever that the early Church entertained the view that the purpose of Christ's death was to disclose the love of God' (*The Death of Christ*, 1959, pp. 147–8). Yet it is surely wrong to reject the 'exemplarist' insight entirely. For it is a simple and glorious fact that many sinners, moved by the teaching and example of the Jesus who laid down his life because of his great love, have learned to love, and even to imitate, him. They also have begun to love and obey God the Father because that death is 'how God showed his love among us' (1 John 4:9). 'God', wrote Paul, 'demonstrates his own love for us in this. While we were still sinners, Christ died for us' (Romans 5:8). And 'Christ's love compels us, because we are convinced that one died for all, and therefore all died . . . that those who live should no longer live for themselves but for him . . . Therefore, if anyone is in Christ, he is a new creation; the old has gone, the new has come!' (2 Corinthians 5:14–17). So Abelard's exemplarist theory has been generated by real Christian experience – which is stronger than sentimentality. As John Knox went on to say, it is the Christian experience that 'in Christ – that is, in the entire event – the love of Christ was not simply made known, as a fact is made known, to our understanding; it was actually "poured into our hearts" (Romans 5:5)'.

Obviously many Christians, and very many people finding their way into Christianity, have felt it to be a problem that Jesus should have been put to death in a way so painful, horrifying, disreputable and isolated. Cicero called crucifixion 'a most cruel and disgusting punishment'. Martin Hengel's study of *The Cross and the Son of God* (in English, 1986) shows in detail how this form of execution was viewed in the ancient world as totally degrading. Its victims were automatically regarded as the worst of criminals. The gospels are full of the disciples' bewilderment about the startling expectation of Jesus that the cross was his destiny and Paul did not have to explain in his first letter to Corinth why the cross of Jesus, who was claimed to be Messiah and Lord, was 'a stumbling-block to Jews and foolishness to Gentiles' (1:23). But neither did he have to explain why the cross was needed in order to deal with sin. He simply reminded Christians that Christ died 'for our sins according to the Scriptures' (1 Corinthians 15:3) or 'was delivered over to death for our sins' (Romans 4:25). It was part of the tradition he had received at his conversion, which seems to have been within five years of that death. And many people who have never gone so far as to be baptised have gone to Calvary in admiring love. A famous example is Gandhi, one of the many millions whose heart-felt devotion has been sung out in the hymn 'When I survey the wondrous cross'.

Some readers may doubt whether a 'liberal' like me can take the cross seriously enough. It may help if I briefly state that I can still remember vividly how moved I was as a boy when I went to church on Good Friday. While I was studying theology I was full of doubts about many doctrines but I always tried to keep my feet on the rock of indisputable history and experience which I had found on Calvary – many years before I saw the actual rock in the church of the Holy Sepulchre in Jerusalem (almost certainly the authentic site of the crucifixion). When I had been ordained I thought I understood enough about the subject to write a book called *God's Cross in Our World*, published a quarter of a century ago. Today I realise how little experience of sin or suffering or sorrow, other people's or my own, I had then; but I can record with utter honesty that the cross of Christ has continued to be the one unconquerable light which has enabled me – as it has enabled so many others – to walk through this dark world.

When I read John Stott's *The Cross of Christ* soon after its publication in 1986, I found that most of it expressed the convictions that had already arisen in my own heart and mind out of my own experience and out of the experience of the Christian centuries (so far as I now know them). But Dr Stott wrote with all the eloquence of a first class preacher whose life is in total harmony with his message – something I can only admire. In particular I admired in his book an emphatic chapter on 'the centrality of the cross'; the great emphasis on the gravity of sin making the cross necessary; the insistence that amid the sin it is God's *love* that we see placarded on the cross; the equal insistence that confronted by sin this is holy, not sentimental, love; the wonder at the bitter cost involved for Christ and at the suffering of the Father; and the description of the Christian fellowship as the community of celebration at the foot of Christ's cross. In all these pages and in many others I found reflected the truths which I have been taught by life and by the gospel. Dr Stott sums it all up in three truths: 'our sin must be extremely horrible, God's love must be wonderful beyond comprehension, Christ's salvation must be a free gift' (CoC, p. 83).

I am sure that this strange wisdom of the cross is wiser than a great deal of philosophy and of theology has been in ancient or modern times. The cross is so central in Christian experience and understanding because it is only on Calvary that we see fully how terrible is the power of the evil in the heart of man and how great is the holy love of the God who forgives, defeats and removes that evil. Too many philosophers, and even Christian theologians, have taken too shallow a view of such realities. Luther in 1518 rightly attacked the 'theology of glory' of the medieval Church by insisting on the 'theology of the cross'. Even in our own century, the century of Auschwitz and Hiroshima, of pollution and starvation, some have remained optimistic that a political or technical solution could be achieved which would one day mean that humanity had got these public problems licked by brain-power and willpower. And even in our cruel age of so many millions of abortions and divorces – an age which has aborted so many hopes of private happiness and has divorced so many from family joys and fulfilling work – the anxiety, loneliness, envy, greed, lust and their evil consequences have been thought conquerable by better education, social arrangements and psychological or physical medicine. The wisdom of the cross, however, is that although the skills of politicians, scientists, social reformers, teachers, doctors and other benefactors of suffering humanity can reduce the problems, basically what is wrong in all history is the heart's inclination to evil. We can so easily be disastrously selfish and short-sighted as individuals and even more aggressive and destructive when herded together in societies. We are often glad to see people who are our moral superiors pulled down. And we love violence or at least are fascinated by its portrayal. We often twist religion itself so that it may justify our self-interest or our depraved passions. And the only answer that has any hope of being completely and permanently successful must come from God. Only if God forgives, only if he exercises his creative and sovereign power, only if he communicates his power so that people doomed by their own crimes and follies can break out of the trap, can there be a human prospect of ultimate victory. Precisely that is found when Jesus, abandoned by his followers, stripped of all his clothes and of all normal dignity, broken down publicly, cursed, is tortured to death by men who act on the orders of the local political and religious leadership. Calvary sees the supreme drama of evil's power – and of God's. When Jesus forgives, we see God forgiving the worst intensity of evil. When Jesus finishes his work, we see how God triumphs. So Jesus does for us sinners something which we cannot do for ourselves. And it is something more significant than anything else – however bad or good – in all history. All this is said by John Stott more effectively than I can say it and I need not expound it further.

Clearly the death of Jesus was a sacrifice in some sense.

Obviously he sacrificed his life in a way tragically familiar to us in the twentieth century, a period which has seen more lives laid down in the cause of patriotism, and also more Christian martyrdoms, than any previous century. And obviously Jesus and the first Christians would compare this self-sacrifice not only with the deaths of human martyrs but also with the sacrifices of the animals in the temple which dominated Jerusalem. The animals were killed in vast numbers because their owners wanted to prove the sincerity of their devotion to God. Deliberately these were costly sacrifices. In the early years after the death of Jesus his followers who like him were Jews, and who now lived in Jerusalem, continued to take part in the sacrificial worship in the temple. But within about forty years of his death the situation had changed radically. Not only was the temple destroyed by the Romans after a revolt which the Christians had refused to support, so that its sacrifices came to a permanent end. Both Jews and Christians ceased to sacrifice – Jews, because their religious law (Deuteronomy) forbade sacrifices outside the temple, and Christians, because the conviction grew that Jesus had already made the perfect and all-sufficient sacrifice (a conviction authoritatively expressed within the New Testament in the letter to the Hebrews). So Christian thinkers had to ask themselves: With which of the old sacrifices should the death of Jesus be compared? In 'pagan' or 'primitive' religion – which of course survived the events of the first Christian century and has been much studied by modern anthropologists and other scholars – sacrifices have been offered for a number of purposes, in order to bribe, feed, placate, thank, eat or simply have joyful communion with the god. Hebrew or Jewish sacrifices were no doubt offered for the same variety of purposes to begin with, and although great efforts were made to purge them of any ideas unworthy of the worship of Yahweh the God of Israel they remained actions with more than one motive. So what was the purpose of the sacrifice on Calvary?

I am particularly grateful that Dr Stott rejects theories

which have been endorsed by many eminent teachers and preachers but which seem incompatible with the faith that God is love. Not only does he criticise all the theories I have already mentioned. He also attacks a theory which is still very much alive and which is still often thought to be *the* Evangelical doctrine. I need call only two witnesses to the content and the vigour of this theory. In her excellent short book on *Sacrifice and the Death of Christ* (1975, p. 11), a British theologian, Frances Young, pointed out that a common interpretation of the death of Christ runs something like this: 'God was angry with sinners. The Jews had tried to placate his anger by symbolically offering the lives of animals to him in place of their guilty selves. But this was inadequate and so Jesus offered a perfect sacrifice. He died as our substitute to appease God's anger.' Dr Young commented: 'With certain degrees of sophistication, this is the general picture one gets from listening to sermons or reading the majority of easily available books.' And in the 1984 *Evangelical Dictionary of Theology* the American contributor of the article on 'Evangelicalism', R. V. Pierard, wrote (p. 379):

God himself provided the way out of the human dilemma by allowing his only Son, Jesus Christ, to assume the penalty and experience death on man's behalf . . . Christ's substitutionary or vicarious atonement was a ransom for mankind's sins, a defeat of the powers of darkness, and a satisfaction for sin because it met the demand of God's justice.

In considerable contrast, Dr Stott teaches plainly that if Christ is pictured as 'intervening in order to pacify an angry God and wrest from him a grudging salvation', or if God is thought of as punishing 'the innocent Jesus in place of us the guilty sinners who had deserved the punishment', such presentations 'denigrate' the Father, who is seen as a 'pitiless ogre' (CoC, p. 150). 'We must not speak of God punishing Jesus,' he says (CoC, p. 151). 'Any notion of penal substitution in which three independent actors play a role – the guilty party, the punitive judge and the innocent victim – is to be repudiated with the utmost vehemence' (CoC, p. 158). He protests against any idea that God is 'subordinate to something outside and above himself which controls his actions, to which he is accountable, and from which he cannot free himself' (CoC, p. 123). He insists that there is in God 'no change of mind or heart secured by Christ. On the contrary, the saving initiative originated in him' (CoC, p. 151). 'It cannot be emphasised too strongly that God's love is the source, not the consequence, of the atonement' (CoC, p. 174). And he says vigorously that God's love is suffering love. God is *not*

> the cosmic sadist who delights in making us squirm. It is this terrible caricature of God that the cross smashes to smithereens. We are not to envisage him on a deck-chair, but on a cross. The God who allows us to suffer, once suffered himself in Christ, and continues to suffer with us and for us today. (CoC, p. 329)

In so emphatically dissociating himself from some of the teachings of fathers of the Church such as John Chrysostom, of many medieval theologians, of the great Protestant Reformers (most notably Calvin), and of many Evangelical writers and preachers since the eighteenth century, Dr Stott is not alone among contemporary Evangelical leaders. I am aware that many Evangelicals simply repeat that 'by becoming our substitute, taking our place and dying our death, Jesus perfectly satisfied both the justice and the love of God' without adding the safeguards on which Dr Stott insists. (I have quoted from his own Presidential Address to the British Isles Conference of the Universities and Colleges Christian Fellowship in 1982, published as *Make the Truth Known*.) But Dr Stott would not be trusted so widely by Evangelicals if many did not completely agree with him. In *The Empty Cross of Jesus* (1984) Michael Green, for example, says that 'God is not anywhere in the New Testament said to be reconciled to us by the death of Christ' (p. 82). 'Though the New Testament does speak of the cross as propitiation, it never says that Christ propitiated God the Father. Though the New Testament does speak of Christ's bearing our sins, it does not call this, as Calvin does, "the penalty which we had incurred" or "the price of satisfaction to the just judgement of God". Indeed, the New Testament does not use the word punishment, *kolasis*, of the death of Christ. Though the New Testament is strong on the wrath of God, it does not apply the verb *orgizomai*, "be wrathful", to God, and certainly does not go so far as Calvin did in saying "God in his character as Judge is hostile to us". Nor does the New Testament talk of the "merits" of Christ being put to our account' (p. 65). 'A great deal of harm has been done by teaching that God is a wrathful Judge, determined to punish somebody, who takes it out of Jesus rather than us' (p. 78).

These are all highly significant corrections to much traditional teaching. They deserve very close and widespread study.

But John Stott also rejects ('respectfully') the explanation of the cross given by (for example) the British Student Christian Movement in its 'Aim and Basis' in 1919. 'It is only when we see on Calvary the price of suffering paid day by day by God himself for all human sin', the SCM then declared, 'that we can enter into the experience of true penitence and forgiveness, which sets us free to embark on a wholly new way of life.' Seventy years or so ago, it was claimed excessively that 'this is the meaning of the atonement'. Dr Stott rightly denies that this can be *the* one and only meaning – and he lays his finger on its defect. The meaning of the atonement is not to be found in our penitence evoked by the sight of Calvary, he says, 'but rather in what *God* did' (CoC, p. 9). So what did God do?

Providing his own summary of *The Cross of Christ* in his Preface, Dr Stott states that 'Evangelical Christians believe that in and through Christ crucified God substituted himself for us and bore our sins, dying in our place the death we deserved to die, in order that we might be restored to his favour and adopted into his family' (CoC, p. 7). And another Evangelical leader, Jim Packer, is quoted as having 'rightly written that this belief "is a distinguishing mark of the world-wide evangelical fraternity"' since 'it takes us to the very heart of the Christian gospel' (CoC, p. 7). Dr Packer's teaching is set out in chapter 18 of his book, *Knowing God*. The chapter is called 'The Heart of the Gospel'.

## The Heart of the Gospel?

This restatement of Evangelical belief seems to me a great improvement both on the theory that 'God punished Jesus' and on the theory that what matters is our response. How right Dr Stott is to say that this is God's action, God's cross in our world, the cross on which the Father loves and suffers in the love and the suffering of the Son! But my question is whether even this improvement is 'the' meaning of the atonement, to the exclusion of all other attempts to explain the self-sacrifice of Christ.

One reason why I ask is that, like Dr Stott himself, I am sure that 'a full-scale atonement doctrine' is missing from 'the apostolic preaching' (CoC, p. 34). Dr Stott wisely says that 'beyond the images of the atonement lies the mystery of the atonement, the deep wonders of which, I guess, we shall be exploring throughout eternity' (CoC, p. 168). What takes place on Calvary is nothing less than the supreme meeting between God in his holiness and man in his sin. No possible formula in human words could be an adequate account.

Teachers of the Church all seeking to be loyal expositors of the New Testament have reached no complete agreement, for the situation in the New Testament is accurately described by Frances Young: 'We find no rationale or explanation of how Christ's blood could purify sin, nor was an explanation sought after' (*Sacrifice and the Death of Christ*, p. 73). At the end of the most sublime and most sustained piece of theology that he ever wrote, the greatest of all Christian theologians exclaimed to the Romans (11:33–34):

Oh, the depth of the riches of the wisdom and knowledge of
  God!
How unsearchable his judgments,
and his paths beyond tracing out!
Who has known the mind of the Lord?
Or who has been his counsellor?

No council of the undivided Church stated 'the' Catholic,
orthodox doctrine of the atonement. None of the fathers of
the early Church wrote a book on the subject that we know
about; we have no ancient equivalent of Dr Stott's *The Cross
of Christ*. The nearest equivalent was written by Athanasius
in about 315, but it contains no full theory of the atonement
and is traditionally referred to as a book on *The Incarnation of
the Word*. Athanasius taught that the law of God was that all
men, having sinned in and since Adam, must die. The
power of this law was 'fully spent in the Lord's body', but
he did not explain this in any detail. He freely referred to
the fragments of other explanations outlined in the New
Testament, as when he declared that

> the Word of the Father was both able to re-create everything
> and worthy to suffer on behalf of all and to be ambassador for
> all with the Father . . . He offered his sacrifice on behalf of all,
> yielding his temple to death in the place of all, in order firstly to
> make men quit and free of their own trespass and further to
> show himself more powerful even than death, displaying his
> own body incorruptible as first fruits of the resurrection of all.

Yet in spite of the richness of this collection of theories, he
reached no clear conclusion: 'it is better not to aim at
speaking of the whole where one cannot do justice even to a
part' (7,20,54).

About the truth that the atonement achieved by Christ's
self-sacrifice is a mystery which should not be reduced to a
formula, all thoughtful Christians are at one. But it is of
course tempting for convinced Christians to express their
convictions in a manner which may suggest that they have
temporarily forgotten that all theories including their own

must be inadequate. Conscious of my own temptations, I ask whether Dr Stott has always resisted his.

Another reason why I question the adequacy of his teaching is that the theory which he expounds is not one which is the plain teaching of the Bible as the Bible can be read by the plain man. I regret that in *The Cross of Christ* Dr Stott, who has been found by many to be a warmly sympathetic pastor, shows little sympathy with attempts to communicate at least something of what the Bible does say to the many people who would find his own theory difficult and even unintelligible. There are passages in this book which I find hard to reconcile with his approach at, for example, the National Evangelical Anglican Congress at Nottingham in 1977. In his *Evangelicals Tomorrow* (1977, p. 40), John Capon recorded that Dr Stott caused some alarm among conservatives. 'Although in himself Christ does not and could not change, we change and the world changes; and therefore the Christ whom we perceive and whom the world needs is bound to change also.' Questioned about this statement which he admitted was phrased 'slightly loosely', he explained: 'In my own ministry I tend to present Christ as Liberator or as one in whom authentic love and humanness are found. Both these understandings of Christ are a response to the current age.' There speaks, as we should expect, the voice of a Christian who wants to communicate.

In *The Cross of Christ*, however, the tone sometimes seems harsher. He says that to honour Jesus as teacher instead of as Lord is to honour him 'for the wrong reason' (CoC, p. 51); that Jesus 'did not die as a martyr' (CoC, p. 60); that 'it is not only anomalous, but actually impossible, to associate our sacrifices with his, or even to think of asking him to draw ours up into his' (CoC, p. 271); that the message that the Holy Spirit can bring 'into focus in Jesus Christ a shape already glimpsed in human experience' – the shape of pain and joy, suffering and security, betrayal and love, winter and spring – 'is not the gospel of the New Testament' (CoC, p. 325). And I have to say that when he writes in this

dismissive manner he is being more 'biblical' than the Bible
– an extraordinary charge for a liberal like me to make, as I
admit.

'Teacher' is an inadequate title for Jesus but Dr Stott has
himself observed that it expresses a 'fundamental reality'
(CtC, p. 209). 'Martyr' is also not enough, but 'greater love
has no-one than this, that he lay down his life for his
friends' (John 15:13). A scholarly introduction to *Pauline
Christianity*, by John Ziesler (1983), notes that while Paul
'never says that the cross was necessary to turn away God's
anger' it is increasingly being suggested that what he *did*
say 'owed a good deal . . . to the idea of the righteous
martyr whose death was believed to have a cleansing effect.'
And 'Paul's major contribution to the theology of the cross
and resurrection is that believers participate in them' (pp.
88–90). Paul wrote to the Philippians about 'the fellowship
of sharing in his sufferings' (3:10) and the letter to the
Colossians even includes the bold idea that something was
lacking in the sufferings of Christ which Christians can 'fill
up' (1:24). The first letter of Peter tells Christians to 'rejoice
that you participate in the sufferings of Christ' (4:13). And
some 'fellowship' with him, however limited, can surely be
experienced by non-Christians. John, the most exclusive of
all the early Christian theologians, was sure that 'the true
light . . . gives light to every man' (1:9), while Acts presents
Paul as building on pagan knowledge or half-knowledge of
that light, in his speech in Athens (17:16–31). Indeed,
unless the Holy Spirit can bring into focus 'a shape already
glimpsed' outside the Bible and the Church, no appeal to
common ground is possible and therefore no evangelism
can be persuasive.

I find it sad that in *The Cross of Christ* so little attention is
given to those who want, as a preliminary to a convincing
account of the work of Christ, some serious reckoning with
scientific and historical knowledge of the human situation.
It seems to be a vital part of Dr Stott's theory that 'Jesus
Christ, who being sinless had no need to die, died our
death, the death our sins had deserved' (CoC, p. 65). This

idea, we are told, follows from the view taken in 'the Bible everywhere' that death is not a *natural* but a *penal* event, not part of God's 'original intention for humankind . . . God seems to have intended for his human image-bearers a more noble end, akin perhaps to the "translation" which Enoch and Elijah experienced, and to the "transformation" which will take place in those who are alive when Jesus comes' (CoC, p. 65). The doctrine that 'the wages of sin is death' because of Adam's fall was certainly held and taught by Paul (Romans 5:12–14; 6:23) and by many of his Jewish contemporaries. And there were many roughly similar doctrines in this field. Although no mention is made of Adam, the book called *The Wisdom of Solomon* (probably written by an Alexandrian Jew in the first century BC) declares that 'God created man for immortality, and made him the image of his own eternal self; it was the devil's spite that brought death into the world, and the experience of it is reserved for those who take his side' (Wisdom 2:23–24 NEB). But the implication there seems to be that the devil caused those on his side to die eternally, while the righteous only seem to die when they die physically. We are told that 'the souls of the just are in God's hand' although 'in the eyes of foolish men they seemed to be dead' (3:1–2). This passage illustrates the variety of meanings which could be given by Jews of Paul's time to the idea that the devil introduces death. The less precise cluster of thoughts that everyone is a sinner, that everyone dies, and that everyone deserves to die in God's sight, was widespread. But the direct link between Adam's fall and all humanity's physical or spiritual deaths is rare. It is not included in the recorded teaching of Jesus and it occurs only once in the Old Testament, in the story of God's curse in the Garden of Eden (Genesis 3:19).

In Genesis (chapter 5) it is said that Adam lived 930 years and that even Enoch, whom God 'took away', was 365 years old – which scarcely suggests a consistent tradition that the patriarchs' lives were cut short. Indeed, the reduction of the human lifespan to a mere 120 years is said in

Genesis to have been punishment for intercourse between bad angels and the beautiful daughters of men (6:1–4). And even within the story of Adam and Eve there are traces of a variety of traditions. 'The tree of the knowledge of good and evil' (2:17) is, as the commentaries show, a tree in whose branches many theorists have built their nests. Probably it is a symbol of the end of innocence with the knowledge of the difference between good and evil. If so, it seems to be implied that the previous obedience to God's command not to touch it was automatic rather than saintly, because 'good' and 'evil' were alike unknown. One consequence of eating this forbidden fruit is the knowledge of good and evil in sexuality – which may be regarded as moral progress rather than as 'the fall'. (If Adam and Eve had had children through shameless sex, would it have been God's will for the sex lives of their children to be shameless? Would incest, for example, have been approved?) And the punishment decreed for the trespass is not only death understood as a return to 'dust' but also a variety of phenomena – the facts that snakes crawl on their bellies and are sometimes poisonous, their appearance of eating dust, pain in childbirth, female heterosexuality, male dominance, the painful toil of tilling the fields in order to eat. But I understand that not many 'Bible believers' have recently blamed all these phenomena on Adam and Eve.

Most people who are able to put such stories in the context of other ancient literature think it obvious that the sagas of Adam and Enoch are mythological and should not be relied on as accurate history. Why, then, should we not be at liberty to regard the whole notion of death as a punishment either for Adam's fall, or for sin in general, as one tradition in the developing Jewish culture which Paul inherited and used but which is not compulsory for us? Dr Stott can write that 'God himself' spoke to the serpent in the garden of Eden (CoC, p. 231) and forbade Noah to eat meat with the blood still in it (CoC, p. 138), but he may not intend these references to mean more than that he is quoting these

Hebrew myths. Certainly many Christians are among those who do not want any account of the human situation to depend on taking ancient myths as straightforward history. 'The fossil record indicates that predation and death existed in the animal kingdom before the creation of man,' as Dr Stott notes (CoC, p. 65), and we have no sound reason to believe that death has been anything other than natural since man's emergence in evolution. All biology says that life is impossible without it. This is 'the way of all the earth' (1 Kings 2:2). It must therefore seem unlikely that Jesus was punished on the cross by being deprived of his exemption from the human lot of death.

However, we can readily understand why the fact that to be human is to be mortal is so often regarded as a tragedy; why Paul's first letter to Corinth proclaims the vision that 'the last enemy to be destroyed is death' (15:26). Death's ignoble reality is obviously alien to man's hopes, specially when it comes painfully or by violence or accident, or by a disease which strikes an innocent person who is not old. None of us needs to be told that. This profound and universal emotion rebelling against the dominion of death has been the theme of poetry without end. It was expressed in the great Genesis myth associating mortality with alienation from the Creator and from paradise. Indeed, because death is so commonly dreaded and hated, as something always inescapable but often evil, in the Bible as in all other records which reflect human experience, it is startling to read in *The Cross of Christ*, without discussion, that throughout Egypt before the exodus of Israel the first-born son in each house was spared by God 'only if a lamb was slain in its place' (CoC, p. 72).

I can see why Dr Stott takes that story (Exodus 12:29–31) literally. Not only does he wish, in principle, to treat historical statements in the Old Testament as factual. He is also, of course, acutely aware of the 'Lamb of God' passages in the New Testament. John's gospel gives us the famous exclamation by the Baptist about Jesus: 'Look, the Lamb of God, who takes away the sin of the world!' (1:29). There are twenty-six references to Jesus as 'the Lamb' in the Revelation of John. Jesus was crucified at Passover time; the Last Supper was in some sense a Passover meal; the exodus of Israel from Egypt was recalled very solemnly at Passover when a lamb was eaten; and the crucifixion and resurrection of Jesus have often been compared with the exodus. Paul's first letter to Corinth, for example, announced that 'Christ, our Passover lamb, has been sacrificed' (5:7). In his own recorded teaching, however, Jesus never spoke of himself as the Lamb and no mention of eating a lamb is included in any narrative of the Last Supper although almost certainly one was the centrepiece of the meal. If we are to go by the recorded self-understanding of Jesus, we have no need to insist that he was slain like a lamb in order to avert God's wrath. And if we are to accept the picture of God given in the teaching of Jesus, we have no right to assert that God really killed all the first-born sons throughout Egypt except where he saw that a lamb had been killed. The God who is proclaimed by the Bible taken as a whole is not a God who is a butcher like Pharaoh (who orders all Hebrew boys to be thrown into the Nile immediately after birth at Exodus 1:22), or like Herod, who arouses horror because he massacres the male infants of just one village (Matthew 2:16–18). He is the God of mercy, the God who can be heard to bless 'Egypt my people' (Isaiah 19:25).

In *The Cross of Christ* John Stott insists that as he was dying Jesus was 'absolutely alone, being now also God-forsaken', for

. . . an actual and dreadful separation took place between the Father and the Son; it was voluntarily accepted by both the Father and the Son; it was due to our sins and their just reward; and Jesus expressed this horror of great darkness, this God-forsakenness, by quoting the only verse of Scripture which accurately described it, and which he had perfectly fulfilled, namely, 'My God, my God, why have you forsaken me?'. (CoC, p. 81)

*Basic Christianity* tells us that 'God turned away his face . . .
Our sins sent Christ to hell. He tasted the torment of a soul
estranged from God' (BC1, p. 93). Accordingly Dr Stott
rejects explanations of that quotation of Psalm 22:1 which to
him are not 'simple and straightforward'. We are told that it
cannot have been a cry of anger, unbelief or despair by one
who imagined that he was forsaken when actually he was
not. To suggest that is 'denying the moral perfection of the
character of Jesus'. It cannot have been a cry of loneliness,
for 'the words of Psalm 22:1 express an expression of *being*,
and not just *feeling*, God-forsaken'. And it is 'far-fetched' to
interpret it as a cry of victory. Admittedly Psalm 22 does
end with 'great confidence, and even triumph' – but 'why
should Jesus have quoted from the Psalm's beginning if in
reality he was alluding to its end?' So Dr Stott asks, being
convinced that the Father abandoned the Son.

I am one of the innumerable Bible students and preachers
who have found it difficult to expound – or to understand –
the meaning of these terrible words. But I want to plead that
John Stott's explanation is not the only one that is possible. I
do not think that Jesus was 'in hell' in the sense indicated
when it is said that God had turned away his face from him,
for I do not believe that the God revealed by Jesus would
keep anyone 'in hell' who cried to him not with a curse but
with a prayer: 'My God, my God . . .' And I do not think
that devout Christians need reject the idea that Jesus felt
emotions which were somewhat like the fears which many
people have when approaching death, particularly death in
agony and defeat. Dr Stott, commenting on the anguish of
Jesus in the garden of Gethsemane, is convinced that the
cup from which he shrank was 'the spiritual agony of
enduring the divine judgement which the sins of the world
deserved'. He finds it 'ludicrous to suppose that he was
now afraid of pain, insult and death' (CoC, pp. 74–6). He
refers to Socrates, who died 'without fear, sorrow or protest', and to the Christian martyrs for whom pain and
rejection were 'a joy and a privilege, not an ordeal to be
shrunk from in dismay'. He asks: 'So was Socrates braver

than Jesus?' Here is loyalty to Jesus, but if I may say so it seems to be misplaced. Dr Stott himself quotes Samuel Johnson: 'No rational man can die without uneasy apprehension' (CoC, p. 243). There is much evidence that many Christians have felt anger, unbelief, despair, utter loneliness and panic when suffering acutely and when about to die. It seems possible that the historical Socrates did; the account of his death to which Dr Stott refers is a piece of fine literature by Plato, a disciple more interested in philosophy than in history. So far as we know, however, most martyrs and other Christians under great stress have conquered their fears (as Dr Johnson finally did), relying on God's grace received through prayer. The author of Psalm 22 did – and Jesus, although he quoted only the first verse of that psalm, prayed to 'my God, my God'. He *felt* forsaken by the Father – but whether he really was forsaken, he did not know at that moment. Deliberately identifying himself with a psalmist, he entered fully the human darkness.

The cry of dereliction is nowhere explained in the New Testament. The earliest of the gospels gives it as the only cry from the cross, the last words from the central figure in the gospel about 'Jesus Christ, the Son of God' (Mark 1:1) – and the reader is not offered an explanation why the centurion who 'heard his cry and saw how he died' said: 'Surely this man was the Son of God!' (15:39). It may be that many of the early Christians refused even to attempt to explain the mystery of the death of Christ, 'because they were afraid' (Mark 16:8). But presumably the writer to the Hebrews had Gethsemane in mind, if not this cry from the cross, when he taught that 'during the days of Jesus' life on earth, he offered up prayers and petitions with loud cries and tears to the one who could save him from death, and he was heard because of his reverent submission. Although he was a son, he learned obedience from what he suffered' (5:7–8). And since on the cross Jesus was supremely obedient, the simple and straightforward conclusion from what the New Testament as a whole says about God is that Jesus when dying in agony because he did the Father's will was *not* forsaken by the Father. In the seventeenth century Blaise Pascal absorbed part of the truth of Calvary when in his distress he heard the silent voice of God: 'Be comforted. You would not seek me if you had not already found me.' Hans Küng seems to me to sum up the thinking – and, far more important, the experience – of countless Christians when he writes: 'Suffering too is encompassed by God; suffering too, even though it seems like being forsaken by God, can become the point of encounter with God. The believer knows no way to avoid suffering, but he knows a way through it' (*On Being a Christian*, in English 1978, p. 434).

Of course I believe that it is not enough to say that Jesus was a man who in his agony felt God-forsaken. I am one of those who believe that the divine 'Word became flesh and made his dwelling among us' (John 1:14). That is why I believe that the cross of Jesus shows the suffering love of the Father. But I am also one of those who are extremely hesitant when offered speculations about the relationships of Father, Son, and Spirit, a subject beyond human understanding, and I console myself with the fact that the New Testament itself is very reticent. As Dr Stott observes, for the practical purposes of the average Christian who is not a speculative theologian

> it would be wiser . . . to say what the New Testament authors said, faithfully echoed by the Apostles' Creed, namely that he who 'was conceived by the Holy Spirit, born of the Virgin Mary, suffered under Pontius Pilate, was crucified, dead and was buried' was not 'God', still less the Father, but 'Jesus Christ, his only Son, our Lord'. (CoC, p. 156)

So I ask whether it is 'the' necessary meaning of the atonement that 'in and through Christ crucified God substituted himself for us and bore our sins' and 'took his own loving initiative to appease his own righteous anger by bearing it his own self in his own Son when he took our place and died for us' (CoC, p. 175). What do the Scriptures say? I cannot find Dr Stott's theory taught plainly anywhere in them. If it is 'the heart of gospel', is it not extremely strange that it is not mentioned in any of the gospels?

Mark (10:45) gives a saying of Jesus: 'For even the Son of Man did not come to be served, but to serve, and to give his life as a ransom [in Greek *lutron*] for many.' Scholars are generally agreed that 'for many' (in Greek *anti pollon*) was a Jewish way of saying 'for all'. In the New Testament the death of Christ is elsewhere referred to as being 'on behalf of' (in Greek *huper*) and not 'instead of' (in Greek *anti*) sinners, so that this teaching which means that Jesus must die 'instead of all' is specially significant. 'Ransom' is not always used in the Bible to refer to the payment of a price. The Lord did not pay Pharaoh a price when he 'ransomed' Israel from Egypt (Exodus 6:6) and no price is expected when a new exodus is predicted (Isaiah 35:9; 41:14; 43:1, 14). When Luke's gospel speaks about the ransoming of Israel by Jesus (1:68; 2:38; 24:21), probably 'liberation' is intended in a general sense. But I accept the conclusion of most scholars that at Mark 10:45 (as at 1 Timothy 2:6; Titus 2:14; 1 Peter 1:18) the price of a death is implied, as a substitute for the continuing imprisonment or enslavement of 'many'. That is not a difficult idea, provided that we do not ask to whom the payment was due. In the world of Jesus and his early followers the freedom of slaves or captives was often purchased either by themselves or by well wishers. Jewish literature then of recent date referred to the Maccabean martyrs' lives being 'ransoms' for others. Greek and Roman literature said much the same about the martyrdoms of other heroes who died 'for' their cities or families. But the ransom idea is not developed by Mark or in any other gospel. In this passage it is given as the explanation of a practical command: 'Whoever wants to become great among you must be your servant' (10:43). No doubt Mark regarded the value of the ransom paid by Jesus in his death as utterly unique, but in the same passage he reported Jesus as saying to James and John: 'You will drink the cup I drink' (10:39). The implication seems to be clear.

This is the cup of human suffering, known to include a martyr's death in the case of James. The suffering which the followers of Jesus must undergo is not wholly unlike the cross of their Lord. As Paul reminded the Corinthians in his second letter, 'the sufferings of Christ flow over into our lives' (1:5).

So Jesus drank his cup of suffering and death in order that 'many' or all might go free. It was literally true at once, for the execution of Jesus was reckoned to be enough by Pontius Pilate and none of the disciples was killed or, we are told, even arrested. The spiritual meaning is also obvious and no Christian who feels liberated by Jesus can be surprised that words which include the idea of a ransom (for example, Paul's word *apolutrosis*, 'redemption') are used nine times in the New Testament. But the idea is of limited relevance to the cross of Christ and Dr Stott seems to acknowledge this limitation when he makes the valid and very important point that 'the New Testament never presses the imagery to the point of indicating to whom the ransom is paid' (CoC, p. 179). Christian theologians ought never to have taught that the ransom was paid either to the devil or to God. That cannot be the meaning of Christ's self-sacrifice.

Mark also tells us that at his last supper with his disciples Jesus took the cup and said: 'This is my blood of the covenant, which is poured out for many' (14:24). The background in the Hebrew Scriptures is further hinted at when Jesus is said to have declared that 'the Son of Man will go just as it is written about him' (Mark 14:21). Paul's first letter to Corinth, which is earlier, gives fewer words: 'This cup is the new covenant in my blood' (11:25). But Matthew's gospel slightly expands Mark's: 'This is my blood of the covenant, which is poured out for many for the forgiveness of sins' (26:28). Matthew is here attributing to Jesus the only saying in the gospels which directly connects the death of Jesus with the forgiveness of sins. Many scholars, noticing these differences, believe that some (at least) of these words do not exactly record what Jesus said but reflect the Church's thought about what he did. I share this belief but see no good reason why the historical Jesus should not have regarded his life, culminating in his death and vindication, as the inauguration of a new covenant or agreement between God and his people, making them 'at one' again, as prophesied by Jeremiah (31:31–34). Nor would there be anything strange in the belief that Jesus could not accomplish his reconciling work without sacrificing his life. That self-sacrifice could be compared with the sacrifice of young bulls killed by the young men on behalf of Moses at the inauguration of an earlier covenant (Exodus 24). But these passages do not explain *why* the sacrifice was necessary and *why* the blood had to be shed. Here is no theory of the atonement.

Those who regard the cross as the payment of a penalty due to God or the acceptance of a punishment by God – either in the senses which Dr Stott rejects, or in the way which he expounds – are right to ask the rest of us to consider seriously the Song of the Suffering Servant in the book of Isaiah (52:13–53:12).

This passage is often quoted in the New Testament outside the gospels, although not every reference to God's 'servant' need refer to this particular passage, and it is almost certain that it was the main Scripture in the minds of those who formulated the gospel which Paul repeated in his first letter to Corinth. 'What I received I passed on to you as of first importance: that Christ died for our sins according to the Scriptures . . .' (15:3). The Song of the Suffering Servant says that this 'man of sorrows' who *was* (it does not lie in the future) despised, rejected, pierced and killed 'poured out his life unto death, and was numbered with the transgressors. For he bore the sins of many, and made intercession for the transgressors' (Isaiah 53:12). Almost certainly this passage was in the minds of Mark and Matthew as they reported the tradition that Jesus said at his last supper that his life was to be 'poured out for many'. I see no good reason why it should not have been in the mind of Jesus. But it does not seem to follow that the passage in its entirety was central to his self-understanding. On the contrary, 'we can say with confidence that it appears only on the margin of the synoptic tradition' – or so C. K. Barrett declared (*Jesus and the Gospel Tradition*, 1967, p. 41).

Jesus seems to have referred to himself as the Son of Man, not as the Servant of the Lord (which seems to have been an early Christian title for him, as in Acts 3:13; 4:30). His recorded teaching includes only one direct quotation from the Song of the Servant. 'He was numbered with the transgressors' is quoted in Luke's gospel (22:37) in comment on the carrying of swords by the disciples, but Luke does not quote 'poured out for many' in his account of the Last Supper. Luke also does not say 'a ransom for many' in his equivalent of Mark 10:45; and in his account of the study of the Song of the Suffering Servant by the Ethiopian eunuch in Acts 8:32–33 he does not quote any of the verses about an atoning sacrifice. If Jesus was reserved in his use of the Song, the explanation is not difficult. An intensely moving poem, inspired by deep emotion about deep suffering, it is the clearest vision in the Hebrew Scriptures of the way of the cross, through suffering to glory. It begins from the fact of a martyrdom. Because innocent martyrs sacrificed their lives they were often regarded in the ancient world, Jewish or Gentile, as 'making atonement' for the sins of others, turning away the wrath of God or the gods. The Song says that the servant of the Lord 'was led like a lamb to the slaughter' (Isaiah 53:7); that 'the Lord has laid on him the inquity of us all' (verse 6); that 'it was the Lord's will to crush him and cause him to suffer' (verse 10); that 'the Lord makes his life a guilt offering' (verse 10). It is not clear, however, whether this suffering servant is an anonymous individual or is the embodiment of the sufferings of the Jewish people. Nor is it clear what will reward this sacrifice. 'He will sprinkle many nations' (52:15) is a translation now generally abandoned by scholars. 'He will see his offspring and prolong his days' (53:10) is hard to interpret since the servant was killed. That he will be given 'a portion among the great' (53:12) is modest. The people who sing this Song are converted as they see the servant's reward after his suffering, but no systematic theology is worked out there or in any Jewish comment on the poetry. And it is hard to see how *all* the ideas in the Song could be pursued systematically without damaging the highest ideas about God taught in the Hebrew Scriptures. The Hebrew consonantal text of verse 10 reads: 'Yahweh was pleased to crush him the sickness.' Already when the Greek translation (the Septuagint) was made, devout Jews felt morally compelled to translate this as: 'The Lord was pleased to cleanse him from sickness.' Nor is this the only difficulty in making calm, rational and moral 'sense' of the turbulent poetry. That the Song of the Suffering Servant has often seemed mysterious is attested by the number of places where the text is a problem, suggesting that copyists made well-intentioned corrections. There is a large literature commenting on the many obscurities and M. D. Hooker's *Jesus and the Servant* (1959) pointed out the New Testament problems.

In the rest of the New Testament we find definite or possible references to the Song but these do not necessarily mean that every word in that passage is taken literally and applied to Jesus. In his gospel, when Matthew has reported that Jesus healed all the sick he quotes from the Song, 'he took up our infirmities and carried our diseases' (8:17). But he does not mean that Jesus was infirm or diseased; he is speaking poetically about a general identification with the sick. Daring new thoughts are mentioned, rather than developed systematically, as Christians meditated on the horror of the death which their Lord had accepted for their sakes. Thus Paul told the Galatians (3:13) that Christ became a 'curse' on our behalf, quoting Deuteronomy 21:23 ('anyone who is hung on a tree is under God's curse'). His second letter to Corinth (5:21) said that 'God made him who had no sin to be sin for us'. However, he did not pause to explain what he meant by such startling expressions. The most likely explanation seems to be that he marvelled that Christ so identified himself with sinful humanity that he consented to be executed as if he had been an accursed sinner. But as D. E. H. Whiteley judiciously observed in his text book on *The Theology of St Paul* (1974, p. 136), 'it is too easy to read this verse in the light of whatever theory we may hold'.

A Greek noun for which the traditional English translation was 'propitiation' (*hilasterion*) was used about Christ's sacrifice in Paul's letter to the Romans (3:25). The corresponding verb (*hilaskesthai*) comes in the letter to Hebrews (2:17). A closely similar noun (*hilasmos*) was used twice in the first letter of John (2:2; 4:10). Such nouns may mean no more than 'place' or 'means' of atonement, since in the only other use of *hilasterion* in the New Testament the word clearly refers not to any particular sacrifice but to the 'mercy seat', the cover of the Ark of the Covenant, on which sacrifices were offered in the Jerusalem temple (Hebrews 9:5). The verb may mean 'to expiate' – that is to deal with sin, to wipe out its guilt and to remove its pollution, not necessarily 'to propitiate', which means 'to appease God'. But these words probably would have reminded those being addressed of the propitiatory sacrifices which, it was hoped, removed the divine wrath, for such sacrifices were familiar to pagans and (to a much lesser extent) to Jews. I acknowledge the truth of this point made by Dr Leon Morris among others. However, 'propitiation' is related to Christ only once by Paul and only by very brief references in two other documents. That seems significant because the word is dangerous. It can suggest that the anger of God can be ended, or his justice influenced, by the gift of an animal or a human being whether or not there is a repentance for sin. As Dr Stott stresses, in the Old Testament the sacrifices were not thought of as magically compelling God to forgive. They 'did not make God gracious; they were provided by a gracious God in order that he might act graciously towards a sinful people. And this truth is yet more plainly recognised in the New Testament' (CoC, p. 174). It is in order to guard against the danger of a less than biblical view of God that Dr Stott so emphatically teaches that the sacrifice of Calvary was not only provided but actually made by the Father. If this sacrifice is thought to propitiate the wrath of the Father who is often referred to simply as 'God', Christians have to guard against some highly misleading ideas.

The letter to Hebrews – the New Testament document which is fullest on the idea of sacrifice – never says that the sacrifice of Calvary is made by God in order to propitiate his own wrath. Its teaching is that the Son of God, although 'the radiance of God's glory and the exact representation of his being' (1:3), was a man, 'not ashamed to call [men] brothers' (2:11). Summoned by God, he became 'a merciful and faithful high priest in service to God', in order that 'he might make atonement for the sins of the people' (2:17). 'He sacrificed for their sins once for all when he offered himself' (7:27) and his blood will 'cleanse our consciences from acts that lead to death, so that we may serve the living God' (9:14). He 'died as a ransom to set them free from sins committed under the first covenant' (9:15). He is thought of as saying to God: 'a body you prepared for me . . . Here I am . . . I have come to do your will' (10:5,7 – which is a quotation from the Greek version of Psalm 40). The teaching is that men's consciences and actions needed to be cleansed and changed – exactly how is not said. Here the author is deficient in comparison with Paul. He is so unclear about the nature of God's forgiveness that in chapter 6 he advances a theory, which the Church rejected, that sins after baptism cannot be forgiven. He dwells on the Day of Atonement because then the Jewish high priest purified the inner sanctuary, the Holy of Holies, in the temple by sprinkling the blood of the sacrificed goat, but he does not mention the other goat in this ritual, the scapegoat. This was driven away into the wilderness, being thought to 'bear' the sins of the people committed during the past year, and it was compared with Christ in the second-century letter of Barnabas and in much subsequent theology and devotion. The important point for us at the moment is that in the letter to Hebrews there is no full atonement theory. It is never mentioned that God's wrath needed to be satisfied or that God himself made the propitiatory sacrifice. What is affirmed is that God's will needed to be done. It was done by the Son of God who as a man had 'learned' perfect obedience. He, the perfect high priest, provided the perfect sacrifice. And in this letter, the idea of 'sacrifice' seems to remain as richly varied in meaning as it is in the Old Testament itself.

Is Dr Stott's theory necessarily implied in the first letter of Peter when in a possible translation (in the New International Version, for example) it is said that Christ 'bore our sins in his body on the tree' (2:24)? In the Old Testament, as Dr Stott points out, 'to "bear sin" means specifically to endure its penal consequences, to undergo its penalty' (CoC, p. 143). He is also right to note in this passage a reference to the Song of the Suffering Servant ('by his wounds you have been healed'). But the passage may also be translated 'he carried our sins to the gibbet' (as in the New English Bible) – and as Dr Stott observes, 'the references to the cross in Peter's first epistle are asides' since here again the concern is 'more ethical than doctrinal' (BC1, p. 87). The emphasis is, indeed, that Christ suffered, 'leaving you an example, that you should follow in his steps . . . so that we might die to sins and live to righteousness' (2:21,24). Certainly there is a comparison between Christ's death and the sacrifices in the temple. Sinners were 'redeemed from the empty way of life . . . with the precious blood of Christ, a lamb without blemish or defect' (1:18–19). But these asides may well mean no more than that Christ was killed as if he had been a sinner. Certainly when this letter says that 'Christ died for sins once for all, the righteous for the unrighteous, to bring you to God' (3:18), it does not add that in consequence 'we enjoy the righteous status which God has conferred on us' – which is for Dr Stott 'the true meaning of justification (CoC, p. 185). It says that 'God's elect' are 'shielded by God's power until the coming of the salvation that is ready to be revealed in the last time' (1:1,5). It says, 'you call on a Father who judges each man's work impartially' (1:17). It urges, 'above all, love each other deeply, because love covers over a multitude of sins' (4:8). It warns, 'it is time for judgment to begin with the family of God' (4:17). So this letter does not teach the theory that Christians can be forgiven because Christ, or God himself, has already endured the just penalty of sin.

The idea of the wrath of God – or 'the wrath', not explicitly stating its divine origin – is biblical. We are told that it can be found in the Old Testament more than 580 times. It is also found in the teaching of Jesus, although the idea is not expounded systematically; it is expressed by pictures of human anger in the parables and by very solemn warnings to repent. An unforgettable example is: 'Fear him who, after killing the body, has power to throw you into hell. Yes, I tell you, fear him' (Luke 12:5). But in his teaching Jesus does not clearly promise that God's wrath will be appeased by his death. His parables leave the warning without detailed explanation. An example is the parable about the unmerciful servant: 'In anger his master turned him over to the jailers to be tortured, until he should pay back all he owed. This is how my heavenly Father will treat each of you unless you forgive your brother from your heart' (Matthew 18:34–5). Here no explanation is offered about how the servant can be expected to accumulate a fortune in order to repay his debt while being tortured in prison. The torture is a touch in the story-teller's art.

In the third century the great theologian Origen devoted a great deal of attention to the purification of this idea in the light of Christ and since then many similar efforts have seemed necessary. For generation after generation of thoughtful Christians it has been vital to 'consider . . . the kindness *and* sternness of God' (Romans 11:22) – and to remember that the sternness arises out of the kindness, as it usually does in a human parent. As Dr Stott repeatedly stresses, God's love, not his anger, must be the controlling idea. It is characteristic of the New Testament that the first letter of John mentions 'propitiation' in the context of a great emphasis on God's love (4:10). And it deserves notice that in John's gospel the Greek words translated as 'forgiveness' and 'forgive' do not occur except in the promise to the apostles that 'if you forgive anyone his sins, they are forgiven' (20:23) – so little is John preoccupied by the need to find forgiveness in order to escape wrath.

Some theologians (C. H. Dodd was among them) have sought to reduce the dangers in the idea of the wrath of God. They have explained that the 'wrath' is not God's personal anger but a more mechanical process, the inevitable and inescapable working out of the consequences of sin. Up to a point, this seems a helpful explanation – for the tragic consequences of human choices of evil must often be taken very seriously indeed, while the picture of an angry God can be ridiculed. The process by which evil steadily leads to disaster surely *is* impersonal. But Dr Stott is, I believe, right to teach that the 'wrath of the Lamb' (Revelation 6:16) is also personal. For God deals with sin personally. Countless sinners have felt that God's forgiveness of that sin is personal. They would say, too, that his condemnation of it is personal. For they have felt that sin is a personal affront to God, as in Psalm 51:4 –

> Against you, you only, have I sinned
> and done what is evil in your sight,
> so that you are proved right when you speak
> and justified when you judge.

There is an element of truth in the dangerous idea of personally appeasing the personal 'wrath of God'. This can be learned by the bitter experience of a disrupted human relationship. A lover, husband, wife, parent, child or friend may grieve that a very precious relationship has been broken by someone else and may be unable to restore the relationship unless that person removes the barrier by admitting what was wrong – for a relationship is a two-way traffic. No doubt every human being is up to a point in the wrong, so that one sinner should never condemn another; but there remains a difference between right and wrong.

One person may be more in the wrong than another; that person may guiltily know it deep down; that person may hold up the traffic of the relationship until the fault is acknowledged; and if the acknowledgement is ever made, that guilty person may rightly think of it as pleasing or even 'appeasing' or 'satisfying' the one who has been wronged. If this can be true of a human relationship between two sinners, how much more may a repentant sinner feel that it is true of a relationship with the God who is 'holy, holy, holy'! A deeply penitent sinner knows what the New Testament is talking about, as when the letter to the Colossians says: 'Once you were alienated from God and were enemies in your minds because of your evil behaviour. But now he has reconciled you by Christ's physical body through death to present you holy in his sight' (1:21–2). Our hostility to God was such that we thought he was our enemy and we could not see that he was our friend, until the dying Christ reconciled us to his Father. This profound experience is at the heart of Evangelicalism as of many other forms of Christianity. Out of it Dr Stott wrote *The Cross of Christ*. I want to make it completely clear that I am not disputing his right to express his experience in his own way. What I am respectfully questioning is his right to claim that he has expressed the 'heart of the gospel' which all his fellow-Christians ought to believe.

But I am aware that I have not yet reached the heart of *The Cross of Christ*, for as I understand it the heart is Dr Stott's conviction that the doctrine which he expounds is the teaching of Paul, which authoritatively expounds the significance of Jesus. And I also acknowledge that in his doctrine there *are* elements of Pauline thought. The scholars who have argued this are neither incompetent nor dishonest. But the plea which I shall submit is that the doctrine is not taught with anything like the clarity and centrality which would be necessary in order to make it compulsory for Christians.

Paul, unlike Jesus, was a professional theologian. Yet even he never explained exactly how God's wrath was ended: for him as for his Lord, the important question was spiritual and ethical, not theological. His use of *hilasterion* comes without discussion in a passage which has rightly been called 'one of the most obscure and difficult in the whole epistle' (Ernst Käsemann, *Commentary on Romans*, in English, 1980, p. 92), but the main thrust of his letter to the Romans (1:18–5:19) is clearer:

> The wrath of God is being revealed from heaven against all the godlessness and wickedness of men who suppress the truth by their wickedness . . . Therefore God gave them over in the sinful desires of their hearts to sexual impurity . . . Because of your stubbornness and your unrepentant heart, you are storing up wrath against yourself for the day of God's wrath . . . No-one will be declared righteous in his sight by observing the law . . . But God demonstrates his own love for us in this: While we were still sinners, Christ died for us. Since we have now been justified by his blood, how much more shall we be saved from God's wrath through him! . . . Through the obedience of the one man the many will be made righteous.

It is not said that God has satisfied his own wrath. What is said is that we 'will be saved' in the future and have already been declared righteous ('justified') by the fact that Christ died for us 'while we were yet sinners', thus demonstrating God's love for us. What interested Paul was not how to understand, but how to escape, the wrath of God.

He tells the Romans that God presented Jesus as a *hilasterion* in order 'to demonstrate his justice, because in his forbearance he had left the sins committed beforehand unpunished' (3:25). In its context this is a celebration of the mercy in God's justice, which already before the life and death of Jesus has left all the sins of the human race 'unpunished' although there has been 'no-one righteous, not even one' (3:10). Another celebration bursts out when Paul says that God sent his Son to deal with sin when the Law of Moses had failed. 'To be a sin offering' is a possible translation of Romans 8:3, as in the New International Version, but the New English Bible's vaguer 'as a sacrifice for sin' more accurately reflects the Greek. And when Paul moves to the climax of his argument, he still dwells on the mercy of God, which we must trust. Quoting Genesis 15:6, he says that the faith of Abraham 'was credited to him as righteousness' (4:3). He seems to mean that Abraham's trust in God's mercy enabled God both to treat him as if he had been righteous and to make him righteous. So Abraham became 'the father of all who believe but have not been circumcised' (4:11). Such Christians believe, Paul says, in Jesus who

> was delivered over to death for our sins and was raised to life for our justification.
> Therefore, since we have been justified through faith, we have peace with God through our Lord Jesus . . . While we were still sinners, Christ died for us.
> Since we have now been justified by his blood, how much more shall we be saved from God's wrath through him! (4:25; 5:1,8–9)

What Paul does *not* clearly say here should be noted. He does not clearly say what Evangelicals have often said. As Leon Morris has observed in his fine study of *The Apostolic Preaching of the Cross* (1965, p. 282), Paul 'never says in so many words that the righteousness of Christ is imputed to believers, and it may fairly be doubted whether he had this in mind in his treatment of justification'. Dr Morris adds that 'it may be held to be a corollary from his doctrine of the identification of the believer with Christ', but if the belief that Christ's righteousness is imputed to believing Christians only, resulting in their (and only in their) salvation, had been as central in Paul's gospel as has often been claimed, surely it would have been taught explicitly. Instead of offering a clear explanation, Paul hurries back to his theme of God's mercy. The Jews became disobedient in order that they might 'all' receive God's forgiving mercy together with the 'full number of the Gentiles'. This is an advance on earlier teaching as recorded in the first letter to the Thessalonians, where the Jews 'who killed the Lord

Jesus and prophets and also drove us out' are said to 'displease God' and to be 'hostile to all men', so that their sins are heaped up to the limit and 'the wrath of God has come upon them at last' (2:15–16). The mature Paul is not content with the idea that only a minority, the Christians to whom Christ's righteousness is imputed, can be saved.

In his final celebration of God's inexhaustibly faithful mercy as he 'justifies the ungodly', Paul echoes his Lord's proclamation of the Father's forgiveness. I regret that Leon Morris, who changed his mind on a number of points in response to criticisms, defended to the end the belief that Christ 'truly suffered to reconcile his Father to us' (the belief set out in the sixteenth century in the Augsburg Confession of Lutheranism and in Article II of the Church of England's Articles of Religion). Leon Morris claimed:

> It is certainly using language which goes beyond that of the New Testament. But it is not giving expression to teaching that is foreign to that of the New Testament. We cannot get a glimmering of an understanding of what the New Testament understands by Christ's atoning work unless we see that God is hostile to every evil thing and every evil person. (*The Atonement*, 1983, p. 138)

Here he seems to contradict Jesus. So does Dr Stott himself when he writes that 'the reason why wrath, revenge and retribution are forbidden us is not because they are themselves wrong reactions to evil, but because they are *God's* prerogative, not ours' (IFCT, p. 87). Of course Dr Stott refers to Paul's exhortation to 'leave room for God's wrath' since God will avenge (Romans 12:19). But that cannot be the end of the matter for a Christian. Whether or not Paul fully possesses the 'mind of Christ' in his own teaching at this point, the teaching of Jesus must take precedence over Paul.

According to the gospels Jesus repeatedly says that God the Father offers his forgiveness to all. Jesus shows this by his fellowship with tax-collectors, prostitutes and other 'sinners' at table as much as by any words. In none of the miracle stories is a demand for the confession of sins and penitence made before the healing act. We read, for example, that Jesus declared that a paralytic's sins were forgiven before that man had uttered a word (Mark 2:1–12). Here, as many scholars have commented, is a major difference between the teaching of Jesus and what was normally taught in the Judaism of that period. Of course the rabbis believed in the mercy of God: that was a central theme of the Hebrew Scriptures. But usually it was thought of as compassion and forgiveness *for the penitent*. According to Mark the climax of the confrontation of Jesus with his critics comes when he declares that all the sins and blasphemies of men will be forgiven them except continuation of the 'blasphemy against the Holy Spirit' which causes spiritual blindness and therefore the incapacity either to receive or to understand God's forgiveness. This blindness is shown when people call the healings performed by Jesus the work of an evil spirit (3:20–30). In saying that about Jesus, they are not merely criticising him. They are implying that he must be killed, for the Jewish religious law decreed that the man who says 'Let us follow other gods' after performing a miracle 'must be put to death' (Deuteronomy 13:1–5). The warning is about spiritual blindness that is utterly hostile to good and completely scornful of its appeal. Where people are not blind to that extent, the message of Jesus is the message that God forgives.

In Matthew's gospel we read that the Father is perfect and shows this by causing his sun to rise on the evil as well as good (5:43–48). Human parents know how to give good gifts to their children – 'How much more will your Father in heaven give good gifts to those who ask him!' (7:9–11). The Father is like a master who cancels his servant's debt simply because he is asked to do so (18:21–35), or who pays a living wage simply because every worker needs it (20:1–15), or who invites to a banquet everyone in the streets (22:1–10). It is the Father's will that all the 'righteous' in all the nations will be admitted to eternal life, although they never recognised the presence of the Son of Man among them (25:31–

46). Those who enter the kingdom of heaven will be those
who do the will of the Father, 'not everyone who says to
me, Lord, Lord' (7:21). In Luke's gospel Jesus, solemnly
beginning his public work, quotes the prophet's words that
he had been sent to preach good news to the poor, etc
(4:14–19), but not the prophet's words (Isaiah 61:2) about
'the day of vengeance of our God'. His teaching is: 'Be
merciful, just as your Father is merciful . . . Forgive, and
you will be forgiven,' for all who love their enemies 'will be
sons of the Most High, because he is kind to the ungrateful
and wicked' (6:32–37). Those who give a banquet to the
poor will be repaid at the resurrection of the righteous
(14:14). Even those whose claim is that they have used their
wealth wisely will be 'welcomed into eternal dwellings'
(16:9). The one who shows mercy, for example a good
Samaritan (10:25–37), is the one who obeys God's law, for
God himself is like the man who seeks the lost sheep or the
woman who seeks the lost coin or the father who runs
towards his lost son 'while he was still a long way off'
(15:1–32). Anyone who simply prays 'God, have mercy on
me, a sinner' is 'justified' (18:9–14) – which is the only use of
the term in the gospels. In Greek the prayer means 'God, be
propitiated for me,' but the means of propitiation is not
mentioned. The Lord's own prayer, taught to his disciples,
adds only one qualification to the petition 'Forgive us our
sins'. It is: 'for we also forgive everyone who sins against us'
(11:4). As he is nailed to the cross, Jesus prays for his
executioners, 'Father, forgive them' – not because he is
about to appease the Father's righteous anger by dying as
their substitute but 'for they do not know what they are
doing' (23:34).

    In the light of this teaching it is strange to be told by Dr
Stott that 'God forgives us only when we repent' (CMMW,
p. 51) and that 'we are not permitted to cheapen forgiveness
by offering it prematurely when there has been no repentance' (CoC, p. 296). The sentence in Luke's gospel (17:3)
quoted by Dr Stott ('rebuke him, and if he repents, forgive
him') is immediately followed by the teaching that 'your

brother' is to be forgiven if 'he sins against you seven times in a day' and 'comes back to you and says, "I repent"' – which scarcely suggests that the repentance has been genuine every time. Matthew's gospel (18:22) drives the real point home by saying that there must be forgiveness 'not seven times, but seventy-seven' times. The teaching of Jesus, taken as a whole, does not make the offer of forgiveness depend on prior repentance. Indeed, the opposite is taught clearly. What seems to have misled Dr Stott is the fact that since forgiveness is the removal of all barriers to fellowship it cannot be *effective* until the barriers have been dismantled on the other side too. So the Father cannot effectively forgive those who by being unforgiving themselves show that they are not willing to pull down the barriers (Mark 11:25; 18:35, etc.). But the Father has a forgiving spirit before his child repents, before the lost sheep is found – and Jesus teaches we must be like the Father, ourselves always willing to forgive whatever the injury, even before the person who has wronged us admits the wrong and seeks reconciliation. That can be crucifying – but that is Christianity.

It seems necessary to add only one point to this piece of critical Bible study which has had to be shorter than the seriousness of the subject requires. Dr Stott (CoC, pp. 154, 181) quotes Acts 20:28: 'Be shepherds of the church of God, which he bought with his own blood.' But as the New International Version notes, many manuscripts read 'the church *of the Lord*'; and this is the reading preferred by the New English Bible. Another possible translation is 'with the blood of his own'. It seems unlikely that the Bible's one reference to God shedding his own blood – a startling idea – should be introduced unobtrusively in the course of an exhortation to the elders of the church in Ephesus. The passage refers to the ransom-like self-sacrifice of Jesus, the supreme martyr.

In the New Testament there is, I conclude, no clear statement that providing the appeasement or satisfaction of the just wrath of God was the mission of Jesus. The gospels tell us that some time before he 'resolutely set out for Jerusalem' for the last time (Luke 9:51) Jesus was already challenging anyone who would 'come after me' to 'take up his cross and follow me' (Mark 8:34) and was pondering scriptures which warned him that he 'must suffer much and be rejected' (Mark 9:12). There is nothing at all unlikely in such expectations. Jesus lived under Roman occupation and could expect to suffer under Roman 'justice' since he was a disturber of the peace who announced the arrival of the kingdom of God. He could also expect to be rejected by fellow-Jews who owed their positions to their collaboration with the Romans. And there is nothing at all unlikely in the idea that Jesus believed that it was within the purposes of his Father that he should accept such a death as an integral part of his mission – indeed, as its climax. Presumably he could have avoided execution, or greatly lessened the risk of it, by abandoning his public mission, by being much more guarded in his teaching or at least by not confronting his enemies by going to Jerusalem at Passover time. But, as Dr Stott rightly insists, he chose to die. It is consistent with the whole known character of Jesus to believe that he drank this cup of suffering because he came to be convinced that it was his Father's will. It is also in keeping with everything known about Jesus to believe that he trusted the Father to vindicate him by making his ransom-like self-sacrifice the prelude to a new covenant with humanity, the crucial event before the coming of the kingdom. We can reasonably believe that all this was in the mind of Jesus even if the 'predictions of the passion' ascribed to him in the gospels and quoted in *The Cross of Christ* have been edited by the Church. (Resurrection 'after three days' is predicted, but the story of the crucifixion contains no hint that either Jesus or his followers then held such a confident hope.) However, Jesus is not said in the gospels to have explained *why* his death was necessary to the Father's purposes. Later, Christians did begin to explain. They had become sure that 'Jesus of Nazareth', 'a man accredited by God' had been 'handed over . . . by God's set purpose and foreknowledge' (Acts 2:22–3). But their explanations were fragmentary and, as I hope I have shown, did not clearly include the explanation said by Dr Stott to be 'the heart of the gospel'. I repeat his own wise teaching that 'a full-scale atonement doctrine is missing from the apostolic preaching' (CoC, p. 34).

Dr Stott is undeniably motivated by the desire to be faithful to Scripture. 'My first anxiety', he writes in his Preface to *The Cross of Christ*, 'has been to be true to the Word of God, allowing it to say what it has to say and not asking it to say what I might want it to say' (CoC, pp. 11–12). This is in keeping with his conviction that 'it would obviously be very misleading to read back into Scripture the notions of a later age', for 'a text cannot with any possible legitimacy mean to me something substantially different from what it meant to its original author and readers' (UB, pp. 171, 175). In his 1982 address, *Make the Truth Known*, he again declared: 'The Evangelical faith is original, biblical, apostolic Christianity. At least that is what we believe it to be, and I for one would not hold it if I were not convinced about this.' But repeatedly the references in Scripture to the meaning of the death of Christ can be interpreted in more than one way. Dr Stott has decided to interpret them in the light of his intense conviction that the wrath of God needs to be propitiated. He believes that God once literally struck Uzzah dead for touching the Ark of the Covenant (CoC, p. 107). In his eyes the sins of the world cannot be taken away except by a propitiation so great that God himself must provide it. But merely to 'provide' this sacrifice in the shape of the innocent Jesus would make God a 'pitiless ogre' – a suggestion which Dr Stott repudiates 'with the utmost vehemence'. So he teaches that God actually makes the propitiation himself, although there he says something which is not said in the Bible. What has happened, I suggest, is that his interpretation of particular biblical passages has been influenced by how the Bible taken as a whole speaks to his reason and his conscience. So now I want to submit some reasons for a conscientious conviction that his own theory cannot be 'the heart of the gospel' in our time.

## Moral Objections

One problem is that we no longer assume that everyone crucified or otherwise executed is under God's curse. In his great *Institutes of the Christian Religion* (11.6–13) Calvin starts his central discussion of Christ's death: 'The cross was accursed, not only in human opinion but by decree of God's law. Hence, when Christ is hanged upon the cross, he makes himself subject to the curse.' From this beginning Calvin concludes that Christ had 'to undergo the severity of God's vengeance, to appease his wrath and to satisfy his just judgement'. But crucifixion was a Roman punishment. It is deeply offensive to reason and conscience to claim that every one of those condemned to death by the rulers of the Roman empire was also condemned by their Maker and Father, and it is doubly offensive to claim this about Jesus, who was condemned by Pontius Pilate although he had never committed or advocated any crime. It also seems monstrous to argue that God himself cursed all those condemned under Jewish law, first stoned to death and then displayed dead on a tree or stake – which is the narrower meaning of the text about the hanged being accursed (Deuteronomy 21:23). That text comes immediately after a law which encourages parents whose son 'will not listen to them when they discipline him' to demand that 'all the men of his town shall stone him to death'. The idea that God always endorses such human 'justice' is particularly abhorrent in a century which has seen miscarriages of justice on a colossal scale. All the blood shed by the cruel tyrants of our time cries out in contradiction. Our solidarity with all the innocent victims of 'justice' compels many of us to apply to the theory that the cross was accursed the great declaration by Paul that 'no-one who is speaking by the Spirit of God says, "Jesus be cursed"' (1 Corinthians 12:3).

Nor is it morally acceptable to say that if an innocent person suffers unjustly it is a sign that God is punishing him in place of the guilty. Every principle of true justice is outraged by the idea that there must be some punishment no matter who is punished. And what is essential in criminal or civil law is also essential when considering the suffering of a whole people. The Jewish people, for example, have suffered very terribly because they were made the scapegoats by evil societies. There is a sense in which their agonies contributed to a happier outcome both for their own people (in that the Holocaust stimulated the establishment and recognition of the state of Israel) and for Europe (in that all sensitive Europeans became ashamed of antisemitism and of any persecution of a racial minority). But no one attempting to comment on these tragedies in the spirit of Jesus, or in the spirit of common morality, would ever say that God punished the Jewish people by bringing about the Holocaust because the penalty for the sins of Europe had to be paid by someone, whether guilty or innocent. All the eloquence of the Song of the Suffering Servant, and of some Christian theories of the atonement, cannot obscure the simple and elementary fact that it is immoral to punish anyone who is not guilty.

Only a minority of people nowadays thinks about the relationship between God and man in terms which include propitiating the wrath of God by any kind of sacrifice. Not even a minority any longer believes in human sacrifices – which are, of course, repeatedly denounced in the Hebrew Scriptures as abhorrent to God. But even a theory which compares the death of Jesus with animal sacrifices is, as Dr Stott often notes, 'unpopular'. The reason needs to be set out. Otherwise people who hold this theory may not appreciate why, as Dr Stott also notes, a distinguished scientist who was 'friendly to all kinds of religious experience' (Sir Alister Hardy) could write that 'the hypothesis that God, in the shape of his son, tortured himself for our redemption' was among the least attractive of religious ideas 'in the whole of anthropology' and belonged to 'quite a different philosophy – different psychology – from that of the religion that Jesus taught' (CoC, p. 111).

In the religion of ancient Israel as purified by the prophets and later by the Scriptures, and in the Judaism which Jesus and his first followers knew, it was always taught that propitiatory sacrifices were of no avail without sincere repentance, and when the Jerusalem temple was destroyed within half a century of the death of Jesus these sacrifices were abandoned (with one small exception, in Ethiopia) – never to be restored. Similar sacrifices do occur among some animists (believers in many 'spirits' in nature) and among some adherents of other religions, but it is significant that they are never condemned when a religion is being advertised in a style which seeks to be educated and reasonable. The contrast is great with the history of the ancient Middle Eastern and European world, and of most other pre-modern societies, where religious sacrifices were universal. So fully has humanity moved out of that world where animal sacrifices seemed normal that in our time not even expert scholars or anthropologists can be sure of the original meaning of all the details in a sacrificial system such as the Hebrews'. The very term 'propitiation' is 'to most of us just plain incomprehensible', as Leon Morris noted in his book on *The Atonement: Its Meaning and Significance* (p. 151). Its usage is particularly problematic in the interpretation of the New Testament, where the meaning 'propitiating God' (or gods), normal in other ancient literature, is always avoided. In the New International Version of the Bible it has to be translated as 'sacrifice of atonement' or 'atoning sacrifice' and in the New English Bible 'the means of expiating sin by his sacrificial death' or as 'the remedy for the defilement of our sins'. People can understand what a 'covenant' or specially solemn and binding agreement is. But the practice in ancient Israel of sacrificing an animal on the occasion of a covenant, cutting it in two and walking between the parts (as illustrated by the story of Abraham's sacrifice in Genesis 15:10–17), requires some understanding and it is significant that scholars are not agreed about how the Hebrews did understand it.

Dr Stott is, of course, aware of all this. Discussing blood sacrifices, he has said:

> today these categories make sense only among Hindus and animists who sacrifice animals, and among the Falasha Jews of Ethiopia who still perform sacrifices. Secular audiences in the West, however, not only lack the background to understand such phraseology, but in addition often feel squeamish at the mention of blood. What I am urging is this. The truth that through Christ's death for us and instead of us we may be forgiven and receive new life is indispensable to the Gospel. But we can proclaim this good news with entire faithfulness without ever mentioning the shedding or the sprinkling of Christ's blood. Only later shall we need to teach converts the meaning of these expressions . . . (ARBMW, p. 12)

But the problem arises not only from unfamiliarity with animal sacrifices but also from a moral revulsion and from the clear conviction that God does not want them. Most Christians and others now feel with a prophet of ancient Israel, Micah. It was not only that Micah 'wondered if he should bring burnt offerings, animals, rivers of oil or even "my firstborn" ', showing that he 'understood the substitutionary principle well', as Dr Stott says (CoC, p. 137); for Micah was sure that God required not sacrifices of any sort but 'to act justly and to love mercy and to walk humbly with your God' (Micah 6:8). Isaiah declared that the word of the Lord was: 'Stop bringing meaningless offerings!' (1:13). Hosea, too, saw that God desires 'mercy, not sacrifice' (6:6) – which is quoted twice in Matthew's gospel (9:13; 12:7). Whether such attacks were aimed at the sacrificial system as a whole or only at sacrifices without sincere piety and morality is debatable. What is not in question is that the sacrificial system was being criticised on religious and moral grounds long before it disappeared. Are modern people who are similarly impatient with all talk of propitiatory sacrifices, who want 'rational worship' (Romans 12:1), to be excluded from any understanding of the heart of the gospel because, as is alleged, they fail to see the permanent significance of Christ's work? If so, the barrier seems somewhat like the barrier which some Christians tried to erect in Paul's day in order to keep out converts who did not understand, and were not willing to accept, the Jewish rite of circumcision.

Even greater is the problem which all but a few Christians and others have with the particular form of the doctrine of the Holy Trinity which is necessary to the argument of *The Cross of Christ*. Dr Stott accepts the orthodoxy of the councils of Nicea, Constantinople and Chalcedon, so that he believes that Jesus Christ was God the Son, 'of one substance with the Father'. Indeed, in *The Authentic Jesus* (1985) he endorsed the words of B. B. Warfield that 'the Chalcedonian Christology is only a very perfect synthesis of the biblical data' (AJ, p. 31). Yet he has to maintain that the Father not only punished but also forsook the Son, quoting the Victorian theologian R. W. Dale to the effect that 'the mysterious unity of the Father and the Son rendered it possible for God at once to endure and to inflict penal suffering' (CoC, p. 159). But as Dr Stott has written, 'precisely *how* God can have been in Christ while he made Christ to be sin for us, I cannot explain' (BC1, p. 94). And I have to say that in common with many other Christians I find the idea of God sacrificing himself to himself not only inexplicable but also incomprehensible. That could be because we are confronted by something that is real but too big for our minds to absorb, like the incarnation itself. But whereas we can begin to see the truth that God was in Christ loving, teaching, healing and dying for our sakes because there is nothing offensive to reason or conscience in the idea of God expressing his love in the morally sublime life of a loving, teaching, healing martyr, Dr Stott's doctrine of the atonement seems far more questionable. I gladly acknowledge that it is far less offensive than the theory that 'God punished Jesus' instead of us, because it says that God, who is love, has loved us so much that he himself has suffered a cruel death for our sakes. But many of us find it impossible to understand the idea of God punishing himself.

Dr Stott's theory suggests that God has done something which would be crazy or wrong for a good man or woman to do. A judge would not be respected if having convicted a criminal and sentenced him to death or imprisonment for life he underwent execution or served the sentence himself. He would be thought to be perverting the course of justice. A father or mother who declared that the children could not be forgiven until he or she had appeased and satisfied his or her wrath by committing suicide might be reported to a society for the prevention of cruelty to children and admitted to a psychiatric hospital. Self-punishment of this sort by a mentally healthy person is inconceivable. Of course God's sense of justice must be both stronger and more justified than any human judge's or parent's. But precisely because God's justice is the justice of holy love, it seems all the more difficult to think that he could do something which would be condemned if done by a good judge or a good parent. Certainly this type of teaching is unlike the style of Jesus, who repeatedly taught the people about the Father by speaking in parables based on everyday experience and by emphasising that the Father is good, is like a good human parent – only more so. The teaching of Jesus did not fall below the level of the psalm which says that God is merciful like a human father pitying his young children (103:13).

In *The Cross of Christ* Dr Stott considers the teaching given to the Colossians that through the Son 'God was pleased . . . to reconcile to himself all things, whether things on earth or things in heaven, by making peace through his blood, shed on the cross' (1:19–20). Rejecting any suggestion that 'all' created things or human beings or 'evil cosmic intelligences' have already been reconciled to God – for in his view 'it is not a universal reconciliation that Christ achieved or that Paul proclaimed' (GNS, p. 98) – he comments: 'We cannot be sure to what Paul was alluding' (CoC, pp. 195–6). And many will sympathise with his puzzlement. This was one of the key texts inspiring the first chapter of F. W. Dillistone's powerful study of *The Christian Understanding of Atonement* (1968), where the cosmic significance of Christ's work was explored with the aid of modern literature. Many of us, however, have moved right away from the world of ideas familiar to the author and readers of that letter to the Colossians. And we cannot be sure to what Dr Stott's own theory of the atonement is 'alluding'. That, too, belongs to a world which we do not know; it belongs to the world where sacrifices propitiated the wrath of gods. The world which we have entered either through education or through daily experience ('culture') insistently teaches us that such ideas are either ridiculous or else actually blasphemous. Do we constitute a public which has to be reckoned with in evangelism – where, as Dr Stott says finely and truly, 'an incarnation means entering other people's worlds, their thought-worlds, and the worlds of their alienation, loneliness and pain' (CoC, p. 291)? Or can the gospel not be understood by us?

The reply may be that sooner or later we simply have to learn to understand these allusions to God's wrath and its propitiation, appeasement or satisfaction by the sacrifice of the cross. So, very briefly, I want to outline an alternative theory. It is not merely my own theory. It has often been expounded by far more authoritative teachers – to give only one example, by Vincent Taylor after his long reflection on the New Testament's evidence (perhaps his clearest summary being in *Forgiveness and Reconciliation*, 1941, pp. 193–4). Although I trust that I have learned from Leon Morris and other critics of Taylor's detailed exegesis, I deliberately refer to a theologian who was convinced that 'the persistence of theories of substitution and satisfaction reveals the immense strength of a felt religious need' (p. 205). It is my hope and prayer that such a need can be met without these theories.

## Atonement

Professor C. F. D. Moule allows me to quote from a very wise letter in which he summarises his conclusions (worked out in, for example, his *Essays in New Testament Interpretation*, 1982):

> It seems to me that dust is thrown in our eyes whenever we forget that sacrifice, ransom, acquittal, cleansing, paying of debts, etc., are all only analogies, each with a limited function. If we forget that, we may try to make them do more than they are meant to do, we may treat them as sacrosanct and be timid about replacing them by other analogies more telling for our day, and we may even elevate the biblical analogies into an authoritative story, turning them into a system independent of the great reality they are meant to illuminate. Once it is realised that forgiveness and reconciliation anywhere and at any time (before Christ and outside the Church, as well as since the incarnation and within the Church) involve an output of forgiving 'energy' met by an output of repentance, such that forgiver and forgiven are bonded together in a work of new creation, then it may be realised that, in Christ, these creative processes are totally implemented (so far as is possible in time and space); and all this ought to deliver us from the tyranny of overgrown analogies, and make the idea of penal substitution unthinkable.

But a few more words can be said about this fathomless mystery.

'God was reconciling the world to himself in Christ, not counting men's sins against them' (2 Corinthians 5:19). The Good News Bible splendidly conveys what Paul means: 'Our message is that God was making all mankind his friends through Christ. God did not keep an account of their sins . . . ' The eternal God inspired, guided, dwelt in and worked in his Son or Word. Jesus, having embodied the divine love and the divine patience in his life and teaching, embodied them supremely as he died. And it cost him not less than everything. 'When they hurled their insults at him, he did not retaliate; when he suffered, he made no threats. Instead, he entrusted himself to him who judges justly' (1 Peter 2:23). Because the Father is also the just Judge, he was not punishing the innocent. The victim of a miscarriage of human justice, Jesus suffered under Pontius Pilate, not under the Father. But the dying Jesus soaked up the evil as a sponge soaks up water. He prayed for the forgiveness of his deluded executioners. He entered the depths of the physical and psychological suffering which evil causes. He became the brother of all the doubters, all the defeated, all the tormented and all the guilty. But he died as he had lived, in obedient dependence on 'my God, my God'. He trusted in '*Abba*, Father' (Luke 23:46). In victory he finished the work which had been given to him by the Father (John 19:30).

That work won the spiritual freedom of all who will accept the Father's constantly offered forgiveness and love. It won it by an apparently powerless patience which perfectly expressed the divine patience of the Creator, a patience revealed in the whole of modern scientific knowledge of the space and time required by evolution. It won it by a self-sacrifice somewhat like the sacrifices with which the twentieth century is entirely familiar when they are made by martyrs, soldiers, rescue and health workers, parents and so forth. This self-sacrifice was also somewhat like the payment of a ransom to free hostages or victims of kidnapping. It did not change God at all. But because it changed the spiritual situation of humanity, because it decisively dealt with human sin ('expiation'), it changed the Father's relationship with the whole of the human race. For the Father can now make his always forgiving love known in the minds and hearts of sinners. Drawn by the Jesus who is 'lifted up' on his cross, and spiritually united with him, people accept that love, are released from the burden of guilt, are declared righteous ('justified'), and are made righteous ('sanctified'). Such people are Christians – who should hope and pray that in the end all of humanity will respond, Christians being only the first fruits of the coming harvest or the spring flowers of humanity's summer. That certainly is the will of God, the Creator of all and the merciful Father and Lover of all.

The cross has been well called 'the meeting place of God and man'. In Christ crucified as in no one else, all can find the glory of man as well as the glory of God. 'Here is the man!' (John 19:5). The life and death of Jesus pray perfectly to the Father for, and on behalf of, all humanity. In penitent humility all can join their own lives and deaths to his. They can know what Paul means when he tells the Galatians: 'I have been crucified with Christ and I no longer live, but Christ lives in me. The life I live in the body, I live by faith in the Son of God, who loved me and gave himself for me' (2:20). So 'Christ crucified' is the supreme representative of humanity – supreme, because in his total outpouring of loving obedience he is nearest to the Father. And when what holds folk back is the thought that the Creator is complacently aloof from the suffering of the world, that he is exempt from the sacrifices which all his creatures must make for each other, age after age, if life is to be continued and fed, that he is not involved in the mess or the pain of it and takes no responsibility for it, then here, too, the cross is the answer. For Jesus, who represents man to God, also represents God to man. The living Jesus interprets the silence of eternity by love. And the dying Jesus shows what it means in such a world of sacrifice to say that God, too, suffers, for God is love. There are clues to the mystery in the words of Donne and Blake:

> God cloth'd himself in vile man's flesh, that so
> He might be weak enough to suffer woe.

> Think not thou canst sigh a sigh,
> And thy Maker is not by;
> Think not thou canst weep a tear,
> And thy Maker is not near.

> O! He gives to us his joy
> That our grief he may destroy;
> Till our grief is fled and gone
> He doth sit by us and moan.

# John Stott's Response to Chapter 3

My dear David,

I was touched by reading your personal testimony to the importance of the cross in your own life, beginning on Good Fridays when you were a boy, keeping your feet on the rock when you were a theological student, and continuing today as 'the one unconquerable light' which has enabled you 'to walk through this dark world'. I could say the same. Although I am afraid our understandings of the death of Jesus diverge widely, we can at least agree that the central reality of the cross is greater than all our human formulations.

I am also grateful for a number of statements you make in your chapter: that, when you first read *The Cross of Christ*, you found that 'most of it' expressed your own convictions (although, in view of the severe strictures you express later, that surprises me); that you liked ('admired' is your gracious word) the 'emphatic chapter' on the centrality of the cross, the insistence on the revelation of God's love, and the equal insistence that his love is 'holy love'; and that in 'any at-one-ment between the Holy God and us sinners' the initiative and achievement must be his. Thank you too for faithfully reflecting, indeed quoting, my sentence that 'any notion of penal substitution in which three independent actors play a role – the guilty party, the punitive judge and the innocent victim – is to be repudiated with the utmost vehemence'.

I agree with you that contemporary Christians should honour the pioneers of Christian thinking about the atonement, even if we do not find their constructions entirely satisfactory. I am sorry, therefore, that you find me 'dismissive' of other viewpoints and even pastorally 'harsh' towards those who hold them. I did not mean to be. You also seem to suggest that I have been unfair in my representation of some of their positions (which I struggled not to be) and have not recognised the element of truth which may be found in each of them. But this last criticism is not, I think, fair to me! I am at pains in *The Cross of Christ* not to oblige people to choose between Anselm, Abelard and Aulen. I write:

> In fact all three of the major explanations of the death of Christ contain biblical truth and can to some extent be harmonized, especially if we observe that the chief difference between them is that in each God's work in Christ is directed towards a different person. In the 'objective' view God satisfies himself, in the 'subjective' he inspires us, and in the 'classic' he overcomes the devil. Thus Jesus Christ is successively the Saviour, the Teacher and the Victor, because we ourselves are guilty, apathetic and in bondage. (CoC, p. 230)

P. T. Forsyth drew attention to this as 'the threefold cord'. Indeed, you may recall that in the book's third section entitled 'The achievement of the cross' there are three chapters called 'the salvation of sinners', 'the revelation of God' and 'the conquest of evil' in which these three themes of the cross are developed.

This leads me to say that it is in this your third chapter that I have felt most acutely the limitations of the methodology we are following. If you felt that I was being unfair to earlier expositors, I have felt that you were being unfair to me! I do not mean that you have deliberately misrepresented me, for you are scrupulous in your endeavour not to, but that a degree of misrepresentation is inevitable because it is inherent in our format. For I am required to respond to your criticisms of me, whereas I wish our readers would read me first (in *The Cross of Christ*) and then you (in this book), instead of reading your critique first and then my response, while the original remains unread! To

begin with, you are selective (again, inevitably because of
space limitations; I'm blaming the way the dialogue is set
up, not you). Thus you make virtually no reference to the
long chapter in which I seek to expound carefully the
meaning of the four images or models of salvation, and
their implications for our understanding of the cross,
namely 'propitiation', 'redemption', 'justification' and
'reconciliation'. You hardly allude to the concept of God
'satisfying himself', or to the biblical foundations of it,
although it is integral to my thesis. And you mention only
as an aside the fact that there are whole chapters on the
relation of the cross to the problems of violence ('Loving our
enemies') and suffering ('Suffering and glory'). Now I fully
understand that you had to concentrate on particular
aspects of *The Cross of Christ*, but the resulting impression
does not do justice to the breadth of horizon which I
attempted to portray in the book.

Then, although you write about 'propitiation' in several
contexts, you nowhere mention the 'three crucial points' I
make, in order to distinguish 'a truly biblical doctrine of
propitiation' from crude, pagan notions. Let me summarise
them. First, the reason why a propitiation is necessary is
not that God is irascible, spiteful, capricious or arbitrary,
but that evil always provokes his 'wrath', which is 'his
steady, unrelenting, unremitting, uncompromising antag-
onism to evil'. Secondly, it is neither we who make the
propitiation (as in a pagan context), nor even Christ (as if by
his death he prevailed on God to pardon us); it is God
himself who took the initiative in his sheer grace and
mercy. Thirdly, the propitiatory sacrifice was not a thing
(whether animal, vegetable or mineral) but a person. 'And
the person God offered was not somebody else . . . somebody distinct from or external to himself . . . In giving his
Son, he was giving himself.' Thus God himself is at the
heart of the divine propitiation. 'It is God himself who in
holy wrath needs to be propitiated, God himself who in
holy love undertook to do the propitiating, and God himself who in the person of his Son died for the propitiation of

our sins.' I conclude: 'There is no crudity here to evoke our ridicule, only the profundity of holy love to evoke our worship' (CoC, pp. 173–5).

Your two major criticisms of *The Cross of Christ* are that my doctrine is (1) unbiblical and (2) uncommunicable. That is, it is neither true to Scripture nor relevant to modern men and women. It is a pretty damning accusation, especially to one whose whole ministry (especially in recent years) has been dedicated to the task of bridge-building, i.e. of relating the word to the world in such a way as to be faithful to the one and sensitive to the other. Nevertheless, I will try to respond to your criticisms.

## Sin, Satisfaction and Substitution

I begin with these three unpopular words, which in combination are calculated to give many liberal theologians apoplexy. Yet they are all indispensable to my own (biblical, as I believe) understanding of the cross. Faced by human sin, God who is holy love, and who must 'satisfy himself', i.e. be true to himself and not contradict himself, identified himself through Christ with our sins and endured their penalty, in order that we might be righteously forgiven. This kind of formulation, you tell me, goes far beyond what Scripture teaches. Do I not myself concede (as you twice remind me) that 'a full-scale atonement doctrine is missing from the apostolic preaching'? Yes, but I was referring only to the earliest kerygmatic sermons recorded in the Acts of the Apostles. Those 'primitive' statements contained only seeds (e.g. 'for our sins', 'according to the Scriptures', 'hanged on a tree' and 'handed over . . . by God's set purpose') which came into flower in the later apostolic letters. Do I not also declare, however, that 'beyond the images of the atonement lies the mystery of the atonement', and imply that a mystery cannot be reduced to a formula? Yes, and I meant it. I am sure that the reality which lies behind the statements that 'God was in Christ reconciling the world' and 'God made Christ to be sin for us' is beyond the powers of resolution of our finite minds, and that we shall spend eternity not only worshipping 'God and the Lamb', but exploring the mystery which inspires our worship. Nevertheless, part of the mystery has been revealed, and we must not shrink from attempting to grasp and formulate this.

Still, however, you chide me that the 'theory' I expound is 'not one which is the plain teaching of the Bible as the Bible can be read by the plain man'. And several times you write that 'Jesus did not teach this' or 'Paul did not clearly teach that'. In fact, you conclude one part of your argument by saying that the New Testament contains 'no clear statement that providing the appeasement or satisfaction of the just wrath of God was the mission of Jesus'. (I would not in any case have used this expression, but I let that pass.) Perhaps you are referring to the gospels? For I would claim that the great references to propitiation in the epistles (Paul's in Romans 3:23–26 and John's in 1 John 2:1–2 and 4:10) are quite plain. At the same time, my case does not rest on proof texts, but on a synthesis of the total teaching of Scripture. After all, there is no plain statement for plain people that 'Jesus was God', but taken as a whole the Scriptures indubitably affirm his deity.

I do not think you have allowed our readers to feel the strength of the sustained and cumulative biblical argument that I have tried to develop in the three chapters of Part Two ('The heart of the cross'), which I have entitled respectively 'the problem of forgiveness', 'satisfaction for sin' and 'the self-substitution of God'. The problem of forgiveness ('to man the plainest of duties, to God . . . the profoundest of problems' – Carnegie Simpson) is constituted by 'the inevitable collision between divine perfection and human rebellion, between God as he is and us as we are'. For God's love is holy love, 'love which yearns over sinners while at the same time refusing to condone their sin' (CoC, p. 88). So I enlarge on the gravity of sin, human moral responsibility, true and false guilt (drawing on modern psychological insights as well as biblical revelation), and on God's holiness, which cannot coexist with evil. And I end this chapter by asserting that

> All inadequate doctrines of the atonement are due to inadequate doctrines of God and man . . . The essential background to the cross . . . is a balanced understanding of the gravity of sin and the majesty of God. If we diminish either, we thereby diminish the cross . . . Before the holy God can forgive us, some kind of 'satisfaction' is necessary. (CoC, pp. 109–10)

It is not a satisfaction of the devil (who has indeed been dethroned by Christ, though not by a bargain as if he had some hold on God, still less by trickery – I don't think you quite grasped my argument here). Nor, I suggested, was it God's law, honour or justice or 'the moral order' which needed to be satisfied – or not at least if these

> represent God as being subordinate to something outside and above himself which controls his actions, to which he is accountable, and from which he cannot free himself. 'Satisfaction' is an appropriate word, providing we realize that it is he himself in his inner being who needs to be satisfied, and not something external to himself. (CoC, p. 123)

'The law to which he must conform, which he must satisfy, is the law of his own being' (CoC, p. 124). Negatively, he 'cannot disown himself' (2 Timothy 2:13), i.e. contradict himself; positively, he must be himself and act in perfect conformity to his divine nature. And what is his divine nature? It is holy love. Moreover, there are some scriptures which express, and some theologians who concede, the legitimacy of talking (though anthropomorphically) of 'a conflict of emotions, a strife of attributes' within God, between his 'compassion' and his 'fierce anger' (e.g. Hosea 11:8–9). As Emil Brunner put it, 'The cross is the only place where the loving, forgiving merciful God is revealed in such a way that we perceive that his holiness and his love are equally infinite . . . [The] objective aspect of the atonement . . . consists in the combination of inflexible righteousness, with its penalties, and transcendent love' (CoC, p. 131).

'How then can God express his holiness without consuming us, and his love without condoning our sins? . . . How can he save *us* and satisfy *himself* simultaneously?' (CoC, p. 132). It is in answer to these inescapable questions that the notion of substitution is revealed, namely that 'in order to satisfy himself, [God] sacrificed – indeed substituted – himself for us'. You say that this is 'not plainly taught anywhere', to which I reply that it is plainly (directly or indirectly) taught everywhere. Marshalling the evidence, I write about sacrifice in the Old Testament, and the significance of the shedding and sprinkling of blood; about the transparently clear substitutionary teaching of the Passover (in which the lamb died in place of the first-born), so that we know what 'Christ our Passover has been sacrificed for us' means; about the Old Testament vocabulary of 'sinbearing', meaning the bearing of sin's penalty, which is applied to Christ crucified in the New; about the two goats of the Day of Atonement, the sacrificed goat and the scapegoat, which together constituted a single 'sin offering', 'the one exhibiting the means, and the other the results, of the atonement' (T. J. Crawford); about the fifty-third chapter of Isaiah, eight verses of which are quoted in the New Testament as fulfilled in Jesus, together with the ransom saying (Mark 10:45) and Jesus' declaration during the Last Supper that his blood would be 'poured out for many' (Mark 14:24), both of which are echoes of Isaiah 53:12; and about the plain, natural meaning of the 'made him . . . to be sin' and 'becoming a curse for us' verses (2 Corinthians 5:21; Galatians 3:13).

You, I know, criticise my interpretation of some of these passages and texts, as indeed I find some of your interpretation of Scripture arbitrary, so that further progress in mutual understanding will be impossible without some careful exegetical work. But it is the steady build-up throughout Scripture of the substitutionary theme to which

I appeal. In my view it simply cannot be set aside in the way you attempt. I note Dr C. E. B. Cranfield's carefully phrased summary, in his great two-volume ICC commentary on *Romans*: 'God, because in his mercy he willed to forgive sinful men, and, being truly merciful, willed to forgive them righteously, that is, without in any way condoning their sin, purposed to direct against his own very self in the person of his Son the full weight of that righteous wrath which they deserved' (CoC, p. 134).

## The Heart of the Gospel

I am not saying that the doctrine of substitutionary atonement is 'compulsory for Christians', if by that you mean that people cannot be Christians without believing it. Nor do I forget Charlie Moule's stricture about 'overgrown analogies'. I have clearly stated that propitiation, redemption, justification and reconciliation are all biblical metaphors or images of salvation, each of which teaches particular truths, although I have added that the substitutionary principle is the reality at the heart of all four models (CoC, pp. 202–3). I am not saying that substitution is *the* one and only meaning of the cross, for the cross speaks also of victory over evil, the revelation of love and glory through suffering. But if you are talking of atonement, the means by which we sinners can be reconciled to the God of holy love, why then, yes, I don't think you or I can escape the truth of the divine substitution.

You respond that this 'theory' (as you – incorrectly, as I think – call the traditional understanding of Scripture) is not only unbiblical, but even 'unintelligible' and consequently uncommunicable. That charge stings, because you know that I am an evangelist at heart and therefore long to communicate the Christian good news meaningfully to my own contemporaries. So I must let you express your criticism in its full outspokenness: 'I find the idea of God sacrificing himself to himself not only inexplicable but incomprehensible', you write. It suggests that 'God has done something which would be crazy or wrong for a good man or woman to do'. 'Self-punishment . . . is inconceivable.' 'Unintelligible', 'inexplicable', 'incomprehensible', 'inconceivable'. Those are strongly dismissive adjectives, David. What can I say in reply?

First, you have not reported me accurately. I have never written *tout court* of 'God punishing himself', or of 'God sacrificing himself to himself'. The phraseology I have used is of 'God satisfying himself by substituting himself for us'. I have summed up my position as 'divine self-satisfaction through divine self-substitution'.

Secondly, this notion does not seem to me to deserve your negative epithets, which declare that it cannot be explained, understood or even conceived. For I am only one of many millions of Christians who believe that Scripture requires us to explain Christ's atoning sacrifice in this way, who find it perfectly intelligible and comprehensible, and who rejoice in it as the greatest possible good news, bringing forgiveness, freedom, joy, peace and hope, and calling forth grateful, wondering worship.

Thirdly, the concept is not meaningless to people unfamiliar with the Bible. The essence of it is the inner necessity for God to be God, to respond to our waywardness and rebellion in a way that is perfectly consistent with his own character of holy love, sacrificing neither his love to his holiness nor his holiness to his love. We see this kind of inner moral conflict in every person (like Sir Thomas More, the 'man for all seasons') who has sacrificed himself rather than compromise his principles. We see it even more clearly in parents who are torn apart with conflicting emotions when their children go astray. They long to forgive, but not in such a way as to condone and so encourage wrongdoing. Sometimes there is the necessity of punishment or discipline which is extremely painful to administer. True parental forgiveness is costly. Incidentally, you do not mention Dr Kenneth Bailey's exposition of this theme in the parable of the prodigal son, which he retells 'through the eyes of

Middle Eastern peasants'. He shows how 'the father bears the suffering instead of inflicting it' (CoC, p. 223). There is nothing incomprehensible here.

At this point I need to say something about penitence as the condition of pardon, with which you disagree. You write not only of God's unconditional love, which I gladly endorse, but also of his unconditional forgiveness, which I do not believe Jesus taught. Perhaps it is only a misunderstanding between us. *Of course* the Father has 'a forgiving spirit before his child repents', and *of course* we must ourselves always be 'willing to forgive' everybody. I have written the same myself. But there is surely a difference between the forgiving spirit or readiness to forgive on the one hand, and on the other the act of forgiveness which restores the forgiven person to fellowship. You say that unlike Judaism, which taught God's merciful forgiveness for penitents, Jesus taught forgiveness for everybody (except those who are blaspheming against the Spirit and in their spiritual blindness cannot receive forgiveness). I wonder if that is accurate. Bishop Stephen Neill wrote, following the Jewish scholar C. G. Montefiore, that, whereas the rabbis promised forgiveness to those who return home in penitence, what was completely new and original in Jesus was his emphasis that the shepherd took the initiative to go out into the desert to seek and find the lost (*Christian Faith Today*, 1955, p. 165).

Your own reconstruction of the gospel of the cross I have read and re-read many times. And I heartily agree with most of what you so eloquently express. The cross was indeed the supreme example of non-retaliation, the acceptance of injustice, the soaking up of human evil, an identification with all the oppressed and defeated, and a revelation of the suffering God. These truths move me as much as they move you, and I think you will agree that I have myself expressed them too.

It is not what you write, but what you omit that troubles me and provokes questions. Does your 'theory' do justice to the biblical doctrines of God's holiness and wrath, and to constantly repeated phrases like 'he died for our sins'? Just how did the cross as you portray it 'deal decisively with human sin'? How does it 'release us from the burden of guilt' and 'win spiritual freedom' for us? And how was the cross a revelation simultaneously of God's justice and love, as Paul clearly wrote in Romans 3 and 5? Further, in what sense could your reconstruction of the cross be a stumbling block to sinners, as Paul said it is? I do not find that your story of Christ crucified offers me a radical enough remedy for my needs. I need more than an example, a revelation, a martyr. You yourself admit the inadequacy of the exemplary interpretation; yet I am not clear what more you are offering.

In the end what worries me about your chapter on the cross, as about your chapter on the Bible, is what I have called your 'biblical selectivity', together with the principle which controls your selection. My own genuine claim, whether it can be substantiated or not, is to have given 'an explanation of the death of Jesus which takes into proper scientific account all the available [biblical] data, without avoiding any' (CoC, p. 83). By contrast, your guide seems to be 'the world which we have entered through education and through daily experience ("culture")', which teaches us that certain ideas are 'either ridiculous or else actually blasphemous'. Perhaps the crucial question between us, then, is whether culture is to judge Scripture, or Scripture culture.

I think I shall need to return to this question later.

Yours as ever,

John

# 4   The Miraculous Christ

## Miracles and Science

Do miracles occur? In *Christ the Controversialist* (1970) John Stott concisely put the questions of the 'modernists':

> Hasn't science demonstrated that the universe is a closed, mechanistic system, and therefore dispensed with any necessity for God? . . . And even if we can still in some sense believe in God as the creator and controller of the natural order, we must surely now give up the old-fashioned notion that this God has ever intervened *supernaturally* in human history, let alone that he still does? (CtC, pp. 50–1)

The answers to these questions have, I gather, seemed so obvious to Dr Stott that he has never felt it necessary to publish any extended treatment of the problem of miracles. His understanding of the inspiration of the Bible is thoroughly miraculous, for he believes that the Bible's human authors were inspired to give an accurate account of events which had occurred and speeches which had been delivered many years previously. It follows naturally from this that the sacred text tells the simple truth about miracles which took place in history. His impatience with doubts came out at the end of *The Authentic Jesus* (1985), for example: 'It seems logically absurd to accept the greater miracle (the incarnation) and jib at lesser ones like the virgin birth and the bodily resurrection' (AJ, p. 88). He was chairman of the committee which drafted the 1982 report on *Evangelism and Social Responsibility*, and in it we read that in the ministry of Jesus the signs of the kingdom of God which gave 'public evidence that the kingdom he was talking about had come' included exorcism and the healing and 'nature' miracles.

For him, the answers are in the Bible. He has felt the full power of the Bible's message that God has intervened in history, supremely in the birth, life, death and resurrection of Jesus followed by the gift of the Holy Spirit but also in the exodus from Egypt and in later events in the preparatory drama of Israel. In the Bible God is the Saviour in history. So he has gladly accepted the Bible's assurance that God is the Sovereign in nature. Faith, he acknowledges, is needed to believe this teaching, for 'by faith we understand that the universe was formed at God's command, so that what is seen was not made out of what was visible' (Hebrews 11:3). Yet faith is, he claims, fully in accord with human knowledge and experience, and is even demanded by them, for as Paul wrote 'since the creation of the world God's invisible qualities – his eternal power and divine nature – have been clearly seen, being understood from what has been made', so that 'men who suppress the truth by their wickedness' are 'without excuse' (Romans 1:18–20). In his books Dr Stott records his conviction that a reluctance to obey God's will – a kind of wickedness – rather than any intellectual difficulty often lies at the bottom of unbelief.

This biblical proclamation of God as Saviour and Sovereign is contrasted in Dr Stott's mind with inferior theologies which in his view have merely encouraged atheism in the long run. Thus he has no wish to defend the belief that every word in the Bible is literally true. Some statements which at first sight appear to contradict science may well have been intended as poetry. Although as we have seen his willingness to deviate from fundamentalism has in practice been limited, this principle means that he has no need to defend the historical accuracy of, for example, the various myths about the creation found in the Hebrew Scriptures (in the Psalms and Job as well as in Genesis).

He also has no wish to defend attempts which have been made to find a place for God merely in the gaps of scientific knowledge. He rejects the picture (associated with Newton as well as with many lesser names) which presents God as a 'hypothesis' necessary to explain things that science cannot yet explain and which suggests that God is active only in creating a machine-like nature and in occasional interventions to put the machine right. He is fully aware of the danger that a God so pictured disappears as the gaps in science are closed. But 'no biblical Christian', he insists,

> can accept the distinction between natural law and divine action which lies at the root of all this misunderstanding. For natural law is not an alternative to divine action, but a useful way of referring to it . . .
> The Bible itself should have protected us from regarding God either as a stop-gap or as a machine-minder, for the God of the Bible dwells not in gaps but in every place. (CtC, p. 59)

I, too, believe that the salvation which committed Christians (at least) have experienced is continuous with the history of salvation related in the Scriptures. My faith in God as the Creator of all that exists flows out of this history of salvation more than out of any observation of nature, which is so often silent or ambiguous when asked our religious questions. With this faith I, too, can understand the signs of God's sovereignty which the eyes of faith can see throughout his creation. I, too, believe that the Bible often expresses this faith poetically, but does magnificently celebrate God's glorious presence and power in the whole of nature, from the stars to the flowers, from the hippopotamus to the ant; and with the authors of the Bible I, too, worship the Saviour and Sovereign.

I also agree with Dr Stott on the point with which we are immediately concerned. C. F. D. Moule put it well when introducing a collection of studies of *Miracles* from Cambridge University (1965). 'If we have reason to believe that the character of God is best seen in Jesus, and that the consistency of sheer moral perfection is the ultimate consistency, then we may have to revise our ideas of what is and is not "possible".' If God is Saviour and Sovereign as the Bible affirms, there is nothing essentially incredible in the idea that for our salvation he will create 'miracles' understood as events which arouse a religious sense of wonder because they seem to be in keeping with God's character but contrary to what is known of nature. Normally the Creator works according to the regularities which can be called 'laws of nature', but this does not mean that his work as Saviour must always be regular. Rudolf Bultmann was not entitled to make his famous claim that no one who uses modern devices developed scientifically, such as electric light, can take miracles seriously. For while thankfully using electricity, I believe that God can switch on a light in a darkened life.

In finding myself in emphatic agreement with Dr Stott about all that, I recall the controversy about belief in a non-interventionist and therefore non-miraculous God ('Deism') in England during the years 1690–1790. That was an age when to many civilised and educated people it seemed imperative to abandon miracles. It was the 'Age of Enlightenment' when modern science was beginning to offer a solid, dependable and fruitful body of knowledge in contrast with the guesswork, credulity, and incompetence of ages which all seemed more or less 'dark'. Even where science was not yet able to provide complete explanations of natural phenomena, it was intellectually and morally essential not to believe reports of miracles. Only if religion and reason could be reconciled would religion cease to be ridiculous. This was the attitude which inspired the historian Edward Gibbon's contempt for the early Christians. David Hume expressed it in a famous essay eventually published in 1748. Reports of miracles, he was sure, came from 'ignorant and barbarous' people. 'A miracle', he declared, 'is a violation of the laws of nature; and as a firm and unalterable experience has established these laws, the proof against a miracle, from the very nature of the fact, is as entire as any argument from experience can possibly be imagined.' And there were theologians who attempted to develop a religion which would be thoroughly at home in that climate of opinion, a *Christianity Not Mysterious* (John

Toland's book in 1696). But they were answered – and not only by stupid conservatives whose wrath Hume had feared (making him delay the public appearance of his essay and hesitate to be too clear about its logical conclusion). Bishop Joseph Butler replied far more wisely and formidably, with the argument that 'natural' religion – without miracles or any special self-revelation by God – had difficulties at least as great as those of biblical, orthodox Christianity. Butler showed that what could be proved rationally from the dispassionate observation of nature fell far short of any demonstration of the existence of a benevolent and mighty Creator. The world, as Butler saw it, was so full of mystery and of evil that if its Creator was in any sense loving he must reveal himself and act in ways such as those reported in the Bible. The core of this argument has always convinced me and has always made me dissatisfied with Deism and with all the movements that have followed it in the history of Christian thought, denying that God is Saviour and Sovereign.

To some extent the climate of educated opinion is now more favourable to the idea of miracle. In 1947 C. S. Lewis was able to attack 'naturalism' or 'materialism' in his book on *Miracles*, knowing both that science was dominant in the culture of the English-speaking world and that the misuse of science, causing the miseries of harsh industrialism and of two horrific world wars, had made many people look for other sources of wisdom. Since then science has not recovered its full prestige as a general guide to life. On the contrary, Theodore Roszak's verdict in *Where the Wasteland Ends*, quoted by Dr Stott, is a judgement which would be shared by many: 'What science can measure is only a portion of what man can know. Our knowing reaches out to embrace the sacred' (IFCT, p. 36). And the continuing advances in science have made many of the more distinguished scientists justifiably proud, confident and determined within their scientific discipline but also humbly sensitive to the limits of science. Not only do they acknowledge that science cannot completely displace religion, art, music, the intuitive emotions and other parts of man's pre-scientific equipment for living. They also acknowledge the limits of the human capacity to understand natural phenomena scientifically – limits which seem likely to be permanent. In quantum physics the dance of the elementary particles seems to be unpredictable and also impossible to measure completely (for example, both position and momentum cannot be measured with absolute accuracy at the same time). The way the world is seems to depend on things which might have gone very differently – in the seconds after the initial 'big bang' or during the long ages of evolution. And no amount of scientific knowledge can answer the question what this immeasurably vast and infinitely complex universe 'means' – whether life arose accidentally or was a programme somehow built into a computer-like universe, whether progress in evolution results entirely from the interplay of 'chance' (for example, random genetic mutations) with 'necessity' (the needs to survive, to feed and to reproduce) or is somehow part of the drive of evolution itself, ever seeking fresh and more complex fulfilment. In this climate of scientific humility, quite a large minority of professional practitioners and teachers of science declares that it is respectably scientific to keep an open mind about the possibility of miracles if God is revealed in history as Saviour and Sovereign. Miracles, some scientists say, are among the phenomena which cannot be accurately predicted or fully understood. If they are thought to be real (on religious grounds, which science can neither strengthen nor demolish beyond the possibility of debate), then the scientist has a duty to accept them, with a sense of wonder to which he is already accustomed in his work.

However, to say that the possibility of miracles should be taken seriously is not to say that all stories about them should be taken uncritically. For the extent to which the climate of educated opinion now favours the idea of miracle (defined by C. S. Lewis as an 'interference with nature by supernatural power') should not be exaggerated. Probably most scientists in the world, and most of those who fully accept science without being professional experts, have an attitude of scepticism rather like David Hume's. While acknowledging that the 'laws of nature' are in fact statistical regularities, they do the kind of science that concerns them (not advanced physics) by assuming that the regularities are stable and consistent. And many religious believers are cautious; 'miracle' is no longer 'faith's favourite child' (Goethe). The conservative Calvinist Benjamin Warfield, who (as I have already noted) more or less defined the creed of the American movement known as fundamentalism, published a massive examination of *Counterfeit Miracles* in 1918, denying that any had taken place since the apostles' day; and since then many Christians have been either outspokenly sceptical or discreetly evasive about some or all of the biblical miracles, which of course Warfield entirely accepted. The 1982 report whose affirmation of the biblical miracles I have quoted recorded a disagreement between Evangelicals: 'Some of us think we should expect miracles as commonly as in the ministry of Jesus and his apostles, while others draw attention to the texts which describe these miracles as authenticating their unique ministry' (ESR, p. 32). For no advance in quantum physics has contradicted the elementary truths of science such as the law of gravity. What we know about nature, after all the investigations, is that it has many statistical patterns, regularities or 'laws' which enable us to understand something of the way it works. That confirms common sense. 'Miracles' are what stands in contrast with understandable regularity and it is inevitable that reports about them are often treated cautiously by educated people.

The Bible includes many sayings such as 'all things are possible with God' and 'everything is possible for him who believes' (Mark 10:27; 9:23). But as the Bible also says, it does not necessarily follow that God performs all the miracles that we should like. The servants of God are not being wise (or biblical) if they rely on the power of their faith to move mountains literally. Nor does it necessarily follow from belief in God as Saviour and Sovereign that he has actually done all the miracles that people have reported. It seems that some accounts of miracles have to be treated as legends if the elementary truths of science are to be accepted, although these accounts may be in the Bible and may read like straightforward history. Thus when considering the authority of the Scriptures I felt it important to separate the Bible's spiritual message from the story that during a war between Israel and the Amorites, in response to the prayer of Joshua, 'the sun stopped in the middle of the sky and delayed going down about a full day' (Joshua 10:13), and from the story that as a sign that King Hezekiah's prayer for healing would be granted the shadow cast by the sun on a stairway 'went back the ten steps it had gone down' (Isaiah 38:8). These quaint and apparently trivial miracle stories matter in the history of Christian thought. The mistaken belief that they must be taken literally compelled many bishops, theologians and preachers to resist the scientific demonstration, basic to any modern understanding of the universe, that our planet circles around a comparatively immobile sun. The Roman Catholic Church's persecution of Galileo has not ceased to be notorious but was matched by a Protestant stupidity equally discrediting to Christianity.

It was, I suggest, a defect in his *Miracles* (sub-titled *A Preliminary Discussion*) that C. S. Lewis never got down to a close examination of the miracle stories in the Bible. It has also been a defect of a good deal of the work of New Testament scholars that they have concentrated on the links between parts of the Bible – for example, on the echoes of the psalms to be found in the New Testament's miracle stories – to the exclusion of serious thought about links with science. That is to eliminate any possibility of conflict with what may be called 'the scientific world-view' or 'common sense' by eliminating any possibility of contact. I am guided by the advice of H. H. Rowley that 'the miracle stories can neither be uncritically accepted as historical, nor uncritically rejected as fantasy. Each example must be examined for itself, in the light of the character of the narrative in which it stands and the purpose for which it appears to have been written' (*The Faith of Israel*, 1965, p. 58). My own approach as an amateur will be to study the miracle stories in some detail, asking not only what they mean in the context of the Bible but also how they relate to what we think we know about the way this world is. At some points I shall accept answers to the second question which seem so probable as to be reliable for most practical purposes. At other points I shall be more hesitant. It can be disappointing when the answer to a question ends up in a probability, not a certainty. But I again recall the wisdom of Bishop Joseph Butler, who pointed out how many of our opinions have to be judgements about probability. Probability, he said, is the guide of life.

## Biblical Miracles

As Dr Stott has observed (CtC, p. 60), the miracle stories are not spread equally throughout the Bible. If we exclude Genesis we can say that they cluster around Moses; around Elijah and Elisha; and around Jesus and his apostles.

When the stories about Moses are considered seriously nowadays, it is often explained that the 'burning bush' where he had his all-decisive vision of God burned with natural electricity, many similar sights having been observed by travellers in those parts. The spiritual miracle that the leader of the Hebrews saw God as 'I am who I am' (or 'I will be what I will be'), and obeyed the will of that God in liberating his people from slavery, does not depend on the bush being a physical miracle (Exodus 3). Nor does the wonder of that liberation, constituting Israel as a federation of tribes, depend on the literal accuracy of the stories of the ten plagues which afflicted their Egyptian oppressors (Exodus 4–11).

The careful study of those stories has disclosed that they come from two sources, called J and P. Only one comes from J alone and only one from P alone. The two sources have not been harmonised in all details, but they are not utterly unrelated to reality as known to scientists. The introductory tall stories – that the magic wand of Moses became a snake, and that his hand became leprous 'like snow' when put into his cloak – are fortunately not typical. The other stories to some extent reflect the facts that the Nile periodically becomes muddy, looks somewhat like blood, overflows its banks and helps frogs, gnats and flies to breed. Cattle do die of plague; Egyptians are troubled by boils; plagues of locusts are highly destructive; hailstorms and cloud formations producing 'darkness at noon' do occur. Such facts were known, even if only by hearsay, to the story-tellers who, however, added many touches of magic while admitting that the Egyptian magicians could perform some similar feats. Thus the Nile is turned into blood by a magic wand, Aaron creates the frogs, the dust becomes gnats.

It is surely not essential to take such magic seriously even when it is attributed to Moses. Nor is it essential to believe that when the Israelites crossed the sea 'the surging waters stood firm like a wall' and 'congealed' (Exodus 15:8). That is a piece of poetry in the Song of Moses. But another strand in the tradition says that 'all that night the Lord drove the sea back with a strong east wind and turned it into dry land' (Exodus 14:21). Elsewhere we are told that it was the Sea of Reeds (Exodus 13:18) and if this was in reality a shallow papyrus marsh on the borders of Egypt the bogging down of the chariots sent in pursuit of the Hebrews is not too hard to explain naturally. Similar natural explanations have been advanced to account for other miracle stories in the Hebrew traditions. The pillar of cloud and the fire at night are said to be volcanic phenomena in the Sinai peninsula; there are other reports of water being made drinkable if a piece of wood is added; *manna* was almost certainly the secretions of a tamarisk tree caused by the sting of a tree-louse; quail are migratory birds and can be caught easily when exhausted; some springs of water in the desert are thinly concealed by rocks which can be broken. I do not reckon that we are being 'unbelievers' if we prefer such explanations to magic. For the true wonder of the exodus is that a group of fugitive slaves found the Egyptian army not strong enough to catch them, and nature friendly enough to support them, as they grew together to form a people which became a unique instrument in the working out of the loving purpose of God.

In the stories about Elijah and Elisha (1 Kings 17–2 Kings 13:20) we meet two of the heroes of Israel's deliverance from Canaanite paganism. But the story-telling has become fanciful. These stories are what a learned commentator (John Gray) has called 'traditions orally preserved' by 'dervish guilds', mostly of 'limited and even trivial interest' and without 'moral tone'. It is possible that 'fire from heaven' or lightning struck both the offerings on an altar to the God of Israel and, later and fatally, Elijah himself; but we have no way of knowing. Obviously there could be a shortage of food, suddenly coming and suddenly going; but the facts behind these tales of miracles during famines cannot be recovered. Obviously children thought to be dead could be resuscitated by artificial respiration, bears could kill other children, poisonous gourds in a stew could be remedied, a skin disease could be cured by the influence of faith on mind and body, an axehead could be recovered after being dropped into a river, and so forth; but the stories are so colourful that we cannot tell exactly what took place in the time of Elijah and Elisha. What is clear is that these legends have little or no connection with the true greatness of the prophets or with the gospel – extremely little when the magic is accompanied by praises of massacres. Luke (9:51–56) reports that when James and John asked Jesus, 'Lord, do you want us to call down fire from heaven to destroy them?' (many manuscripts reading 'even as Elijah did'), Jesus rebuked their lack of mercy on a Samaritan village. And Mark (15:34–37) records that although 'some of those standing near' thought that the crucified Jesus was calling on Elijah for a miracle, in fact the Christians' Lord suffered and died along with the millions who have known no miracle.

Should scepticism be entirely banished when we read the stories told about Jesus himself or about his apostles? We are told that before his own 'exodus' (Luke 9:31, the NIV uses 'departure') from life to death and glory, Jesus was strengthened by a mystical experience during which the figures of Moses and Elijah were seen in 'splendour'. Mark tells us that he was popularly thought to be a reincarnation of Elijah (6:15). According to Luke his sermon in the Nazareth synagogue referred to the miracles of Elijah and Elisha (4:24–27) and the healing of the widow's son at Nain (7:11–17) was closely similar to the miracle performed by Elijah in nearby Shunem. All Christians agree that Jesus shared the spiritual splendour of Moses and Elijah as courageous and vastly influential witnesses to the power and holiness of the one true God. But in modern times there has been no such agreement about the real connection of Jesus with the images of Moses and Elijah as miracle-workers. One of the most elaborate of the recent studies of *The Miracle Stories of the Early Christian Tradition* by Gerd Theissen (in English, 1983), begins its analysis with a very simple statement: 'Today we can no longer regard miracle stories as evidence of divine intervention in the normal course of things' (p. 34). Rudolf Bultmann is quoted: 'Diseases and their cures have their natural causes, and do not depend on the action of evil spirits or on their casting out. This puts an end to the New Testament miracles as miracles.'

One reason why the matter is, I think, somewhat more complicated than Bultmann and Theissen suppose is that it is generally agreed that Jesus was a faith healer and exorcist. As a Jewish scholar, Geza Vermes, showed us afresh in his *Jesus the Jew* (1973), there were a number of charismatic healers and exorcists at work in Galilee in that century. A hostile echo of the tradition that Jesus 'practised sorcery' has survived in the later *Tractate Sanhedrin* in the Talmud, but more important is the evidence provided abundantly from many sources including the New Testament that the ability of charismatics to cure diseases and drive out devils was then taken for granted both in Jewish circles and in the pagan world. It was commonly believed that even a Roman emperor could perform miracles of this kind. If the traditions about Jesus had declared that he had lacked this ability, or had not exercised it, that would have been more remarkable than the claims which were made. Jesus and his first followers lived in an age whose character we glimpse when we read what Paul wrote. He criticised the cult of miracle ('Jews demand miraculous signs . . . but we preach Christ crucified'), but saw no need to justify his claim to have performed miracles while preaching 'from Jerusalem all the way around to Illyricum' (1 Corinthians 1:22–23; Romans 15:19). His first letter to the Corinthians reminded them that some of them had this power (12:28) before putting the emphasis on love. Similar power was present in the churches of Galatia (3:5), but Paul's second letter to the Thessalonians included another reminder – that Satan, too, could perform 'miracles, signs and wonders' (2:9). The Acts of the Apostles provides many more glimpses of the acceptance of these 'miracles'. There it is claimed that the sick could be cured even by handkerchiefs and aprons that had touched Paul (19:12) or by Peter's passing shadow (5:15). In Jerusalem, we are told, 'many wonders and miraculous signs were done by the apostles' (2:43) in response to their prayers (4:30). In Lystra another healing miracle made the people shout: 'The gods have come down to us in human form!' (14:11). But such power was not thought to be confined to Christians. Among the Samaritans, Simon the sorcerer was already famous as 'the Great Power' before he tried to buy extra power from Peter and John (8:9–24). Against that background, it is not surprising to hear the cry of Jesus in Luke's gospel: 'I will drive out demons and heal people today and tomorrow, and on the third day I will reach my goal' (13:32).

About a third of the earliest surviving gospel tells of the miracles of Jesus and the character of the gospels of

Matthew, Luke and John is not very different. Matthew, for example, groups ten miracles together in chapters 8 and 9. Most are healing miracles similar to those in Acts. As with the Acts stories, it is impossible to be sure of the authentic medical situation. Obviously these stories may have grown in the telling during their long journey – between thirty and sixty years long – from a Palestinian village to the pen of the evangelist. This may be true of reports of healing a Gentile from a distance (Mark 7:24–30; Matthew 8:5–13, paralleled in Luke). Sometimes we seem able to watch a story at different stages. Thus Mark (14:47) tells us that a man in the service of the high priest had his right ear cut off during the arrest of Jesus; Luke (22:50–51) that the man was promptly healed by Jesus; and John (18:10) that his name was Malchus. It is also obvious that there was nothing like a modern medical diagnosis. Not all 'the sick' are said to be possessed by 'demons' but demon possession was so commonly thought of as the cause of sickness that the anonymous author of the third gospel – traditionally identified with Luke, 'our dear friend . . . the doctor' (Colossians 4:14) – could explain the cure of Peter's mother-in-law (Mark 1:31): 'Jesus bent over her and rebuked the fever, and it left her' (Luke 4:38–39). The detail with which the symptoms are given in the story of the boy healed after the transfiguration, suggesting epilepsy, is not usual (Mark 9:14–32). It has often been explained that people said to be 'blind' may not have lost all power of vision; that people called 'lepers' may have been suffering from any one of a number of skin diseases; that people thought to be 'dead' may have been in a coma. All such explanations reduce the apparent contradictions between these miracle stories and what is known scientifically of the natural healing processes. The contradiction is further reduced if it is recognised that it is sometimes possible to heal by the power of suggestion. There seems no good reason to doubt that Jesus communicated a spiritual power which, if believed in, had physical effects, including the effect of calming and healing persons convinced that they were possessed by demons. The woman subject to bleeding for twelve years touched the cloak of Jesus and was healed, to be told: 'Daughter, your faith has healed you' (Mark 5:34). Luke's special material includes a similar saying (17:19). Nor is it surprising that the acutely sensitive Jesus 'realised that power had gone out from him' (Mark 5:30), particularly when he healed by laying on hands or by a command to the demon. It is not incredible that the influence of an atmosphere of trust in this miracle-worker, not necessarily a clear personal faith, could effect the cure (as in Mark 2:3–5; 7:24–30). Nor is it incredible that what some patients needed was to be assured that their sins were forgiven, since sickness was believed to be a punishment for sins (Mark 2:5). But when Jesus was amazed to find little faith during a return to his home town, 'he could not do any miracles there, except lay his hands on a few sick people and heal them' (Mark 6:5). All this can be understood in the context of a large body of evidence about the successful practices of 'faith' or 'psychosomatic' healers in many ages and cultures. It is widely agreed that a calmed, cleansed, strengthened, confident mind can affect the body – that 'faith' can sometimes 'heal'. Probably every general practitioner of scientific medicine would agree with that.

These stories about Jesus are far removed from the magical atmosphere of the tales about Moses and Elijah. Jesus wields no wand. So far from uttering an incantation such as the conjurer's *Abracadabra*, he is reported to have been very simple in his words; thus Mark quotes in the original Aramaic not a magical formula but 'Little girl, I say to you, get up!' (5:41) and 'Be opened!' (7:34). When instead of merely touching 'blind' eyes Jesus uses spittle (8:23) as the commonly accepted means of dealing with eye diseases, the atmosphere is somewhat more magical – but not decisively so, since the spittle can be regarded as a sign of faith in the healing power of God. And according to the gospels Jesus does not make his work as a healer his supreme mission. He does not cure as many people as he can; his cures seem to be compassionate responses to emergencies which come his way. It is noticeable that the number of healings decreases as the gospels move to their climax. Jesus is said to have declared that no miraculous 'sign from heaven' would be given by him (Mark 8:11–12) and to have lamented that 'a wicked and adulterous generation asks for a miraculous sign! But none will be given it except the sign of the prophet Jonah' (Matthew 12:39). About the nature of this 'sign of Jonah' the gospels differ. Since Jonah was raised from death in order to preach, Luke (11:29–32) confines the 'sign' to preaching which produces repentance, although Matthew (12:40) interprets it as the sign of the resurrection of Jesus. Luke (16:31) reports a parable which says that people 'will not be convinced even if someone rises from the dead'. Certainly the impression is given by the gospels apart from John's that the healing miracles of Jesus prove very little. Korazin, Bethsaida and Capernaum are unimpressed (Matthew 11:20–24). Very few of those cured are said to 'follow' Jesus. Herod hopes to see a miracle done by Jesus without listening to a word he says (Luke 23:8). Those who do 'follow' are warned that at the last judgement it will not be enough to say, 'Lord, Lord, did we not prophesy in your name, and in your name drive out demons and perform many miracles?' (Matthew 7:22). Indeed, it is expected that 'false Christs and false prophets will appear and perform signs and miracles' (Mark 13:22). Already the critics of Jesus can themselves drive out demons (Matthew 12:27).

The healing miracles are, however, 'signs' (John's great word in his gospel) that the messianic age, or the age of the Spirit, or the kingdom of God, has dawned. Jesus casts out demons by God's 'finger' (Luke 11:20) or 'Spirit' (Matthew 12:28). In Matthew's gospel (11:1–6), paralleled in Luke's, it is reported that when John the Baptist sends messengers from prison to ask whether Jesus really is the Messiah, the reply points to the signs of the messianic age in the poetry of the books of Isaiah (29:18–19; 35:5–6; 61:1). 'The blind receive sight, the lame walk, those who have leprosy are cured, the deaf hear, the dead are raised, and the good news is preached to the poor' (Matthew 11:5). Yet the deepest insight into the central purpose of Jesus is provided by his silence. He does not promise John that he will be delivered miraculously from prison. And he does not rely on a miracle to save him from his own death. This silence arises from the decision, made in the depths of his personality and after a great struggle, that it is not the will of his Father that he should compel faith by performing miracles (Matthew 4:5-7, paralleled in Luke). And Paul, when he prays for a healing miracle for himself, receives a silent answer – silent apart from the message: 'My grace is sufficient for you, for my power is made perfect in weakness' (2 Corinthians 12:9).

This reserve about the importance of healing miracles prepares us for the problem of those miracle stories which present Jesus not as healing people but as interfering with the course of nature. Such stories are particularly prone to grow in the telling. Thus it must arouse suspicion when Luke (5:1-11), and he alone, adds to the story of the calling of the first disciples a story of a miraculous catch of fish. This may well be a story told in order to draw out the meaning of the promise: 'from now on you will catch men'. A similar story is told by John in the epilogue to his gospel (21:1-14) before the risen Jesus turns Peter from the fisherman into the pastor. Matthew (17:24-27) alone tells the story that Jesus paid the temple tax by contributing a coin found miraculously in the mouth of a fish. This may well be a legend originating in the simple thought that fishermen could pay the tax out of their profits. The story of the fig tree which is withered by the curse of Jesus is found more widely, but it is suspicious that Mark (11:20) says that the tree was found withered next morning while Matthew (21:19) claims that the miracle occurred 'immediately'. This may well be a misunderstanding of a parable comparing the opponents of Jesus with a fruitless fig tree (Luke 13:6-9). At least that explanation seems more in keeping with the character of Jesus than Matthew's, which suggests that Jesus was angry because 'hungry' although it was not the season for fig trees to bear fruit.

Other problems are presented by the stories of the feeding of the thousands and of control over storms on the Lake of Galilee. These stories occur in all the gospels. Indeed, Mark and Matthew occupy much of their space by telling of two feedings, of five thousand and four thousand, with a number of repeated details. It has often been suggested that the Church understood the first story as a drama of the spiritual feeding of Jews, while the second is a drama of the spiritual food of the Gentiles, for it takes place in the region of the Decapolis where many Gentiles lived (Mark 7:31). But this is far from certain since Mark does not say that any Gentiles were fed and Luke, who is specially interested in the Gentile mission, includes only the first feeding (9:10–17). It has also often been suggested that the feeding was no more than a speeding up of the natural processes which produce grain and fish. But the stories emphasise the miracle by implying that the bread was baked and by not saying that the fish was raw. We are asked to imagine that complete new loaves – so many that 'seven basketfuls of broken pieces' were left over when 'about four thousand' had been 'satisfied' – were multiplied from the seven loaves placed in the hands of Jesus (Mark 8:1–10). And this is very hard to imagine as a piece of accurate history. It is far more likely to have been a story which developed out of a tradition about a large meeting full of excitement and including a common meal in anticipation of the banquets traditionally believed to belong to the messianic age. As the story was passed on, it may well have been compared with the stories of *manna* in the wilderness and of the miraculous creations of food by Elijah and Elisha – and it may well have acquired colour from those sources. The uncertainty about the numbers involved may well have resulted in two reports being available to Mark and being copied by Matthew.

The story of the walking on the water after the feeding of the four thousand is not included in Luke's gospel. This may have been because he thought it unfit for his readership, which was more educated than Mark's. (He did not recount the story of the cursing of the fig tree.) It is obvious that if Jesus really did multiply the loaves and fish miraculously, he was capable of crossing the lake on foot. It is, however, equally obvious that the disciples have not been the only people to be 'completely amazed' (Mark 6:51). The miracle too closely resembles the story of Elisha's stick which made an iron axe-head float in the river (2 Kings 6:1–7). Another story tells that Jesus 'rebuked the wind and said to the waves, "Quiet! Be still!"' so that the sea was 'completely calm' after a 'furious squall' (Mark 4:35–41). But just as the story of the feeding of the thousands would have appealed particularly to preachers at Christian Eucharists, so these stories must often have been preached as illustrations of the power of the Lord to control the storms of the Christian's life. The probability appears to be that miracle stories developed when, as was almost inevitable in that world, the spiritual message was taken literally. The addition by Matthew (14:28–31) of the story that Peter as well as Jesus walked on the water suggests that the tradition did develop.

What are we to make of these stories? In his *Interpreting the Miracles* (1963, pp. 122–3), R. H. Fuller concluded a careful examination with a plea for agreement about the religious significance of a story such as the miraculous catch of fish.

> Whether we take its historicity for granted (as the evangelist did) or not, the real point lies, *as it did for the evangelist*, elsewhere. It is over that real point that the fundamentalist and the modern critical believer can agree. For the evangelist, the real miracle was not the draught of the fishes, but the call of Peter to the apostleship and his apostolic ministry. This interpretation is not a modern subterfuge, a *solution d'embarrassment* for a sceptic whose faith has been corroded by the acids of modernity. It represents the true intention of the evangelist.

My own plea, for what it is worth, is the same as Professor Fuller's. I do not doubt that the writers of the gospels were far less sceptical about the historicity of these miracle stories than are people who are inclined to scepticism because of their whole education and culture. But the intention of the evangelists was not to satisfy modern sceptics with proof that Jesus did perform precisely these miracles. If that had been their aim, they would have had to provide many more medical details of the patients before and after the cure and much more evidence about the miracles of control over nature (although even to suggest this necessity is to move out of their pre-scientific world). Still less was it their aim to prove the 'divinity of Jesus' (which is not a biblical phrase) by his miracles. Many of the contemporaries of Jesus who were emphatically not divine were reported to perform miracles. The real intention was to strengthen the faith of those who read or heard these stories, in order that these Christians might be delivered from the evils ('demons') which they faced in situations far from Palestine. The power of Jesus to conquer fear and anxiety could have healing effects: that they knew and that they preached. And even when it did not cure the ills of the body, even when the Christian had to undergo sufferings like the Lord's own, the Lord's power could calm the storms of life. John's gospel provides a profound meditation on the spiritual significance of seven miraculous 'signs' – the new wine means a new age (2:1–11), the healing of a boy means a new life (4:43–54), the healing of a lame man means a new freedom from sin (5:1–15), the feeding of the thousands means that Jesus is the bread of life (6:1–15,25–59), the walking on the water means that Jesus banishes fear (6:16–21), the healing of a blind man means that Jesus is the light of the world (9:1–41), the raising of Lazarus means that Jesus already is 'the resurrection' or 'eternal life' (11:1–44).

That was the gospel. Is it not the gospel now? And if it is the gospel to be proclaimed within a scientific culture, is not belief in it compatible with scepticism (or an open mind) about the historicity of parts of the miracle stories? May not faith in God through Christ be held together with an inclination to give the stories of healing miracles explanations which are acceptable to those medical scientists who are prepared to make room for the evidence about 'faith' or 'psychosomatic' healing?

## The Birth of Jesus

I ask these questions hoping that Evangelicals such as Dr Stott will agree to make some distinction between the essential gospel and the miracle stories of the Bible. But I am fully aware that many conservatives are highly suspicious of – or hostile to – the 'liberal' attitude to the two most important miracles in the Christian Scriptures, the virginal conception and physical resurrection of the Saviour. In 1986 I wrote a booklet (*Bishops and Beliefs*) about the controversy which erupted in the Church of England after publicity given to sceptical remarks by the new Bishop of Durham, David Jenkins. There I showed that this controversy had many precedents in theological conflicts in England and many other countries throughout the twentieth century. In response to these arguments, belief in the 'virgin birth' and bodily 'resurrection' is stated to be essential for Evangelicals in many definitions of belief by groups and individual teachers around the Evangelical world. Dr Stott has claimed that the doctrine of the virginal conception, for example, is plainly taught in the gospels of Matthew and Luke and 'has been the virtually unanimous belief of the universal Church ever since. This teaching and tradition cannot lightly be set aside. Besides, it is entirely congruous that a supernatural person (who was simultaneously God and man) should enter as well as leave the world in a supernatural way' (AJ, p. 56).

It might seem that a very careful book of some six hundred pages by a Roman Catholic scholar, Raymond Brown, *The Birth of the Messiah* (1977), left nothing more to be said about the virginal conception of Jesus. The book certainly was an almost completely exhaustive study of the first two chapters of Matthew's gospel and of Luke's. But theologically it left everything to be said, for it did not answer the question whether Jesus truly was conceived by the power of the Holy Spirit without the intervention of a human father. Professor Brown rightly said that both Matthew and Luke assumed that the basic historical question had been answered by the traditions which they received. He added, rightly, that those who compiled the summaries of belief commonly called the Apostles' and Nicene Creeds took it for granted that the gospels of Matthew and Luke were true history, a point very seldom disputed in the ancient or medieval Church. But he also showed that it is very difficult indeed for minds accustomed to weigh evidence in the modern manner to accept everything in these gospels as historically accurate – despite the teaching of Dr Stott that Matthew and Luke were writing 'prose not poetry, history not myth' (AJ, p. 58). This problem is relevant to the historical question, since in the whole of the New Testament there is no other reference to the virginal conception.

Paul's surviving letters do not refer to it. They do not even name the mother of Jesus. Instead they accept that Jesus, 'born of a woman' (Galatians 4:4), 'as to his human nature was a descendant of David', presumably through his father (Romans 1:3). Mark's gospel, beginning with the Baptist and the baptism of Jesus, also does not mention this miracle. It does not even record the name of the legal father of Jesus. John's gospel is also silent about a miraculous conception, except that all Christians are 'born' not through sex but 'of God' (1:13). Far from incorporating the story that Jesus was literally born of a virgin in Bethlehem, it reflects the tradition that Jesus and his followers had faced the difficulty of origins in Nazareth, a village never mentioned in the Hebrew Scriptures. No historical answer is given within this gospel to Nathanael's question, 'Nazareth! Can anything good come from there?' (1:46). Nor are 'others of the people' answered historically when they ask: 'How can the Christ come from Galilee? Does not the Scripture say that the Christ will come from David's

family and from Bethlehem, the town where David lived?'
(7:41–42).

Even more damaging to the historicity of these early
chapters of Matthew and Luke is the fact that none of the
gospels shows any signs of a tradition that the sensational
events surrounding the birth of Jesus were recalled by his
family or other contemporaries. On the contrary, Mark tells
us that his family attempted 'to take charge of him, for they
said, "He is out of his mind,"' and that when the mother
and brothers of Jesus were outside the house looking for
him he replied that his true family was the circle seated
attentively around him (3:21,31–35). Later Jesus lamented
that he was a prophet without honour 'in his home town,
among his relatives and in his own house' (6:4). Matthew's
own gospel reports the saying of Jesus which appears to
exclude his mother from the circle of 'whoever does the will
of my Father in heaven' (12:46–50), while Luke reports that
the adult John the Baptist doubted whether Jesus was the
Messiah (7:19) although we are told that his own mother
had fully shared Mary's experiences before the miraculous
birth. Matthew adds that the Herod whose father had met
the Magi was utterly puzzled by reports about Jesus: was
this John the Baptist risen from the dead? (14:1–2). And in
both gospels the story of the Messiah's birth – of the
miraculous star or the appearance of the angels to the
shepherds – is said to have been known widely in Jerusalem
or in Bethlehem (only five miles away). Yet the story is
apparently not known by anyone who meets the adult
Jesus.

But the final damage to the historicity of these stories is
done by a close examination of their details, many of which
are impossible or improbable. There are, for example,
contradictions. The family trees of Jesus given by Matthew
and Luke do not agree with each other or with the Old
Testament. Matthew says nothing of any association with
Nazareth until the family is back from Egypt (2:19–23); on
the contrary, the Magi are received in a 'house' in Bethlehem (2:1–12), apparently some two years after the birth.

Luke, in contrast, locates the parents of Jesus in Nazareth until a census of the entire Roman world decrees that everyone must go to his own town to register (2:1–7) – a decree which is not mentioned in any other surviving document. Joseph and Mary return to Nazareth after presenting the child in the temple in Jerusalem according to 'the Law of the Lord' (2:21–24) – a law or custom for which, again, there is no other evidence. Matthew says that Joseph is so dismayed by Mary's pregnancy that he intends to divorce her (1:18–19), but Luke claims that her pregnancy has already been explained to Mary by the angel Gabriel (1:26–38). If we believe that both stories are historically accurate, we must suppose either that Mary never told Joseph or that, although a 'just man', he thought that she had invented the story of the angel.

Matthew's stories of Joseph's dreams (1:20–24; 2:13–15) are suspiciously like the stories told in Genesis of the dreams of another Joseph (37:2–11). He claims that a 'star in the east' announced the birth of the Messiah to Gentile astrologers (2:1–2) but does not explain how any star could do such a thing, let alone how it could guide them first to Jerusalem and then, moving ahead of them, to the particular house in Bethlehem where Joseph and Mary were living. He also says that King Herod, although presumably well aware of the popular expectation of a greater king, the Son of David, had to ask 'all the people's chief priests and teachers of the law' where the Messiah was to be born (2:4). Then he made no effort to investigate the family to which the Magi went. The later massacre of 'all the boys in Bethlehem and its vicinity who were two years old and under' (2:16) is not out of keeping with Herod's known character but is not mentioned in the indignantly careful list of Herod's atrocities given by the Jewish historian, Josephus. It is suspiciously like the story of Pharaoh's massacre of Hebrew boys in Exodus (1:22). In Luke's narrative the characters, saying and experiences of John the Baptist's parents (1:5–25; 57–80) are suspiciously like those of Abraham and Sarah in Genesis and Mary's Song

(1:46–55, the *Magnificat*) resembles the song of Hannah (1 Samuel 2:1–10). For all its beauty, it celebrates not the birth of the Messiah but the deliverance of the humble and poor in Israel, only one sentence being a personal reference. Zechariah's Song (1:68–79, the *Benedictus*) is similar. Many scholars believe that these are Jewish or Christian hymns which Luke has incorporated. And they do *not* believe that Dr Stott is right to claim that 'ultimately the facts must have come from Mary and Joseph themselves, whether in written or spoken form' (AJ, p. 61). Joseph seems to have died when Jesus was young. This seems to be the simplest explanation of his absence from the gospels and of the reference to Jesus as 'Mary's son' (Mark 6:3, an expression avoided by Matthew and Luke). If Mary told these stories as facts, she described many events at which she was not present and which are not compatible with each other. According to Jewish custom at that time, she would have been between twelve and thirteen years old when pledged by her family to marry Joseph. Dr Stott thinks that Luke probably 'received her story from her own lips' when he was in Palestine during Paul's imprisonment in Caesarea (AJ, p. 61). But the probable chronology suggests that Mary would then be aged almost eighty and it was very rare for people to live so long.

It seems highly probable that both Matthew and Luke knew of a tradition that an angel had announced that the birth of Jesus would be miraculous, but that to this tradition they added other current stories and their own pious fiction with such success that the imaginations of countless people, including great saints, artists, poets and musicians, have been captured and spiritualised. Apparently the two evangelists did not know of each other's work. Had Matthew known the story of the boy Jesus in the temple in Jerusalem, listening to the teachers of the Law of Moses and asking them questions, it would have fitted in very well with his picture of Jesus as the teacher of the Sermon on the Mount. Had Luke known the story of the Magi, we may guess that he would have delighted to use it as the first great sign that this child was to be 'a light for revelation to the Gentiles' (2:32). But there are enough similarities between their independent narratives to suggest that they inherited a common basic tradition. This tradition may also be reflected in Jewish and pagan charges (of which evidence survives) that Jesus was illegitimate. But it seems more probable that such charges were replies to the stories of Matthew and Luke.

Our answers to the historical question about the virginal conception must therefore depend on our estimates of the probability that this common tradition of an angelic annunciation of a virginal conception is factual rather than fictional. My own answer is that it is probably fictional. As the angel says to Mary in the story, 'nothing is impossible with God' (Luke 1:37). But we have to consider what is probable. Many legends of miracles surrounding the births of heroes exist in the world's literature. We should not link the spiritually beautiful and elevated stories of Matthew and Luke with the pagan myths of girls being impregnated by gods, often against their wills or without their knowledge, but it is striking that within the Christian Church (clearly from the fourth century onwards) the legend developed that Mary was a *perpetual* virgin. This was thought fitting although Mark's gospel speaks plainly of four brothers of Jesus (James, Joseph, Judas and Simon) and of unnumbered sisters (6:3) and Matthew says that Joseph had no sexual intercourse with Mary until after the birth of Jesus (1:25). It seems clear, although tragic, that births avoiding human sex were thought of as being purer and more wonderful than the mystery of the sexual creation of a new human being.

It is also certain that the ancient world knew nothing of the modern science of genetics, which has done something to unravel the mystery. The mother was commonly but mistakenly thought to contribute nothing to the physical basis of the new personality. She appeared to be a mere tube in which the father's seed became a child. A remarkable illustration of this attitude is the insistence of both

Matthew and Luke on tracing the ancestry of Jesus through Joseph although Jesus was only 'the son, so it was thought' of his human father (Luke 3:23). The claim that Jesus was descended from King David could not be supported by claiming that his mother was. But we now know that his mother must have contributed to the genetic equipment which made Jesus a man. Therefore some at least of the theological assertion, familiar in the Church in ancient and medieval times, that his human nature was a new creation, the miraculous work of the Holy Spirit and therefore sinless, resulted from their ignorance of genetics. We live in a different world – a world with which Dr Stott attempts to communicate when he writes that the humanity of Jesus was derived from Mary, while his sinlessness and deity were derived from the Holy Spirit (AJ, p. 65). Within this world we have to think out the gospel which Luke expressed poetically by saying that the Holy Spirit would 'overshadow' Mary (1:35).

There has been a long modern controversy about the suitability of the virginal conception – about its compatibility with the rest of what we know of God's character and methods. It has been generally agreed that the doctrine that Jesus was the Son of God or God the Son incarnate, born as a man through God's loving initiative for our salvation, does not depend logically on the belief that he was conceived by the Holy Spirit, although it is no doubt for many people easier to believe that Jesus was spiritually the Son of God if it is also believed that he was not physically the son of Joseph. This agreement is surely correct. It is well known that like Paul, Mark and John in the New Testament, many Christians in modern times have fervently believed in a gospel about the Son of God which does not include the virginal conception, while some eminent non-Christians (the Prophet of Islam among them as the Koran attests) have believed that Jesus was born of a virgin without believing that he was in any sense divine or even the supreme prophet. Luke himself does not deduce a full trinitarianism from the virginal conception. He presents a

Jesus who is indeed now exalted as the Messiah, the Son of God, the Lord and the Saviour, but who was 'a man accredited by God to you by miracles, wonders and signs' (Acts 2:22). For Matthew, too, the divinity of Jesus is not proved by his miraculous birth. And all that I am now asking Evangelicals and other conservatives to agree is that in order to believe that the glory of God shone 'in the face of Christ' (2 Corinthians 4:6), that the ultimate truth about the birth of Jesus is not that Joseph so loved Mary but that God so loved the world, it is not necessary to believe that Joseph had nothing to do with the conception of Jesus.

## The Resurrection of Jesus

To be a Christian, is it necessary to believe in the supreme miracle reported in the Christian Bible, the physical resurrection of Jesus? The question is so important that I may be forgiven for offering an answer in my own simple and blunt words, although I try to be aware of the sophisticated discussion summarised in, for example, *The Structure of Resurrection Belief* by Peter Carnley, Archbishop of Perth (1987). My own answer to this question is that this belief that the tomb was empty because the corpse was transformed is not necessary although I hold it (or, rather, it holds me despite much puzzlement and doubt). What I believe *is* essential if one is to be a Christian is that one should share the faith expressed in the popular chorus:

> He lives! He lives!
> Christ Jesus lives today.
> He walks with me,
> He talks with me,
> Along life's narrow way.
> He lives! He lives!
> Salvation to impart.
> You ask me how I know he lives?
> He lives within my heart.

Dr Stott does not like this chorus. He thinks that 'some very orthodox Evangelicals are to blame' when they sing it, because 'to affirm the living presence of Jesus by his Spirit in our hearts is not the same as to affirm his resurrection' (AJ, p. 37). Certainly it is not the same as to affirm his physical resurrection as a fact in history. But to affirm that one who was crucified almost two thousand years ago, feeling God-forsaken, is the living Saviour in my life is to affirm that he has been 'raised from the dead' in some sense – in the sense that matters most to me in my life. Here is the reality which often makes Paul say (in language which is confusing in detail) that Christ is now present and active as Spirit. And I believe that what makes a Christian is a bit, however small, of the experience that 'he lives'. Certainly I know that what keeps me a Christian is the conviction that 'he walks with me' through all the changing scenes of life.

Dr Stott insists on belief in the physical miracle. 'Christianity', he tells us, 'is in its very essence a resurrection religion. The concept of resurrection lies at its heart. If you remove it, Christianity is destroyed' (CtC, p. 61). He is clear that about thirty-six hours after Christ's death his soul and body were reunited and he was 'raised'. 'In this resurrection body Christ burst from the tomb, passed through closed doors, appeared to His disciples and disappeared, and finally, in defiance of the law of gravity, ascended out of sight' (CtC, p. 61). And he is clear that this resurrection

> supplies both the proof and the pattern of the resurrection of our body at the last day. As He rose, so shall we – in fact and in manner. The apostle Paul is quite clear about it: 'Just as we have borne the image of the man of dust [*i.e.* Adam], we shall also bear the image of the man of heaven [*i.e.* Christ]' (1 Corinthians 15:49). And, when Christ returns He 'will change our lowly body to be like his glorious body' (Philippians 3:21). On that great day of Christ's return and our resurrection we shall be given bodies like His. (CtC, p. 62)

Dr Stott devoted the fourth chapter of *Basic Christianity* to assembling the historical evidence for the resurrection of

Christ. 'We may not feel able to go so far as Thomas Arnold, who called the resurrection "the best attested fact in history"', he says, 'but certainly many impartial students have judged the evidence to be extremely good.' Indeed, there 'can be no doubt' that the tomb was empty. It is very unlikely that the women went to the wrong tomb, that Jesus revived naturally after swooning on the cross, that thieves stole the body leaving the grave clothes, that the disciples removed it (and then were prepared to go to prison, flogging and death for a resurrection gospel which was a deliberate lie), or that the Roman or Jewish authorities took it into their own custody but were unable to produce it in response to the apostles' story. 'The authorities' silence is as eloquent a proof of the resurrection as the apostles' witness.' The appearance stories are not deliberate inventions: 'that is as plain as could be'. These narratives are 'sober and unadorned' although 'enlivened by the detailed touches which sound like the work of an eye-witness'. Anyone inventing them would have been careful to avoid both the 'complicated jigsaw puzzle of events which the four gospels together produce' and mention of the apostles' doubts and fears. Also, Mary Magdalene would not have been chosen as the first witness. And it is 'impossible' to dismiss 'ten' appearances, with their 'variety in the circumstances of person, place and mood', as 'the hallucinations of deranged minds' inspired by wishful thinking. Above all, the disciples were transformed into 'men who would hazard their lives for the name of the Lord Christ and turn the world upside down'. 'There is', Dr Stott concludes, 'no adequate explanation of these phenomena other than the great Christian affirmation that "the Lord is risen indeed" . . . The cumulative weight of this evidence is all but conclusive.'

I have quoted this teaching at length because it is an eloquent and very influential exposition of the resurrection of Jesus in terms which are familiar in most Christian – not only conservative Evangelical – evangelism. It presents the physical miracle as the 'pattern and proof' of our own destiny and argues for its truth on historical grounds. Here is an attempt to argue that we can reach a decision about our destiny, and therefore about the reality of the loving and sovereign God, not by the 'leap of faith' which (as Kierkegaard said) feels, even when one has plunged into faith, like swimming in an alarming ocean, and not by any reasoning of a philosophical kind, but by weighing *historical* evidence. Our attitude to the great questions of religion is to be settled by what we decide most probably took place one Sunday morning almost two thousand years ago. And my own presentations of the Easter faith in preaching and writing have for many years made some of the same points. Yet on some points I am compelled to disagree profoundly. For I believe that the tone of Dr Stott's talk about 'proof' does not do justice either to the difficulty of the problems involved or to the character of the message given in the New Testament. I am convinced that what is essential in that message cannot be communicated to real sceptics unless the problems are faced with total honesty.

Many people find it extremely difficult or impossible to believe that one day they will be given bodies which although physically identical or continuous with their corpses will be able to burst from the tomb, etc. This belief involves the idea that one day God will cancel *all* the laws, regularities or patterns which have made up the framework of this universe, so far over about twenty thousand million years. The implications are that bodies will be reassembled from whatever fragments may remain long after burial or cremation, and will then be reanimated and released to walk around a planet which like these bodies will never be subject to any further decay, making everything unimaginably like our present bodies and the earth on which we walk. And unless this stupendous, all-transforming miracle is to include only a tiny fraction of the human race there seems to be the prospect of inglorious overcrowding. Is such scepticism about the physical side of the New Testament's pictures of our 'resurrection' compatible with the full acceptance of the message that our personalities can be raised from death by the power of God? I believe that it is and that unless it is seen to be, the message itself – the gospel – will be believed by fewer and fewer people.

A physical picture of heaven does not seem a reasonable expectation to hold within the framework of normal reasoning – the framework to which Dr Stott appeals in his historical arguments for the resurrection of Jesus. And many people also find difficulty in these arguments about 'the first Easter'. It is not only fools incapable of understanding historical evidence who wonder whether the resurrection of Jesus was physical. In order to show this I am compelled to examine Dr Stott's arguments from a strictly historical point of view.

There certainly can be doubt that the tomb of Jesus was miraculously empty. The improbability of a body coming to life after brain-death is very great and very obvious. And there are other problems. W. G. Kümmel stated some of them in his *Theology of the New Testament* (in English, 1974, p. 100):

> In view of the Palestinian climate, it is not conceivable that the women intend to anoint a corpse on the third day after death. Nor is it comprehensible that the women go to the tomb with the intention of anointing the body although they do not know who will roll away the heavy boulder in front of the tomb. Besides, among the Jews it was not the custom to use spices in caring for the dead. In view of these improbabilities, it is hardly possible to regard this account as historically reliable.

These are problems although it is (whatever Kümmel says) possible that the women who loved and followed Jesus were willing to be very unconventional in order to honour him. Although Dr Stott does not mention it, the most likely alternative to such a miracle is that the corpse of Jesus was thrown into the same grave as the corpses of other crucified criminals (presumably in the nearby valley of Hinnom, Jerusalem's rubbish dump) and was beyond recovery and recognition by the time that the story of the resurrection reached the ears of the authorities – a time which may have been many months or years after the death. Almost all Christians will find this alternative distressing to contemplate; I do. But from a strictly historical point of view, excluding all religious faith or emotion, it, too, is possible. Logically it is not necessary to insist on the accuracy or near-accuracy of the evidence given in the New Testament that Jesus was buried in a special tomb known to his followers and that the tomb was known to be empty soon after his burial. There is an alternative.

From this strictly historical point of view, it is not plain that the stories of the appearances of the risen Jesus are so unadorned in their sober accuracy that no non-miraculous explanation of the phenomena can be adequate. Although the task is uncongenial, in all honesty I must point out the difficulties which are familiar to many.

The earliest list of the appearances to have survived is found in 1 Corinthians 15:1–11, probably written about twenty-five years after the death of Jesus. Paul recalls that about five years earlier he had preached in Corinth what he had 'received', presumably soon after his conversion within a few years of Christ's death. This was the gospel that Christ died, was buried and 'raised on the third day according to the Scriptures'. The reference to the Scriptures appears to point to Hosea 6:2 –

> After two days he will revive us;
> on the third day he will restore us,
> that we may live in his presence.

Acts 2:26–27 shows that the early Christians also quoted Psalm 16:9–10 in this connection:

> My heart is glad and my tongue rejoices;
> my body also will live in hope,
> because you will not abandon me to the grave,
> nor will you let your Holy One see corruption.

But the original meaning of the Hosea passage was an exhortation to Israel to hope for God's forgiveness after chastening – and the original meaning of the psalm was a prayer of hope for the recovery of 'your faithful servant' (the probable meaning of the Hebrew, as in the New English Bible translation) from sickness. The relevance of these passages to a resurrection believed to have occurred about thirty-six hours after a death depends on a method of interpreting Scripture which, as we have seen, is ancient rather than modern. The permanent significance of the reference to 'the Scriptures' seems to be that the Old Testament finally encouraged belief in a resurrection at the end of 'this age' – 'Multitudes who sleep in the dust of the earth will awake: some to everlasting life, others to shame and everlasting contempt' (Daniel 12:2). It was the Christian conviction that the age to come, the age of the resurrection, the End, had dawned some days after the death of Christ.

Six appearances are then listed by Paul – to Peter; to the Twelve; to 'more than five hundred of the brothers at the same time, most of whom are still living'; to James; to all the apostles; and 'to me also, as to one abnormally born'. The appearances to women, so important in the gospels, either are not known or are ignored. Three other problems are whether the suggestion that Judas Iscariot had been replaced among the Twelve was deliberate or a slip; whether the Twelve were deliberately distinguished from 'all the apostles'; and whether the accounts of the appearance to Paul given in Acts (9:1–9; 22:4–11; 26:12–18) suggest that it was abnormal in that no physical body appeared or whether it was in this respect like the earlier appearances. The list given to the Corinthians does not explain the connection between 'was buried' and 'appeared' and the long dispute of the scholars shows that it is uncertain whether or not Paul believed in the physical resurrection of Jesus. My own belief is that he did, but that he insisted that his own 'vision from heaven' (as it is called in Acts 26:19) fully entitled him to equality with the other apostles, so that he could write to the Galatians that 'God . . . was pleased to reveal his Son in me so that I might preach him among the Gentiles' (1:15–16). What mattered decisively for Paul was the internal, spiritual experience although that experience was connected with the historical Jesus who was buried and who was raised in a 'spiritual' or 'glorious' body. The minor differences between the accounts of Paul's Damascus Road experience in Acts shows that details about history did not matter decisively to the early Christians.

Of course the claim that Jesus appeared physically after his death does not refer to a mere detail. But the narratives in the gospels, said by Dr Stott to be 'a complicated jigsaw puzzle', produce many problems. Mark recounts that early in the morning Mary Magdalene, Mary the mother of James and Salome saw 'a young man dressed in a white robe', in the empty tomb and were told: 'He has risen! He is not here. See the place where they laid him. But go, tell his disciples and Peter, "He is going ahead of you into Galilee. There you will see him, just as he told you."' The women 'fled from the tomb. They said nothing to anyone, because they were afraid' (16:1–8). Matthew says that during the evening and during an earthquake 'Mary Magdalene and the other Mary' met an angel whose 'appearance was like lightning' and whose 'clothes were white as snow'. He had already terrified and concussed the guards by rolling back the stone at the entrance to the tomb and sitting on it. The women were 'afraid yet filled with joy'. The exit of Jesus from his tomb is not described (28:1–10). The only claim to provide a description occurs in the Gospel of Peter which dates from about AD 150. (There not only Jesus, who is now taller than the heavens, but also his cross, come out of the tomb and not only the soldiers, but also the Jewish elders, marvel at the spectacle.) In Matthew's gospel as the women 'hurried away . . . suddenly Jesus met them. "Greetings," he said. They came to him, clasped his feet and worshipped him,' to be told: 'Do not be afraid. Go and tell my brothers to go to Galilee; there they will see me.' And the 'eleven disciples' did see him on a mountain there, although 'some doubted'. They received from him the great promises about his authority and continuing presence and the great commission to 'make disciples of all nations, baptising them in the name of the Father and of the Son and of the Holy Spirit'. So Matthew and Mark do not agree about the number of the women witnesses. It has never been explained why Mark mentions a young man, who is not explicitly angelic. Mark, like Paul, does not tell us of any appearance to a woman. His authentic gospel stops at verse 8 and by then the women have left the vicinity of the tomb, saying 'nothing to anyone'. Matthew narrates an appearance to the apostles to which Paul also refers – but disturbingly he adds a baptismal formula which (according to Paul's letters and Acts) was not used during the first years of the Church.

Luke (24:1–53) does not name or number 'the women'. In the empty tomb they meet not one 'man' or one 'angel' but 'two men' in gleaming clothes. They report the resurrection 'to the Eleven and to all the others'. Peter alone checks that the tomb is indeed empty apart from the grave clothes. Then Cleopas and another disciple converse with Jesus as they walk to Emmaus. Although their conversation with him is about himself and their destination is seven miles from Jerusalem, they do not recognise him during the long walk. They tell him that 'some of our companions' saw that the tomb was indeed empty, just as the women had said after their 'vision of angels'. When Jesus is recognised as he begins supper with a grace, he disappears. By the time that these two reach the Eleven Jesus has appeared to Peter. He then appears to 'the Eleven and those with them', invites them to touch him and eats a piece of broiled fish in their presence. He tells them to 'stay in the city until you have been clothed with power from on high' and leads them out to the neighbourhood of Bethany, where after blessing them he is taken up to heaven. The disciples then 'stayed continually at the temple'. No mention is made of any appearance in Galilee; on the contrary, had the disciples gone to Galilee it would have been against their risen Lord's explicit command. No explanation is given about the timing of the final appearance in the gospel (called 'the Ascension' in the New International Version) in relation to the beginning of Acts, which is clearly a sequel to Luke's gospel.

Since it is 'nearly evening' at Luke 24:29 and the disciples have to walk seven miles back to the city before the next meeting with Jesus, the gospel reads as if Jesus took his farewell by night, some twenty-four hours after his resurrection. But Acts 1:3 says that 'he appeared to them over a period of forty days'.

The appearances related in John's gospel (20:1–21:24) combine Jerusalem with Galilee. Here only one woman, Mary Magdalene, goes to the tomb. She does not at first meet any man or angel but when she finds the tomb empty she tells Peter and 'the disciple whom Jesus loved', who both investigate. When they have gone back to their homes, she talks with two angels and then meets the risen Jesus, at first mistaking him for the gardener. In the evening Jesus appears to the disciples, having come through locked doors. A week later he appears to a circle which now includes Thomas and he invites him to feel his body. Later he appears to Peter and six other disciples in Galilee, creates a miraculous catch of fish, cooks breakfast and talks with Peter.

John's stories, like Luke's story of the road to Emmaus, possess undying spiritual beauty, fascination and force, but the need to believe that the disciples returned to their fishing trade in Galilee only briefly before going back to Jerusalem is not the only problem in fitting together the pieces of what Dr Stott calls a 'jigsaw puzzle'. Indeed, it has proved impossible to construct a fully harmonised version of the resurrection stories, despite many attempts to do so. It is curious that the gospels in the New Testament contain no stories of the appearances listed by Paul as being to Peter, to more than five hundred and to James (who presumably is James the brother of Jesus). Nor is there any story of an appearance to Mary the mother of Jesus, although in Acts (1:14) she appears with James and her other sons among the disciples. But the stories as given constitute not a jigsaw puzzle but an insoluble mystery.

The incompatibilities in numbering the women and the angels, or in locating and timing the appearances, are less

significant than the problems about the physicality of the
risen Jesus. A body so normal that it can be clasped, can be
thought to be a stranger's, and can cook and eat, is also said
to be unrecognisable by disciples, to pass through walls or
locked doors, and to disappear at will. Another problem,
less noticed by commentators, is that it is said to have
acquired clothes which seem to have looked normal (unlike
the robes of the angels). It seems difficult to classify the
reported phenomenon as either physical or psychic. And
what was physical in the glorious Easter body is reported to
have ceased when the appearances ceased. It is for ever
beyond our understanding.

This difficulty would matter greatly if belief in the physicality of our own future resurrection bodies, said to be
promised by the physicality of Christ's risen body, is to be
regarded as essential to Christian faith. But we read that
Jesus taught that 'at the resurrection they will neither marry
nor be given in marriage; they will be like the angels in
heaven'. The possibility of a glorious resurrection depends
entirely on 'the power of God' – and on the love of God.
God's will is that he should continue to be the God of
Abraham, Isaac and Jacob, who are dead. So he is the God
of all who, although dead, are 'the living' because God
raises them above death (Mark 12:24–27). And Paul expected that the 'spiritual body' – imperishable, glorious and
powerful – would not be the same body, for 'flesh and
blood cannot inherit the kingdom of God, nor does the
perishable inherit the imperishable' (1 Corinthians 15:50).
The 1982 report on *Evangelism and Social Responsibility* tells
us that this international gathering of Evangelical leaders
found itself united in the belief that God is going to re-create
'our bodies', and not create another body *ex nihilo*, 'for the
principle of continuity is evident in the resurrection of
Jesus. Although, as Paul expresses it, our new body will be
as different from the old as a flower differs from the seed,
nevertheless there will be a continuity between the two.'
This report cites another sentence in Paul's first letter to
Corinth: 'God raised the Lord and will also raise us up by

his power' (ESR, p. 41). But it is important to remember that in the ancient world it was believed that a seed *dies* in the ground (1 Corinthians 15:36; John 12:24). The continuity between 'our bodies' and heaven as pictured by Paul is a continuity through death, which is why Paul also dwells on the contrast. He compares it with the difference between human flesh and the flesh of fish, or between the sun and the moon.

An examination of Paul's teachings about the resurrection of Christians shows that here, as in the teaching about the closely linked subject of the end of this present age, he used pictures which cannot be fitted into each other exactly and which should not be treated as literal descriptions of the future. The Philippians are encouraged to await eagerly a Saviour from heaven 'who, by the power that enables him to bring everything under his control, will transform our lowly bodies so that they will be like his glorious body' (3:20–21). It is a picture of the End. So is the picture in the first letter to the Thessalonians of the meeting with the Lord in the clouds after 'the trumpet call of God' (4:16–17). A similar vision is shared with the Romans: 'he who raised Christ from the dead will also give life to your mortal bodies' (8:11). Indeed, the whole universe is being 'liberated from its bondage to decay and brought into the glorious freedom of the children of God' (8:21). Until the glory of that End, the dead 'fall asleep' (1 Thessalonians 4:13,15). Yet 'if the earthly tent we live in is destroyed, we have a building from God, an eternal house in heaven, not built by human hands' and in it we shall be 'at home with the Lord' (2 Corinthians 5:1,8). It seems purposeless to ask whether the glorious bodies of the saints who survive to see the End are to be made on the earth or in the clouds, or whether those who die before the End are merely to sleep in their spiritual tents which will later be replaced by spiritual bodies. 'Someone may ask, "How are the dead raised? With what kind of body will they come?"' If so, Paul comments: 'How foolish!' (1 Corinthians 15:35–36). For it is foolish to ask about the age or the life to come questions which are relevant only to this life. Perhaps not all of the speculations of Paul himself were entirely wise.

To some extent the historical question about the resurrection of Jesus is similar to the historical question about his virginal conception. In common with more expert scholars I have suggested that the birth stories of Matthew and Luke can be shown to contain at least elements of fiction and that the tradition which they both reflect, of an angelic annunciation of a virginal conception, is probably also legendary. Reflection on the resurrection stories leads me to a partly sceptical conclusion about the historical accuracy of these stories as we have them. The narratives are indeed, as Dr Stott says, 'sober and unadorned' in comparison with some legends, but some or all of the detailed touches in them may well be the work of a story-teller. We know from the parables in his gospel as well as from the Acts of the Apostles that Luke, for example, was a story-teller of consummate skill, able to combine restraint and brevity with vividness. Many Christians, perhaps most, can trace the hand of a story-teller in the reports that at the hour of the death of Jesus 'the curtain of the temple was torn in two from top to bottom' (Mark 15:38), that there was an earthquake during which 'many holy people' came out of their tombs and later 'appeared to many people' in Jerusalem, and that the guards at the tomb of Jesus were so afraid of a resplendent angel who appeared during another earthquake that they became 'like dead men' (Matthew 27: 52–53; 28:2–3). But we have to ask whether these are the only legends in the Easter traditions. The difference of details in these resurrection stories is best accounted for, in my view, by holding either that the stories were handed on in different communities or that the evangelists had different imaginations. But although the opinion which I reach about literary and historical probability cannot endorse the Christmas or Easter stories as all literally true, in my honest view the probability seems to be that the central claim behind the Easter stories *is* reliable. I believe that contrary to what is known of nature Jesus appeared alive and triumphant after his death, his tomb being empty and his glorious body having some recognisably physical characteristics. It was a miracle.

I say this because I believe that miracles, however rare, are possible in principle and because the evidence for this one seems strong enough to appeal to a person who already believes in this possibility. Like the report that Jesus was a wonderful healer, the report that he appeared alive and triumphant after being buried comes to us from a number of sources. It was taught to Paul within a few years of the crucifixion and he could tell the Corinthians that most of the eye witnesses were alive when he wrote to them. It is common ground amid the differences between Matthew, Luke and John. Mark's gospel may be the one exception to this consensus. The puzzle of its enigmatic end is sometimes solved by saying that Mark did not know of any resurrection appearances and believed that they would be postponed until the time when 'men will see the Son of Man coming in clouds with great power and glory', as predicted at 13:26 and 14:62. But this solution seems improbable, since the reference in his Easter story is to a future appearance in Galilee, not in the clouds. It seems more likely that Mark believed that such an appearance had taken place but that his gospel does not include it, either for a reason unknown to us or because its end was soon lost after 16:8. If so, Mark's gospel is not really the exception and all the gospels testify, as does Paul, to the appearances of the risen Lord.

With our modern inclination to minimise the divine or supernatural interference in the processes of nature known to be normal, we may prefer to classify these appearances along with the psychic phenomena commonly called 'ghost stories'. Not all 'ghost stories' deserve a complete scepticism although many do. The evidence about *post mortem* experiences is always debatable, but it is quite widely believed by serious investigators that the very large body of evidence in this field does not rest entirely on fraud or self-deception. However, I am convinced that if the tradition about the appearances of Jesus is to be placed among *post mortem* psychic phenomena, its place must be unique. For these appearances transformed the disciples. Luke, who appreciated the power of the resurrection in the history of the progress of the gospel from Nazareth to Rome, was emphatic that the disciples did not see a mere ghost (24: 37–39). He deduced that the risen Jesus must have had 'flesh and bones'. What can be said with more confidence is that the *post mortem* appearances had the power to evoke in the Christian community poetic celebrations with the thrill of triumph. 'The trumpet will sound, the dead will be raised imperishable, and we will be changed' (1 Corinthians 15:52). 'He placed his right hand on me and said: "Do not be afraid. I am the First and the Last. I am the Living One; I was dead, and behold I am alive for ever and ever! And I hold the keys of death and Hades"' (Revelation 1:17–18). It can also be said confidently that the Christian celebration of this triumph took place on the first day of the Jewish week, the day associated with the event of the resurrection of Jesus. This 'Sunday' gradually replaced the seventh day ('Saturday') as the holy day of the Christians, the climax of their celebration being a memorial of the *death* of Jesus. Those who belong to the community of Christian faith know how terrible would have been the memory of the totally humiliating death without the memory of the appearances of the risen Lord. So I conclude that these appearances were real and really powerful. Far from being hallucinations, they were uniquely real. I note that this was the conclusion of a recent book by an orthodox Jew, Pinchas Lapide, on *The Resurrection of Jesus* (in English, 1983). It was also the upshot of the scholarly discussion in the book by Archbishop Peter Carnley to which I have referred.

For many a modern mind it would be simpler to leave it at that, for so far I have said no more than that the appearances were like psychic phenomena, although far more triumphant than other events behind authentic 'ghost stories', far more powerful in transforming people from a state of defeat, normal collapse and despair. But the evi-

dence does not permit me to consider only the tradition that
'he appeared'. The message which Paul and the gospel-
writers conveyed was that Jesus appeared *after being buried*.
The deduction that his tomb was empty is less probable
than the deduction that his appearances were real, for it is
further removed from the world known to science. We are
reminded of that by the uncertainty about whether Paul
himself accepted or knew this tradition. Many thoughtful
modern people therefore confine their own Easter faith to
the convictions that 'he lives' and 'he appeared', excluding
the empty tomb. For example, Pinchas Lapide wrote: 'I
cannot believe in the empty tomb nor in the angels with
white garments . . . All that belongs to the pious fraud of
later generations which themselves no longer felt the direct
impact' (p. 12). But the empty tomb is a tradition in all the
gospels and, as it seems to me, can reasonably be accepted
on such evidence as exists by people who thoroughly
appreciate what it means to say that physical miracles are
possible for God who is the Saviour and the Sovereign – and
what it means to say that Jesus was and is the utterly unique
Lord, the Son or Word of this sovereign God.

The empty tomb, if accepted within this faith, was an
astounding demonstration of the power of the Creator to
cancel the processes of death and decay. It was a miracle
utterly unique and therefore beyond our understanding –
for we can understand only what we can classify. It involved the dematerialisation of a corpse, for nothing less
than that could assure the disciples that the death of Jesus
was followed by triumph rather than survival and that they
must now share the joy of the triumph. That miracle did
not, I think, provide information about the precise future of
the universe, of the earth or of any member of the human
race other than Jesus. It did not even mean that Jesus
himself was always to keep a body that was physical. He
'ascended'. I am aware that Dr Stott is among those who take
at least some of the New Testament's pictures of the ultimate destiny literally. One day, he writes, 'Jesus Christ will
appear in full magnificence. He will raise the dead, judge

the world, regenerate the universe and bring God's Kingdom to perfection. From it all pain, decay, sin, sorrow and death will be banished, and in it God will be glorified for ever' (IFCT, p. 35). But I am among those who believe that these are only imaginative pictures, not blueprints of the future of this planet. Although the 'spiritual' or 'glorious' body in which Jesus appeared is a sign pointing to God's will for all humanity – for it leads to the hope that our joyful end will be 'spiritual' and 'glorious' – it seems highly improbable that all the tombs of humanity will ever be emptied. The emptiness of the tomb of Jesus, and of Jesus alone, was (it seems) a sign given by God because of the uniqueness of his embodiment of God, because of the uniqueness of his work, because of the uniqueness of the evil which judicially murdered him, and because of the uniqueness of the danger that his cause would be lost as his disciples crept back to Galilee in despair. So I believe. However, if further reflection by myself within my own limited capacity, or by others, were to sway the argument the other way (against the empty tomb), I should not feel that the heart of the Christian faith had been destroyed. I cannot regard it as the absolutely decisive question, whether the physicality of the life of Jesus was ended on the first Good Friday or a few days, or forty days, later. The essential belief, it seems to me, is that God the Saviour and Sovereign has shown the power of his love by raising Jesus from the dead, so that Jesus appeared to his disciples after being buried. He met them as the Living One. That is what makes Christianity a resurrection religion.

I do not claim that the conclusion that the tomb was empty ought to be accepted merely because no other explanation is adequate and the cumulative weight of the evidence in this direction is all but conclusive. Here is a conclusion which is likely to seem reasonable and probable only to people who are prepared to take the step of faith into the post-resurrection community – a community which is formed by the trembling acknowledgement (not understanding) of a mysterious act by the God who is the ultimate reality but also the ultimate mystery. Amid the welter of discussion about the 'Easter faith' and history, I have found no words wiser than these:

> This is an affirmation about God which historical evidence as such cannot demonstrate (or, for that matter, disprove). Yet it is not unrelated to history, for the affirmation began to be made at a particular point of time, which can be dated by historical means, and it was motivated by occurrences which can be described in historical terms . . . It is evident that these appearances, vitally important as they were in the origins of primitive Christianity, cannot prove more than that, after the crucifixion, certain persons believed that they had seen Jesus again; they cannot prove the Christian doctrine of the resurrection, since this involves a statement about the action of God incapable alike of observation and demonstration. (C. K. Barrett, *The First Epistle to the Corinthians*, 1971, p. 341)

The first messengers of the empty tomb in the gospels are women. Their evidence would not have been admitted in any court of law in that male-dominated society and they 'were afraid'. But they believed, we are told, because of their direct experience. The gospels do not claim that Pilate, Caiaphas, the other enemies of Jesus or the mob repented because they found the weight of the evidence for the empty tomb overwhelming: the direct experience was essential before there could be faith. Frequently Paul insists on the absolute necessity of a trusting faith and of the spiritual rebirth. I have found in my own experience, and in all that I know of other people's, that the empty tomb almost always seems incredible unless one has this felt, active, all-transforming faith in the utter uniqueness of the one Lord – the Lord whom one must follow in his suffering before one glimpses his victory. One has to belong to the company of those whose hearts, in so far as they are attached to the world known to the passions or to science, history and normal everyday experience, have been broken. One has to know something of what Paul meant when he said that 'if only for this life we have hope in

Christ, we are to be pitied more than all men' (1 Corinthians 15:19). And after that knowledge of death and defeat through our knowledge of the death and defeat of Jesus, we have to be ready to say – again out of our own experience – that 'surely this man was the Son of God', that 'our hearts were burning within us while he talked with us on the road', that he knows us by name and is our Teacher, that he is our peace, that he is our divine Lord, that he forgives our betrayals because he knows that we love him, that he commands us to feed his sheep, that he goes before us as we follow him into the unknown, that he 'will be with us always', that he is the miraculous Christ.

# John Stott's Response to Chapter 4

My dear David,

I am glad you have included in your book this chapter on miracles, because clearly Evangelicals (indeed, conservatives of all sorts) and liberals react differently to miraculous claims, and Christian attitudes to them have ranged from uncritical endorsement through doubt and embarrassment to outright rejection. I wonder if you will have seen what is certainly the most thorough scholarly treatment of miracles yet written by an Evangelical, namely Colin Brown's *Miracles and the Critical Mind* (1984)? It is a well-documented historical survey and evaluation, and Dr Brown followed it in 1985 with a more popular book covering very similar ground, entitled *That You May Believe*. In both books he quotes this rather telling statement of Reinhold Seeberg: 'Miracle was once the foundation of all apologetics, then it became an apologetic crutch, and today it is not infrequently regarded as a cross for apologetics to bear.'

There are two reasons why this chapter (both your essay and my response) differs from the previous three. The first is that, as you rightly comment, I have never attempted a full discourse on this topic. In consequence I am in a better position to respond to you, than you are to me! The second difference is that in this area I find myself caught in the crossfire between credulity and scepticism, that is, between those who not only accept the biblical miracles but believe they are continuing today and every day, and those who deny not only contemporary miracles but the biblical ones as well. I feel I need to address myself to both positions if I am to clarify the traditional stance of Evangelicals on this topic.

## Signs and Wonders Today?

During the last few years a 'signs and wonders' movement
has developed, as you will know, within charismatic circles. Its origin is associated with John Wimber and his
Vineyard Fellowship in California, but it has now spread to
several other countries, including ours. John Wimber (with
Kevin Springer) has summarised his position in two books
called *Power Evangelism* (1985) and *Power Healing* (1986).
Although I cannot attempt to do justice to them here, he
argues in *Power Evangelism* as follows:

(1) Since the kingdom of God has come, life is an unremitting battle with Satan, in which we conquer territory for
Jesus Christ, evidenced by signs and wonders.
(2) Signs and wonders were 'everyday occurrences in New
Testament times' and 'a part of daily life' (*Power Evangelism*,
p. 117).
(3) They should therefore be part of 'the normal Christian
life' for us too (pp. 11, 101), since God 'has given us the
authority to work the works of Jesus' and 'his power is
available to us to do the same works' (pp. 102, 105).
(4) Church growth in the Acts of the Apostles was due
largely to signs and wonders, and still is today. 'Power
evangelism is a spontaneous, Spirit-inspired, empowered
presentation of the gospel' (p. 46).
(5) Resistance to this emphasis is due to a 'western world-
view' dependent on logic and rationalism (pp. 74–85).

I think I was particularly struck by the repeated phrase
'the normal Christian life', partly because it reminded me of
an earlier book with that title by the Chinese author Watch-
man Nee, and partly because I am convinced that miracles
cannot be described as 'normal'. Indeed, any definition of
miracles must include the fact that they are abnormal, and
are deviations from God's normal mode of working. This,
then, is a good place for me to begin my response to you.
You and I are fully agreed, I am sure, that the overriding
biblical revelation of God is of the living Creator who,

having made the universe, holds it in his power and sustains the life of all its (i.e. his) creatures. He causes his sun to rise, and sends rain upon the earth. The sea is his, and so is the dry land. He makes the rivers flow and the grass to grow. His trees are well watered. He feeds the birds and clothes the flowers. And 'he himself gives all men life and breath and everything else' (Acts 17:25; cf. Matthew 5:45; 6:25–30; Psalm 95; 104). Moreover, included in life is health. All healing is divine healing. God has put in the human body remarkable therapeutic and recuperative powers, so that, for example, antibodies are formed to fight infection, and energy is restored in sleep. God is ceaselessly active not only in nature, but also in history, working out his purposes in all the nations of the earth. In both spheres (nature and history) we echo the triumphant cry of the psalmist: 'Yahweh reigns!' It is very important for all of us to recover this biblical perspective, for some charismatic Christians are inclined to discern God only in miraculous happenings, which is to turn him into a magician and miss the principal spheres of his operation. This is the biblical witness to those observed normalities or regularities which are usually called 'natural laws'. It was the Christian insistence on the uniformity of nature which provided the essential basis for the scientific enterprise. As Professor R. Hooykaas argued, 'Metaphorically speaking, whereas the bodily ingredients of science may have been Greek, its vitamins and hormones were biblical' (*Religion and the Rise of Modern Science*, 1972, p. 162).

As a corollary to this, we have to say that the Bible is not primarily a book of miracles, since the God of the Bible is not primarily a God of miracles. Of course the Bible contains miracle stories, as we know, but they do not occur evenly throughout the books of the Bible, and whole tracts of biblical history are devoid of them. It is because they appear in significant clusters that it is possible to propose a biblical doctrine of miracles. For the clusters relate to the four major epochs of God's redemptive revelation, and are associated with the major figures of those epochs – first

Moses, the exodus and the giving of the law; secondly, Elijah and Elisha, pioneers of the outburst of prophecy during the monarchy, and champions of the contest between Yahweh and the Canaanite deities, not to mention some of the later prophets; thirdly our Lord Jesus and his inauguration of the kingdom of God; and fourthly the apostles, whom he appointed and authorised to found and teach his Church. That is why we refer to the Acts correctly as 'the Acts of the Apostles', and why Paul called his miracles 'the things that mark an apostle' (2 Corinthians 12:12; see also Acts 1:2; 2:42–43; 5:12; 14:3–4, etc.; Hebrews 2:1–4). This authentication by miracles of the great figures of salvation history and the great organs of revelation has been recognised throughout Christian history, beginning in particular with Augustine. Calvin, in his preface to the first edition of his *Institutes* (1536), replied in these words to the Roman Catholic criticism that the Reformers' doctrine was a novelty unsupported by miracles: 'In demanding miracles of us, they act dishonestly. For we are not forging some new gospel, but are retaining that very gospel whose truth all the miracles that Jesus Christ and his disciples ever wrought serve to confirm', (p. 5). for the 'legitimate end and use of miracles', according to Scripture, was to confirm, seal and magnify both the law and the gospel.

Does this mean that miracles died out with the apostles? No, not necessarily. This is the mistake which B. B. Warfield made in his otherwise important book *Miracles Yesterday and Today*, which was first published in 1918 as *Counterfeit Miracles*. He was right in his affirmation that miracles were 'part of the credentials of the Apostles as the authoritative agents of God in founding the church', but wrong in his deduction that miracles were 'confined . . . to the Apostolic Church and . . . necessarily passed away with it' (p. 6). Those of us who believe (as I do) that the major function of miracles no longer exists, because we are not living in a fresh epoch of revelation or redemption, and that therefore we have no liberty to expect miracles to occur with the frequency with which they occurred in such epochs, should nevertheless be entirely open to them. We believe that God the Creator is free, sovereign and powerful. We must not attempt to domesticate God, or dictate to him what he is allowed to do. Especially on the frontiers of mission, where a power-encounter may be needed to demonstrate the lordship of Christ, miracles have been and are being reported. So if our expectation is limited, we must ensure that this is due to the biblical doctrine of miracles, and not to our unbelief or to a Western rationalistic mind-set.

As a church historian, David, I expect you have come across Baron George Lyttelton's little book *Observations on the Conversion and Apostleship of St Paul* (new edition 1769)? Lyttleton refers in it to certain recent and 'famous miracles supposed to be done at Abbé Paris's tomb' in France which were enthusiastically claimed by the Jansenists. The authorities were determined to suppress them, however. So first they walled up that part of the church where the tomb was situated, and then they fixed on the wall this peremptory order: *De par le roy défense à Dieu de faire miracle en ce lieu*, which Lyttelton translated: 'By command of the king, God is forbidden to work any more miracles here'!

## The Argument against Miracles

Three main arguments seem to have been developed against miracles in general and against the biblical miracles in particular. Perhaps it would be appropriate for me to attempt a response to them, even though you do not elaborate them all.

The first is that miracles cannot and therefore did not happen, and that in the modern world it is impossible to believe in them any longer. You quote Bultmann's famous statement to this effect. But the roots of such scepticism go back at least to Spinoza in the seventeenth century, who plainly declared that nothing in nature can 'contravene nature's universal laws'. This conviction about the mechanistic uniformity of nature was given a further push by

Newton's brilliant exposition of the laws of physics (died 1727), and found in David Hume in the same century its best-known champion. You quote Hume's definition of a miracle as 'a violation of nature' and his consequent rejection of them. In the nineteenth century Strauss and Renan published their *Lives of Jesus* from which everything miraculous had been expunged. Coming to our own century, I will quote only from a lecture in 1937 by Max Planck, the distinguished German physicist: 'the faith in miracles must yield ground, step by step, before the steady and firm advance of the forces of science, and its total defeat is indubitably a mere matter of time' (*A Scientific Autobiography*, 1950, p. 155). I imagine that all this is what you mean by 'the climate of educated opinion'.

But there still remains a large (even growing?) number of educated people who do not share the contemporary climate of scepticism. They do more even than 'keep an open mind about the possibility of miracles' (your phrase); they actually believe in them! I think, for example, of those fourteen scientists, most of whom were university professors in different disciplines, and whose spokesman was the geneticist Professor R. J. Berry, President of the Linnaean Society, who wrote to *The Times* on 13 July 1984 as follows: 'It is not logically valid to use science as an argument against miracles . . . We gladly accept the virgin birth, the Gospel miracles and the resurrection of Christ as historical events.' I doubt if these scientists would be comfortable with Hume's definition of a miracle as 'a violation of the laws of nature', for it implies a violent contradiction. C. S. Lewis' 'interference' is better. But better still, instead of a violation of (or interference with) the natural, would be a deviation from the normal. Professor Donald MacKay emphasised this in his *The Clockwork Image* (1974): 'Biblical theism insists that any breaks with scientific precedent that have occurred were but a further expression of the same faithfulness (of God) to a coherent overall purpose which is normally expressed in the day-to-day reliability of nature on which we depend as scientists.' He then instanced the resurrection of Jesus as something not incredible but inevitable, 'because it was not possible for death to keep its hold on him' (Acts 2:24). 'In other words, it would not have made sense for the Creator, when he came into his own drama, to have been destroyed in any ultimate sense by characters in that drama' (pp. 65–6). In all this I am not suggesting that miracles are an adequate basis for theism. But, once we have come on other grounds to believe in God, indeed in 'a real, living, active, creative, loving, serving God' (as you beautifully describe him), it becomes logical to affirm, and illogical to deny, the possibility of the miraculous. For 'natural laws' describe God's activity; they do not control it.

The second argument against the biblical miracles follows; it declares that such stories are legends. You yourself mention the parallels which some scholars have discerned either in Greek tales of healers, exorcists and 'divine men', or in the 'charismatic' Jewish teachers and miracle-workers (of whom Geza Vermes has written), or in the fanciful prodigies of the apocryphal gospels, which Archbishop Trench called 'a barren and dreary waste of wonders without object or aim'. (Dr Craig Blomberg has a useful section on these supposed 'parallels' in his *The Historical Reliability of the Gospels*, 1987, pp. 81–92.) But in contrast to these, the miracles of Jesus in the canonical gospels are sober, restrained, unsensational and spiritually significant, as we will see later. Moreover, they are evenly distributed through the four gospels and their sources, so that they are widely attested; the time elapsing between the public ministry of Jesus and the publication of the gospels was not long enough for the development of legends; and many eyewitnesses would have been still alive to refute (if the stories were not true), for example, the restoration to Malchus of his right ear and to Bartimaeus of his eyesight.

Thirdly, a standard objection to miracles has been the argument that the evidence for them is inadequate. This is not just Hume's general point that the witnesses of miracles are either incompetent or gullible or prone to exaggeration or lovers of gossip, or 'ignorant and barbarous', or impelled by ulterior motives. It is rather his emphasis on the principle of analogy. That is, all testimony has to be evaluated in the light of our regular experience. Since we did not ourselves experience a past event, we have to ask if it is in any way analogous to events which we have experienced. Ernst Troeltsch, the early twentieth-century German theologian and philosopher, developed this argument further. He wrote: 'Agreement with normal, ordinary, repeatedly attested modes of occurrence and conditions, as we know them, is the mark of probability for the occurrences which criticism can acknowledge as having really happened or leave aside' (quoted by Colin Brown in *Miracles and the Critical Mind*, p. 129).

It is not valid, however, to make the principle of analogy determinative of truth and to reject as unhistorical any event of which we have had no analogous experience. John Locke told the story of the King of Siam, repeated by Hume and others of 'an Indian prince', who, when the Dutch ambassador told him of water in northern countries which becomes so hard that elephants could walk on it, refused to believe in ice: 'Hitherto I have believed the strange things you have told me, because I look upon you as a sober, fair man; but now I am sure you lie' (quoted by Colin Brown in *That You May Believe*, p. 33, and in *Miracles and the Critical Mind*, p. 84). But the fact that ice was beyond the king's own experience was not a reasonable ground on which to refuse to believe in it. Similarly, as those fourteen scientists said in their letter to *The Times*, 'Miracles are unprecedented events . . . It is important to affirm that science (based as it is upon the observation of precedents) can have nothing to say on the subject.' The incarnation and the resurrection, for example, were both *sui generis*, without precedent or parallel. If anybody could claim an analogy in his own experience, it would be a reason for disbelief, not faith.

I realise that these general points are not a complete answer to the commonest philosophical, scientific and historical objections to miracles, but perhaps they show in what direction answers may be sought and found.

# A Fresh Look at the Gospel Miracles

I do not have space to comment on the Old Testament miracles which you mention, although, as you say, the portrayal of some is certainly poetic rather than literal (e.g. 'By the blast of your nostrils the waters piled up,' Exodus 15:8); others may be explained by natural phenomena (e.g. the quails and the manna), in which case the miraculous element was only the timing; and a number are important because they belong to the context of God's judgement and salvation (e.g. the exodus) and to the public contest between Yahweh and Baal (e.g. the fire consuming Elijah's sacrifice on Carmel).

Instead, I will concentrate on the miracles of Jesus recorded in the gospels. A good place to begin is with the three commonest words which are used to describe them. 'Powers' (*dunameis*) seems to refer to their origin and nature: they were expressions of supernatural power, though in other people the power could be satanic, not divine. 'Works' (*erga* is similar.) The second word 'wonders' (*terata*) refers to their effect; they evoked amazement in the people who witnessed them. More important than either of these, however, is 'signs' (*sēmeia*), which indicates that they signified something. They were more than power-packed, wonder-working events (which is all they are in the apocryphal gospels); they had a message. They were sermons, parables, even sacraments, which pointed beyond themselves to another and greater reality. So their purpose was to arouse in the beholders not just astonishment but understanding, and indeed an understanding faith. John is of course the evangelist who emphasises that Jesus' miracles were 'signs' (seventeen times in his gospel), and many commentators have suggested that the first half of his gospel, because it deliberately focuses on seven major signs, could be called 'the Book of Signs', while the second part is 'the Book of Suffering'. To John Jesus' signs belonged to the category of testimony, whose purpose was to lead to faith and so to life: 'Jesus did many other miraculous signs in the presence of his disciples, which are not recorded in this book. But these are written that you may believe that Jesus is the Christ, the Son of God, and that by believing you may have life in his name' (20:30–31). The order is clear: testimony (through words and signs)—faith —life. John is not the only evangelist, however, who calls miracles 'signs'; so do the three synoptists (especially in the phrase 'seeking a sign'), and so did Peter in his Pentecost sermon, namely that Jesus of Nazareth was 'a man accredited by God . . . by miracles, wonders and signs [he used the three words together], which God did among you through him' (Acts 2:22). Indeed, it is the sign-character or significance of the miracles, and the teaching which they embody, which is their distinguishing characteristic. For false prophets can also do miracles which exhibit power and excite wonder (Deuteronomy 13:1–3; Mark 13:22), but they perform them according to 'the energy of Satan' (2 Thessalonians 2:9; cf. Matthew 12:24–28). Such miracles could even be called 'signs', as in Deuteronomy 13 and Mark 13, but what they signify is different. The signs must be judged by the teaching, not the teaching by the signs.

This biblical emphasis on miracles as meaningful 'signs' seems to offer the most fruitful way forward in our dialogue. It explains Jesus' refusal to perform miracles on demand or for show, merely to satisfy curiosity or create a sensation (e.g. Matthew 12:39; 16:1–4; Luke 23:8). It is true that in these verses what people were requesting was precisely 'a sign', yet all they meant by this was an authenticating display of power (cf. 1 Corinthians 1:22). Jesus had decisively rejected that way of securing a following before his public ministry began (Matthew 4:1–11). In this John and the synoptists are agreed, and Alan Richardson was surely right to draw attention to it:

> We would draw no . . . clear distinction between the Synoptists and St John. In all the Gospels Jesus is unwilling to work miracles as mere displays . . . In the Synoptists no less than in St John the miracles are evidence (. . . to those who have eyes to see) as to Who Jesus is. This, we shall maintain, is their *raison*

*d'être* in all four Gospels. (*The Miracle-Stories of the Gospels* by Alan Richardson, 1941, p. 31)

If it is right, then, always to bracket the teaching and healing of Jesus, his words and works, his sayings and signs, what did his miracles signify? John's statement, in the context of his first sign, was that 'he thus revealed his glory' (John 2:11). But, since his 'glory' is the visible manifestation of his being and character, this leads us to ask a supplementary question, namely: 'Which aspects of his person, or what kind of "glory", did his signs display?' Some will immediately reply 'his compassion', and indeed the evangelists several times say that his motive (e.g. in healing the sick and feeding the hungry) was compassion for the needy. 'He saw, he was moved with compassion, he took action' is a regular sequence in the miracle-stories. But such compassion lay behind all his works of mercy; it was not uniquely displayed in his miracles.

Essentially the mighty works of Jesus were signs of the inauguration of the kingdom. We are agreed about this, although I would want to add that their miraculous nature was inherent in this claim. Preaching and healing went together because the former was the proclamation, and the latter the demonstration, of the kingdom's arrival. Why was this so? Partly because, as Jesus implied in his message to the imprisoned Baptist, the prophetic vision of the coming kingdom included the blind seeing, the lame walking, leprosy sufferers being cured, the deaf hearing, the dead receiving life and the poor hearing good news (Matthew 11:2–5, echoing Isaiah 35:5–6). Partly because the coming kingdom would coincide with a liberal effusion of the Spirit (e.g. Ezekiel 36:26–27; Joel 2:28–29), and the Spirit was evidently upon Jesus in both his words and works (e.g. Luke 4:18–19; Matthew 12:28). And partly because (here is where we part company, I think) the *shalom* of the kingdom would include the subservience of all nature to God's rule. That is why Jesus walked on the turbulent waters and stilled the storm on the lake (for wind and waves were widely seen as symbolising the primeval chaos and the hostility of demonic forces); turned water into wine (the water standing for Judaism and the wine for the gospel); multiplied loaves and fishes (setting forth the messianic banquet). That also is why Jesus is said to have 'rebuked' both the fever of Peter's mother-in-law (Luke 4:39) and the tempest on the lake (Mark 4:39), just as he 'rebuked' the demons. His nature-miracles were signs of the overthrow of Satan's kingdom, and of the establishment of God's. They gave a dramatic preview (which we cannot, and should not expect to, replicate) of the final subjugation of the whole material order to the gracious rule of God.

I think we must say, however, that the signs of Jesus revealed the glory of his deity as well as of his kingdom. For they visibly set forth judgement and salvation, both of which are the prerogative of the Father, although entrusted to the Son (John 5:19–23). At least John saw things this way. Perhaps the only judgement-sign was the cursing of the fig tree (an Old Testament symbol of Israel), although this story is limited to the synoptists. The cleansing of the temple is another (non-miraculous) sign – and warning – of judgement, told by all four evangelists, although the synoptists put it at the end, and John at the beginning, of Jesus' ministry. The salvation-signs predominate, however. John plainly sees the 'I am' affirmations dramatised in the accompanying miracles, as the Bread of life feeds the hungry crowds, the Light of the world gives sight to the man born blind, and the Resurrection and the Life restores life to Lazarus. These are signs of the saving sonship of Jesus. Colin Brown, at the end of his thorough study and survey, goes further, and sees the three persons of the Godhead manifest in Jesus' works:

From one standpoint, the miracles of Jesus are the work of the Spirit or divine breath in and through him. From another, they are wrought by the Word of God that he uttered and that, according to John, was made flesh in him. From yet another standpoint, both these activities were the work of the Father.

For the Spirit is the Spirit of the Father and the Word is the Word of the Father . . . The question of miracles is really a question of the Trinity. (p. 325)

So, then, you and I are agreed that, as you say, the works of Jesus had 'religious significance', and that this is their real point. But you want if possible to detach the thing signified from the sign, or at least from its miraculous character. Is this feasible, however? Certainly 'miracles are not to be severed from the accompanying teaching', to quote Colin Brown again (p. 98). But can the teaching be severed from the miracles? Well yes, in the sense that the teaching can stand on its own without the necessity of any signs. But no in the sense that the miraculous nature of the signs is intrinsic to their meaning. Thus, reverting to John 20:30–31, the signs bear witness to the glory of Jesus, in order to elicit faith in Jesus, so that readers of the gospels may receive life from Jesus.

## The Virgin Birth and the Resurrection

The virginal conception and bodily resurrection of Jesus are both said to be 'essential to Evangelicals', you write, as may be seen from their various 'bases of faith' in different parts of the world. What you write is true. But two queries arise in my mind as I reflect on your statement. First, are you meaning to imply that these two doctrines are distinctive to Evangelicals? If so, I must respectfully dissent, for both are to be found in the Apostles' Creed and therefore belong to the universal Church. On the one hand, our Lord Jesus Christ 'was conceived by the Holy Ghost, born of the Virgin Mary', which is unambiguous. On the other, 'the third day he rose again from the dead', which in its wording may be ambiguous (since it is not explicitly stated whether he rose 'bodily') but in its intention is not (since we know the beliefs of those who framed the creed). Moreover, the Apostles' Creed is the minimal faith which new converts are asked to express at their baptism; it is not the fuller statement which candidates for the presbyterate (the official teaching office of the Church) are expected to make before and at their ordination (the Thirty-Nine Articles in the case of the Church of England). So the proper question is not whether Evangelicals are peculiar in holding fast to these doctrines, but whether liberals have liberty to depart from the catholic faith.

My second query, when you ask whether a particular tenet is 'essential for Evangelicals', is to respond with the counter-question, 'Essential for what?' I think the virginal conception and bodily resurrection of Jesus are essential if the faith we profess is legitimately to be termed 'Evangelical', 'catholic', 'original', 'apostolic' or 'biblical'. If, on the other hand, you are asking me to pronounce whether those who deny these doctrines *ipso facto* forfeit the right to be called Christians, then I would say 'no' or at least 'no, not necessarily'. For only God knows those who belong to him (2 Timothy 2:19); it is not for us to make such judgements. Personal faith in Jesus Christ as 'God and Saviour' is certainly essential. And one can go on to argue that, in order to be biblically consistent, this faith should include the virginal conception and bodily resurrection of Jesus. But in all of us our heart may be better than our head, and salvation is by faith not by orthodox formula, even though 'faith' must have some solid Christian content.

With regard to the virgin birth, I confess that I do not experience the difficulties that you do. Perhaps you will regard my faith as more simplistic than simple. But the birth and infancy narratives seem to me to be much more cogent and compelling than you concede. Let me make a number of points briefly (they are somewhat elaborated in *The Authentic Jesus*, as you know). Whatever case may be made for the idea that Matthew was writing *midrash* (commentary-as-story), Luke's account of the virgin birth must surely be understood in the light of his gospel preface, in which he claims to 'have carefully investigated everything from the beginning', to depend on sources traceable to the first eyewitnesses, and so to be writing history, not myth, which will help establish Theophilus in 'the certainty of the things' he has been taught. It is, of course, true that Mark and John do not refer to the virgin birth. But that is neither here nor there. For both evangelists choose to open their narrative with John the Baptist, although John begins his gospel with his marvellous prologue about the eternal Word. The argument from silence is notoriously precarious. Mark and John do not mention the birth or boyhood of Jesus at all; are we to conclude from this that they thought he had neither? Besides, there is no evidence (beyond their silence) that these evangelists did not believe in the virgin birth. There is indirect evidence that John did. He refers so often to the pre-existence of the Son, who 'came down from heaven' or 'was sent into the world' and indeed 'became flesh', that he is likely to have had some notion as to how these things took place. There was also the persistent rumour that Jesus' birth had been illegitimate (Mark 6:3; John 8:41; 9:29), which led Bishop John Robinson to write:

> the first and most indisputable fact about the birth of Jesus is that it occurred out of wedlock. The one option for which there is no evidence is that Jesus was the lawful son of Joseph and Mary. The only choice open to us is between a virgin birth and an illegitimate birth. (*Twelve More New Testament Studies*, 1984, pp. 3–4)

You offer as evidence against the virginal conception the fact that Jesus' family did not at first recognise or acknowledge his identity. But this is a problem for all of us, whether we believe in the birth and infancy stories or not. For those denying the virginal conception are not also denying his deity and sinlessness, on account of which he must have been unique in boyhood and youth. How, then, is it that his relatives doubted and even opposed him? One can only guess the reasons. It may be that Mary still 'treasured up all these things and pondered them in her heart' (Luke 2:19), and felt free to share them only with one or two confidants.

Or, if all the family knew, they may have been motivated either by fear of the reaction of the Jewish authorities or by their own prejudice, because Jesus did not fit the messianic style they were expecting. You then go on to give a longish list of apparent discrepancies between Matthew's and Luke's accounts. But as with other gospel discrepancies, so with these, they really are not so baffling as you make out. Every one has been given a plausible explanation. Indeed, most of them are due to independent pieces of information, which cannot reasonably be said to contradict each other, but simply do not overlap. Whether we react to them in faith or in scepticism depends largely, I think, on whether we approach them in a believing or a sceptical frame of mind.

I agree with you that the incarnation 'does not depend logically [I would prefer the word 'necessarily'] on the belief that he was conceived by the Holy Spirit'. In theory, at least, God could have chosen some other 'mechanism' by which the incarnation took place. There have been and are Christians (yourself among them) who firmly believe in the incarnation, while doubting or denying the virgin birth. So I accept your statement that 'in order to believe that the glory of God shone "in the face of Christ" . . . it is not necessary to believe that Joseph had nothing to do with the conception of Jesus'. I agree further that, though the death and resurrection of Jesus were integral to the apostolic *kerygma*, as summarised in Peter's speeches in the Acts and in Paul's statement in 1 Corinthians 15, his virgin birth was not. At the same time, I am bound to add that I find your doubt and denial strange and indeed (if I may say so without appearing obnoxiously patronising) regrettable. For it seems to me (1) that it is inconsistent to affirm the greater miracle (the incarnation) while denying the lesser (the virgin birth), and not to perceive the congruity between them; (2) that you are quite unnecessarily negative towards the Matthean and Lucan birth narratives; (3) that you reject the only account we have of how the incarnation took place, without offering any alternative explanation;

and (4) that you do not sufficiently feel the seriousness of breaking away not only from Scripture but from the way the universal Church has understood and accepted its witness on this matter.

Turning now to the resurrection, I am extremely thankful for your conclusion (though you describe it only as 'reasonable and probable' and not 'absolutely decisive') that the tomb was empty, that the body in which Jesus appeared was 'a sign given by God because of the uniqueness of his embodiment of God', and that 'he is the miraculous Christ'. Despite all your caveats and hesitations, I really rejoice with you that 'Christianity is a resurrection religion'.

I have to concede that in my summary in *Basic Christianity* of the historical evidence for the resurrection of Jesus my single use of the word 'proof' was a slip. For to 'prove' something is to establish its truth. The way I end that chapter, however, is to speak of evidence, not proof: 'the cumulative weight of this evidence is all but conclusive'. I then add that, in consequence, 'it makes eminently reasonable that last step of faith which brings us to our knees before him and puts on our lips the mighty confession of a doubting Thomas "My Lord and my God"' (pp. 59–60). But if my claim for the evidence was somewhat exaggerated, your long list of supposed discrepancies is exaggerated too. Yes, I have written that the resurrection narratives form 'a jigsaw puzzle'. But it is of the essence of jigsaw puzzles that their various bits and pieces can be fitted together. I really cannot agree with you that this 'has proved impossible', and that the stories 'constitute not a jigsaw puzzle but an insoluble mystery'. G. E. Ladd in *I Believe in the Resurrection* (1975) and Murray Harris in *Raised Immortal* (1984) both address these problems, while John Wenham in *Easter Enigma* (1984) has proposed the fullest, most careful and cogent harmonisation yet. My own view is that the resurrection narratives contain enough discrepant material to show their independence, but not enough to destroy their credibility, let alone to establish their falsehood.

The *kerygma* of 1 Corinthians 15:1–7, which Paul claims to be both the original (verses 1–4) and the universal (verse 11) faith of the Church, has seemed to most commentators to include an affirmation of the objective, bodily character of Jesus' resurrection. The reference to the preceding burial (which definitely referred to his body), the apparently trivial detail that he was raised 'on the third day' (which makes it a datable event), and the fact that elsewhere he distinguishes his 'visions' (e.g. 2 Corinthians 12:1–10) from the resurrection appearance in which he had 'seen Jesus' (1 Corinthians 9:1), all point to the physical or quasi-physical nature of both the resurrection and the appearances. Yet, I agree, my statement that the resurrection of Jesus supplies 'the proof and pattern' of ours is a little bit (though not much!) too emphatic. Because 'proof' means 'conclusive evidence' it is slightly too strong a word, although Paul's use of 'firstfruits' (1 Corinthians 15:20,23) clearly implies that the harvest will follow. And, although 'pattern' is accurate, since Paul more than once says that our resurrection bodies will be like Christ's (1 Corinthians 15:49; Philippians 3:21), our knowledge of his resurrection body is scanty, being pieced together from the resurrection narratives. It would therefore be wise not to be too dogmatic about its precise character, remembering John's frank admission that 'what we will be has not yet been made known', except that we shall see him and be like him (1 John 3:2).

At the same time, I am anxious to be true to what has been made known. This includes Paul's statement in Romans 8, which you quote, that one day the whole creation, now groaning as if in the pains of childbirth, is going to be 'liberated from its bondage to decay and brought into the glorious freedom of the children of God', and in addition that our own bodies are going to be included in that redemption (verses 18–25). Is it not legitimate to identify this hope with the 'regeneration' or 'renewal' of the universe (Matthew 19:28), the time when God will 'restore everything' (Acts 3:21) and make 'a new heaven and a new earth' (2 Peter 3:13; Revelation 21:1–5)? It is not just 'heaven' to which the New Testament looks forward, but a renewed universe, from which pain, sorrow, disease and death have all been eliminated, indeed destroyed. It is a more *material* expectation than popular visions of 'heaven'. Was William Temple not right in emphasising that Christianity is 'the most materialistic religion in the world' – with its doctrines of creation and resurrection, and its use of water, bread and wine? That's surely why our affirmation of the resurrection of *the body* (his and ours) is so important. A year or two ago Bishop David Jenkins kindly spent a couple of hours with five of us Evangelicals who wanted to engage in questioning and discussion with him. He has given me permission to quote my recollection of one part of our conversation. He was willing to concede that the bodily resurrection of Jesus, although in his view 'historically unverifiable' (because the story of the empty tomb was probably not published until twenty years or more after the event), could nevertheless be termed 'theologically appropriate'. There, I think, was a man speaking out of his catholic tradition, but we Evangelicals endorsed it.

In conclusion, is not the most helpful way to approach the gospel miracles to place them within the familiar and inescapable tension between the already and the not yet, kingdom come and kingdom coming, the new age inaugurated and the new age consummated? To the sceptical (who doubt all miracles) I want to say 'but *already* we have tasted the powers of the age to come'. To the credulous (who think that healing miracles are an everyday occurrence) I want to say 'but *not yet* have we been given resurrection bodies free from disease, pain, infirmity, handicap and death'. In this interim period between the beginning and the end we both look back to the outburst of miracles in the ministry of Jesus and his apostles, and on to the final resurrection of both body and universe.

Further thought about the implications of the 'already – not yet' tension would, I suspect, be profitable to us all.

Yours as ever,
John

# 5 The Bible and Behaviour

## Christian Morality Today

How is a Christian supposed to get guidance from the Bible about the perplexing or agonising problems of daily life, personal and social? It is not an easy question to answer, for the sixty-six books of the Scriptures were written in a world very different from the one we see when we open the front door or look at the news on TV – and the moral instruction which they give, although plentiful, is very varied and often seems to be inclined to be either disturbingly ideal (rather than practical) or else disturbingly primitive (rather than modern). The answers supplied by countless church leaders, preachers, priests, theologians and lay people such as parents and teachers have often seemed unsatisfactory to the Christian who, often in an emergency and under confusing pressures, has to decide whether or not 'to do it'. But the answers given by John Stott are among the best that I know. He was chairman of the drafting committee which produced the report of the 1982 international consultation of Evangelical leaders on *Evangelism and Social Responsibility*. In it I read this key sentence: 'Because mankind is made in the image of God, every person, regardless of race, religion, colour, culture, class, sex or age, has an intrinsic dignity because of which he should be respected and served, not exploited' (ESR, p. 17). And he has summed up his own mature teaching on social and moral questions in two recent books.

*The Message of the Sermon on the Mount*, first published in 1978, has already had many editions. Originally it was called *Christian Counter-Culture* because it arose out of a great desire to present the teaching of Jesus to those seeking an 'alternative society' – a search which Theodore Roszak described in his book of 1969, *The Making of a Counter-Culture*. Particularly Dr Stott had in mind students who were anti-war ('make love not war'), 'repudiating the greedy affluence of the West which seems to grow ever fatter either by the spoliation of the natural environment or by the exploitation of developing nations or by both at once'. He wanted to present a Christian alternative and he did so with such authority that his book survived with a new title when the talk of a 'counter-culture' had died down.

In *Issues Facing Christians Today*, first published in 1984, he achieved another success by exploring at some depth the issues which would not go away. These were not only the global issues which had preoccupied the would-be makers of a counter-culture – the nuclear threat, the environment, North-South economic inequality, human rights, employment, industrial relations, apartheid and other forms of racial prejudice, and the liberation of women. The book also dealt with moral questions which the radical protesters of the 1960s had tended to brush aside – divorce, abortion, homosexual relationships. And it carefully considered issues which trouble those who seriously try to form a 'Christian mind' about social and moral questions – but which to that minority certainly are troublesome. Many earnest Christians have been 'solafideists', believing that faith not behaviour is essential to salvation, or they have belonged to various 'holiness' movements whether Catholic or Protestant, believing that the individual's behaviour ought to be a perfect imitation of Christ but that politics is too dirty to be touched. Or they have committed themselves wholeheartedly to one or other political crusade that turned out to be mistaken in one way or another. So successive chapters in Dr Stott's survey asked: Is it our concern, can we think straight amid the complexity, should we try to impose our views, do we have any influence, what is needed for Christian leadership? The book was a powerful plea for a specifically Christian involvement and the title of its American edition was *Involvement*.

These two books by John Stott are full of wisdom. Whether they study the text of Matthew's gospel or the facts of a social problem belonging to a world very different from Matthew's, the study is always done in enough detail to feed the mind but also with enough clarity to enlighten it. Always Christians are urged to be 'salt' in the world. They are warned against reducing the gospel and abandoning the identity of the followers of Jesus: their message must not be the mere endorsement of some fashionable contemporary ideas. But they are also warned against the temptation to be 'pure' by being detached from contemporary perplexities and agonies: salt, light and yeast work by being used. Although the authority with which John Stott writes seems effortless, in fact his decisiveness must have been achieved by great intellectual labour including not only research but also the work of thinking things through to the point of clarity. And as I stressed in my first chapter, his own willingness to be publicly involved in these complicated and contentious discussions represents a courageous departure from the pietistic atmosphere of the student group to which he belonged in the 1940s. At many points it also differs bravely from the political and moral positions characteristic of American fundamentalism, still vocal and powerful in the 1980s.

There would be no point in my attempting to follow him in every step of his journey through a large minefield of problems. Here it will be enough to offer a few comments on the points he makes and on the reasons for which he makes them.

It does not worry me to think that the Sermon on the Mount as we have it – which would have taken no more than ten minutes to preach – has been edited quite substantially by Matthew or the community behind him. Jesus is said to have given instructions about 'when you fast' at 6:16 although later in the gospel, at 9:14, we are told that in his lifetime the disciples of Jesus did not fast. It is no accident that within the gospels the Greek word *ekklesia*, in English 'church', occurs only twice, at Matthew 16:18 and 18:17. The latter instance seems a clear example of an instruction which is unlikely to have come from the historical Jesus: 'if your brother sins against you . . . tell it to the church; and if he refuses to listen even to the church, treat him as you would a pagan or a tax collector'. So I am sure that the Sermon on the Mount as we have it is an edited document.

I welcome the far more important point that it presents with unforgettable force teaching which is characteristic of the Teacher. This teaching combines depth and simplicity. It fascinates because it challenges us to be content with nothing short of the divine perfection, yet its feet are on the ground of village life in Galilee, where people are as prone to be angry, vindictive, lustful, dishonest, hypocritical, materialistic, arrogant, unforgiving, anxious, gullible, and so forth, as humanity normally is. This sermon gives us 'impossible possibilities', as Reinhold Niebuhr quipped. And its force is not lost in John Stott's exposition, which could only have been done by a Christian who is both holy in himself and pastorally experienced in the difficulties of sinners. It is an exposition which brings before us the essence of what Jesus commands about a distinctive right-eousness and piety, and about new attitudes to material needs and to other people. 'That is to say,' John Stott sums up, 'our supreme ambition must be the glory of God' (CCC, p. 25).

Rightly he corrects those who are so superficial in their praise of this sermon that one wonders whether they have read it. The sermon is not meant to encourage easy opti-mism about the human capacity to be good in a conven-tional style. On the contrary, the person who really hears its challenges will be tempted to a hopeless despair. So the sermon is addressed not to the crowds who have come to see Jesus heal the sick but to 'his disciples' (Matthew 5:1). It is 'on the mount' because it is high above the heads of the crowds. 'Jesus spoke the sermon to those who were already

. . . the citizens of God's kingdom and the children of God's family,' John Stott explains.

> The high standards he set are appropriate only to such. We do not, indeed we could not, achieve this privileged status by attaining Christ's standards. Rather by attaining Christ's standards, or at least approximating to them, we give evidence of what by God's free grace and gift we already are. (CCC, p. 29)

Many sermons are unhelpful because they hold aloof from the journey which is necessary if the Christian is to move from the Sermon on the Mount to everyday problems. As a preacher, I do not find this surprising. We who stand in the pulpit are often immobilised by our sense of inadequacy as we contemplate humanity's distresses. There is a bewildering and terrifying descent from the mountain peak and its visions to the valley, desert or abyss in which the crowds are trapped. No doubt that has always been the case but the descent is particularly frightening in an age well characterised by two words prominent in Dr Stott's books – disillusionment and complexity.

That is what makes so much that is said in *Issues Facing Christians Today* so helpful. Having spoken out of his own tradition by reminding us of the great Evangelical heritage of social concern, and having confessed honestly that Evangelicals retracted from that involvement ('the great reversal'), Dr Stott does more than lament the decline. He provides answers to social and moral problems which do far more than merely repeat pleas for involvement – pleas which have come from many publications and conferences. He clearly urges not only 'social service' (relieving human need) but what a conference over which he presided called 'social action' (removing the causes of human need). God's children must care about God's whole creation and supremely about these 'human but godlike' creatures whose evil passions have caused most of the trouble. Obedient faith must be shown in active love and practical action must be guided by informed thought. 'What is needed', John Stott writes, is more conscientious group study in which (1) we learn to pray together, (2) we listen attentively to each other's positions, and to the deep concerns which lie behind them, and (3) we help each other to discern the cultural prejudices which make us reluctant and even unable to open our minds to alternative viewpoints. This kind of discipline is painful, but Christian integrity demands it. As a result, we shall refuse to acquiesce in superficial polarizations, for the truth is always more subtle and sophisticated than that. (IFCT, p. 34)

The agreements that emerge out of such Christian thought should not be imposed on others, but it is rightly hoped that they will have influence as they are contributed to the public welfare.

Most of the policies which Dr Stott suggests as the result of his own research, reflection and discussion seem to me to deserve influence. Indeed, although they will not be accepted by everyone they seem almost always wise. Having stated the nuclear threat, he totally condemns the use of nuclear weapons but very reluctantly accepts the need to keep some of them temporarily in order to deter aggression by uncertainty until disarmament can be negotiated. That may well be less dangerous than a total renunciation by one side unilaterally. Having outlined the threats to the environment through population growth, resource depletion, industrial pollution and runaway technology's hunger for fuel, he advocates practical steps. 'We learn to think ecologically. We repent of extravagance, pollution and wanton destruction. We recognise that man finds it easier to subdue the earth than he does to subdue himself' (IFCT, pp. 119–20). Having repeated the Brandt Commission's analysis of the global North-South divide and its dangers, and having also accepted that the commission was too hesitant to criticise some cultures of the South which keep their peoples in poverty by discouraging development, he emphatically supports the principle of global economic co-operation while saying that he lacks the expertise to comment on detailed proposals. Having lamented the violations of human rights in so many countries, he urges that we should keep ourselves informed and take what action we can – for here, too, we are responsible; 'we *are* our brother's keeper'. Having argued that work is intended for the fulfilment of the worker, he protests vigorously against the acceptance of widespread unemployment and against the lack of participation in decision-making at work. Similarly he protests against the racism or 'cultural imperialism' which denies mankind's essential unity in diversity. He ends this section by pleading for a simple lifestyle and a growing generosity as two signs of protest against the division of humanity into gross affluence and dehumanising poverty.

In his guidance on sexual issues, he welcomes much in the rise of feminism but rightly ponders the obvious truth that 'although men and women are equal they are not the same'. The traditional 'headship' of the husband is interpreted as being 'more of care than of control, more of responsibility than of authority'. Divorce for serious sexual immorality, or on the desertion of an unbelieving partner, is permissible and in those two cases (only) a Christian is 'not bound' to remain unmarried; but all divorce is contrary to God's purpose, which is the permanence of marriage. All abortions are contrary to the norm of the inviolability of the foetus and 'human life ought not to be taken except in cases of urgent necessity' which must be specifically and rigorously argued. The risk, however substantial, of a handicap, however severe, is not enough to justify the foetus that will become a child being killed in the womb. Dr Stott agrees with a fellow-Evangelical that 'the destruction of the unborn on this massive, deliberate scale is the greatest single offence regularly perpetrated in Britain today' – and could have noted that the position is far worse in some other countries (women in the Soviet Union have, on average, more than six abortions). He concludes with a condemnation of all relationships which involve homosexual practices, combined with a plea for the loving support of homosexuals who courageously practise self-restraint.

It would not be very interesting to any reader if I were to

explain at length why I disagree with a few of these judgements on pragmatic grounds. There may be more profit in a discussion of the biblical basis which Dr Stott offers for all his policies. Inevitably my criticism of his use of the Bible is sharpened when I do not like its practical consequences, but I want to attempt a fairminded analysis of his method of arguing even when I welcome the result of the argument. I ask three questions.

## The Old Testament's Relevance

My first is whether his appeals to the authority of the Old Testament are entirely convincing. On the one hand, it is admirable that he discerns in the Hebrew Scriptures some principles which are permanently valid. He expounds a biblical basis for social concern in general. God is the God of nature as well as religion, the God of creation as well as of the covenant, the God of social justice as well as of personal justification – and man is a 'body-soul in community', endowed with conscience to discern between alternatives and freedom to choose between them. These are all great Old Testament themes and they are all, I believe, profoundly true and important. And other Old Testament principles are expounded rightly by being related to specific issues of our own period. Thus the horror over the shedding of innocent blood is related to nuclear weapons and abortions. The truths that God gave man 'dominion' over nature but that it must be a co-operative, responsible and laborious control are related to the practical problems of conserving natural resources and obtaining full employment. The truth that the human race was created to be a single people on a single planet is contrasted with the injustices of North-South inequality and with racial discrimination. The true dignity of human beings, created by God 'male and female' and 'in his own image', is contrasted with the denial of human rights, the exclusion from decision-making and the oppression of women. The Creator's blessing on heterosexuality, permanent marriage and loving companionship is contrasted with the contemporary realities of easy divorce and the 'gay' lifestyle.

On the other hand, Dr Stott's style of citing Scripture reduces the value of these appeals to permanent principles by sometimes appearing to depend on a naive understanding of stories which are in fact mythological. In the society to which *Issues Facing Christians Today* is addressed, Adam, Eve and the snake are usually treated as comic characters. It therefore lessens the seriousness of Dr Stott's account of the human tragedy when he claims that 'all our human alienation, disorientation and sense of meaninglessness stem ultimately' from the fact that Adam and Eve 'listened to Satan's lies, instead of to God's truth' (IFCT, p. 34). The creation of Adam from dust, and of Eve from one of Adam's ribs, is also often treated humorously. It therefore reduces the impact of Dr Stott's accounts of man's place in nature, and of the equality of male and female, when he quotes the first two chapters of Genesis without a word about evolution (IFCT, pp. 111–12, 242–3). And the serious assertion of the unity of mankind, amid tensions caused partly by population growth, is not strengthened when he writes too simply: 'God said, "Be fruitful and increase in number; fill the earth and subdue it"' (IFCT, p. 128).

Sometimes Dr Stott seems to be reluctant to admit that some of the moral teaching given in the Old Testament falls far below the heights to which he rightly directs our attention. In the Old Testament

> the Lord said to Moses, 'Take vengeance on the Midianites' . . . Moses was angry with the officers of the army . . . who returned from the battle.
>
> 'Have you allowed all the women to live?' he asked them. 'They were the ones who followed Balaam's advice and were the means of turning the Israelites away from the Lord . . . so that a plague struck the Lord's people. Now kill all the boys. And kill every woman who has slept with a man, but save for yourselves every girl who has never slept with a man.' (Numbers 31:1–18)

Dr Stott only glances at the fact that genocide is repeatedly urged in the Old Testament as God's will in the punishment of the Canaanites. The Canaanites, like the Midianites, are said to have been especially wicked, but it is hard to feel that this justifies the idea that God wanted a whole people to be massacred. It gives the wrong answer to the question which Abraham asks on one of the moral peaks of the Old Testament, before he suggests that there may be ten righteous people in Sodom and therefore the city does not deserve to be destroyed: 'Will not the Judge of all the earth do right?' (Genesis 18:25). And it ignores the vision of God's compassion conveyed in the lovely story of Jonah, where the city of Nineveh, which God refuses to destroy, includes more than 120,000 innocents and many cattle (4:11). Still less does humanity's wickedness at an earlier stage seem to merit being drowned by the flood, apart from the few refugees in Noah's ark, together with all but a small fraction of the animal kingdom. And the Hebrew penal code, although humane in comparison with many contemporary codes, does not strike the modern conscience as being wholly civilised. To see this one has only to reckon how many offences incur the death penalty. Not everything in the Old Testament is morally speaking the permanent word of God.

## Jesus the Legislator?

My second question is whether Dr Stott is entirely convincing when he quotes the teaching of Jesus as if it were a religious law. On the one hand, he is very impressive when he appeals to the authority of Jesus in advocating the defence and service of the poor. As he reminds us, Jesus himself taught that 'our attitude to him will be revealed in, and so judged by, our good works of love to the least of his brothers and sisters' (IFCT, p. 23). He is equally impressive when he quotes Jesus on other issues – for example, when he repeats that husband and wife should be 'one flesh'.

On the other hand, he seems not to take full account of the fact that the moral teaching of Jesus was often clothed in deliberate exaggeration (hyperbole is the technical term) in order to provoke a repentance, an aspiration, a resolve and a whole life which would be more than conventionally righteous. An example is the challenge to 'hate' parents, wife, children, brothers, sisters and even one's own life as the cost of discipleship (Luke 14:26). Experts have reconstructed the teaching in the styles and the very language which were original, Palestinian and Aramaic – the kind of work which Joachim Jeremias brought to a climax in his treatment of *The Proclamation of Jesus* which formed the first volume of his *New Testament Theology* (in English, 1971). Jeremias understood Jesus's teaching as nothing less than 'the call of God'. I find it curious that not all scholars whose tendency is conservative see the real differences between this call and other voices heard in Palestine at that time. It is, for example, very curious that Dr Stott gets the contrast between Jesus and the Pharisees wrong. He claims that the Pharisees 'made the law's demands less demanding and the law's permissions more permissive' (CCC, p. 79) although their very name almost certainly means 'the Separated'. Elsewhere, as I have already noted, he alleges that the Pharisees 'thought an external comformity to the law would be righteousness enough' (CMMW, p. 75) – which scarcely suggests permissiveness. In the gospels Jesus repeatedly attacks them for a harshly inhumane legalism and Paul's letters (for example Philippians 3:5–6) record the memory that while a Pharisee he had kept the Jewish religious law zealously. And the truth about the Pharisees, as it has emerged from modern scholarly debate, seems to be that they were groups of laymen so devout that they felt themselves obliged to live at the standard of ritual purity normally expected only of priests on duty in the temple.

There is a tendency in Dr Stott's exposition to suggest that Jesus, too, was a legislator, different from the Pharisees in that he was less 'permissive'. Thus the saying of Jesus that 'whoever says, "You fool!" will be in danger of the fire of hell' is treated as if it implied that God is a judge unable to discriminate between minor and major crimes, since 'angry thoughts and insulting words are tantamount to murder in God's sight' (CCC, p. 85). In his *Basic Christianity* (BC1, pp. 65–9) Dr Stott expounds the ten commandments of the Old Testament in the light of the teaching of Jesus. Much of this exposition would be accepted by most Christians. But he states, as if it were a law made by Jesus, that 'every loss of temper, every outburst of uncontrolled passion, every stirring of sullen rage, every bitter resentment and thirsting for revenge – all these things are murder'. He claims that the seventh commandment 'has a far wider application than just to unfaithfulness in marriage. It includes any sort of sex outside the marriage relationship for which it was designed. It includes flirting, experimenting, and solitary sexual experience'. Such teaching surely does not reflect the real intention of Jesus. The purpose was not to blur the distinction between anger and murder, or masturbation and adultery. It was by the use of hyperbole to challenge the disciples to 'be perfect . . . as your heavenly Father is perfect' (Matthew 5:48). One of the differences between Jesus and the Pharisees was that Jesus was not a legislator but a poet.

Here is, I suggest, a failure to see that Jesus taught by stating a vision not a law, and by exaggerating rather than modifying the practical consequences of that vision. And this failure seems to lead Dr Stott into some interpretations of the teaching which are probably wrong – although these interpretations do not come down on the side of the rigorists.

In both the books we have been considering he insists that the version of the teaching on divorce given twice by Matthew (5:31–32; 19:1–9) is authentic and that therefore divorce after sexual immorality is permitted to the Christian. But most scholars take the more probable view that this 'Matthean exception' to the general condemnation of divorce derives from Matthew or the community behind him, not from Jesus, who is elsewhere reported to have made no such exception (1 Corinthians 7:10–11; Mark 10:11; Luke 16:18). If Jesus taught what Matthew says, it is hard to understand why his disciples exclaimed: 'If this is the situation between a husband and wife, it is better not to marry' (Matthew 19:10). He would have done no more than to repeat the interpretation of Deuteronomy 24:1–4 already given by the stricter rabbis such as the famous Shammai. The declaration that *all* divorce is against God's will was evidently remembered widely as one of the most surprising things in the teaching of Jesus. Many scholars believe that Matthew took one of his passages about this problem from the collection of sayings called Q (Luke has a parallel passage) and the other from Mark's gospel, before amending them to reflect the teaching given in his own community.

However, it does not necessarily follow that Jesus intended his own absolutely simple vision of permanent marriage to be legislation. Paul evidently thought not, for he makes the exception about desertion by an unbelieving spouse. And the two contexts of the teaching in Matthew's gospel do not suggest that legislation is being enacted. In the Sermon on the Mount the teaching is given after a passage of hyperbole about lust: 'If your right eye causes you to sin, gouge it out and throw it away . . . If your right hand causes you to sin, cut it off and throw it away . . .' (5:29–30). In the second passage the teaching about divorce is admitted to be hard and therefore acceptable only to those 'to whom it has been given. For some are eunuchs because they were born that way; others were made that way by men; and others have renounced marriage because of the kingdom of heaven. The one who can accept this should accept it' (19:11–12). Such talk about the people who accept the total condemnation of divorce as being sexless ('eunuchs') sounds like another example of hyperbole. The probability seems to be that the Matthean community, like Paul, had found it pastorally essential not to treat the vision of Jesus as a legal prohibition of all divorces. Some Christians after some tragedies, which certainly were not what God willed, should be allowed second marriages, for 'a believing man or woman is not bound in such circumstances; God has called us to live in peace' (1 Corinthians 7:15).

At times Dr Stott does see that Jesus used hyperbole, getting a message across by what everyone knows to be exaggeration rather than by an attempt to be precisely accurate. Thus he does not interpret 'do not judge' (7:1) as the prohibition of all moral judgements or 'ask and it will be given to you' (7:7) as a promise that all petitions to God will be granted, and when he considers the agonising moral problems posed by nuclear weapons he does not treat the Sermon on the Mount as legislation. I happen to agree with his views on nuclear weapons (as well as with his views on divorce). I also agree with his non-pacifist insistence that the state has a role – employing the minimum necessary force, or the threat of it, where necessary for the sake of justice – which is different from the duty of a private individual. But as pacifists healthily remind all Christians, there remains an enormous contrast between the Sermon on the Mount and the possession of nuclear weapons; for the possession would be pointless if it did not imply some threat of use. This contrast between the world of the cross and the world of the Bomb is a special challenge to Christians in government or the armed forces who control nuclear weapons. They cannot plead that they leave religion and morality behind at the door when they enlist in the service of the state. That plea did not save Nazi war criminals – a fact which ought to have made Dr Stott pause longer before praising the theory of an earlier German, Martin Luther, that there are two realms, the kingdom of Christ and the realm of the emperor. The solution which argues that 'the duties and factions of the state are quite different from those of the individual' (CCC, p. 111) is not a perfect solution, for individuals consent to serve as officers of the state. We have also to remember that in a democracy individual voters accept some responsibility for the defence policy of a country. If wrong, they incur some guilt. I mention such familiar problems in order to make the point that the moral dilemmas associated with the possession of nuclear weapons would be totally intolerable if Jesus had been legislating either for states or for individuals when he taught: 'Do not resist an evil person. If someone strikes you on the right cheek, turn to him the other also . . .' (Matthew 5:39).

One of the many merits of *Issues Facing Christians Today* is that it treats with equal seriousness the question of nuclear weapons and the question of abortion. It is not always that these two large-scale contemporary insults to the sanctity of human life are considered together. Dr Stott states with the right passion an absolute rejection of the extreme 'liberal' position on abortion: 'we reject as totally false and utterly abhorrent the notion that the foetus is merely a lump of jelly or blob of tissue, or a growth in the mother's womb, which may therefore be extracted and destroyed like teeth, tumours or tonsils' (IFCT, p. 284). But his own position is (I think, sensibly) not completely absolutist. It would disappoint many Catholic or Evangelical 'prolife' campaigners in the USA and elsewhere. 'Is abortion, then, never justified?' he asks. 'To answer this question in a way that is both faithful and realistic theologians and doctors need each other' – for, he says, 'the most exceptional cases' do exist (IFCT, pp. 294–5). And of course some of the doctors and nurses who may rightly perform abortions in these rare cases are Christians.

## The Bible and the Cultures

My third question is whether it is right to take as authoritative teaching in the Bible which, as I read it, reflects the surrounding society and its culture. Such teaching, I believe, ought not to be decisive in the discussion of modern problems.

In the nineteenth century it was extremely important to establish that the Bible's consistent acceptance of slavery reflected the surrounding culture and did not reveal the will of God. William Wilberforce and other Evangelical campaigners against the slave trade, and the later Evangelical crusaders against slavery in the USA, had to face and overcome much argumentation which defended that iniquitous institution as 'biblical'. I ask whether one lesson to be learned from that controversy is not this: whether we like it or not, the Bible often is culture-bound. Behind this question is my inability to accept the tendency of the 1982 report on *Evangelism and Social Responsibility* to see faults in us but never in the Bible. 'It is not that God's Word is unclear in itself,' this report assures us, 'nor that its meaning is captive to any culture. The problem lies rather within our minds as we read. The assumptions we bring with us, which are often insufficiently examined and converted in the light of God's Word, distort our understanding of it' (ESR, p. 10). I do not wish to repeat my discussion of the authority of the Scriptures, but that statement seems to me true only if 'God's Word' is understood as what the Bible taken as a whole affirms – which may be only loosely connected with, or may contradict, the natural, original meaning of a particular passage in the Bible. If 'God's Word' means the Bible, then I have to say that it is sometimes unclear and sometimes culture-bound. Indeed, the 1982 report appears to admit this. 'When the teaching of Scripture seems unclear, and human reason has to seek to develop a position out of biblical principles, then the Church should make a pronouncement only after thorough study and consultation' (ESR, p. 52).

The question about a culture-bound Bible is, of course, raised whenever the Bible is quoted in the debate about nuclear weapons. The idea that a state governed by Christians would possess a weapon capable of destroying a whole city if a button was pressed, and would threaten the possible use of it if only to deter aggression by creating uncertainty, was inconceivable in an age when the most powerful weapon was the sword. The question must also, I believe, be asked whenever the Bible is quoted in the debate about Christian responses to the situation created by modern attitudes to marriage and divorce. So I return to that subject.

In modern societies marriage is a relationship between equal partners who are lovers. It does not need the consent of parents except in the rare cases where the lovers are not adults. It does need registration by the state. It may be dissolved by the state if the relationship has broken down in the eyes of either partner. If a woman and a man have intercourse before or after an engagement to marry (which is not legally binding), but before marriage, most people do not disapprove. In fact many people think it is a good idea because if the emotional relationship is made legal before it has been thoroughly tested it may end in the tragedy and trauma of divorce. In a society which contains many citizens who do not guide their lives by Christian convictions, it is generally held (by Christians among others) that the state is right to legislate on the basis of this widely accepted understanding of the partnership between the sexes. But the attitude of society to marriage in biblical times was almost entirely different. It was customary for almost everyone to be married and the plight of widows and orphans was so pitiful that the married were often exhorted to be charitable towards such unfortunates. The prostitutes' profession seems to have been recruited from widows and divorced women who could not find husbands. It was, it seems, assumed that after divorce a woman would remarry if she found a man. When a woman without children lost her husband by death she was thought to be lucky if her brother-in-law would agree to do his duty by marrying her, and it was not impossible to imagine that in this way seven brothers might marry the same woman (Mark 12:18–23). The custom was for a girl to be betrothed by the gift of a bride-price of her father. This occurred after puberty, often between the ages of twelve and thirteen but sometimes as late as seventeen. The man betrothed to her, but no other man, might then have intercourse with her. A girl not found to be a virgin on betrothal was to be stoned to death according to the Law of Moses, as was any adulteress or any man committing adultery with another man's wife (Deuteronomy 22:13–22;

Ezekiel 23:43–47; John 8:1–5). The betrothal usually lasted for a year but it might be longer. Then the woman was taken to the groom's house amid the many festivities of the 'wedding feast'. These customs make it clear that although affection and love may become normal between the partners, the arrangement is made between the man and the girl's parents. The state is not involved in it. It is made partly because of the man's needs for sex and companionship, partly because of society's needs for many children, some of whom will survive infancy, and partly because the woman is needed to work in the house and the fields. All this is implied when we are told in the Adam and Eve story that 'it is not good for the man to be alone', so that he needs a suitable 'helper' (Genesis 2:18). The only question about divorce was in what circumstances, if any, the husband might end this relationship with the approval of those around him and without consulting any officer of the state. Although Mark's gospel has been edited so as to reflect the Roman law by considering the possibility that a woman might divorce her husband (10:12), such a possibility was very rare among the Jews. In the Jewish tradition the subordination of the wife to the husband was such that polygamy was never censured when practised by patriarchs such as Abraham and heroes such as David and Solomon – and disappeared only slowly and without any great moral protest that is on record. It is also significant that the Greek word for sexual love, *eros*, does not occur in the New Testament.

The teaching of Jesus was addressed to this situation in which marriage was a male-dominated, sexual, procreative and economic relationship which might or might not be supported by love but which was not registered by the state. And Jesus and his followers seem to have accepted this practical basis of marriage although they gave the relationship a new spiritual depth and therefore permanence. The first letter of Peter (3:7) typically instructs husbands to treat their wives' with respect as the weaker partner and as heirs with you of the gracious gift of life, so that

nothing will hinder your prayers'. Paul's letters show that
he, too, assumed that the wife was 'weaker'. In the letter
to the Ephesians (CCC, pp. 22–32) 'wives, submit to your
husbands as to the Lord' comes before 'husbands, love
your wives'. An acceptance up to a point of the ancient
understanding of marriage is also the impression left by the
evidence about Jesus. Although he taught that according to
the will of the Creator 'a man will leave his father and
mother and be united to his wife, and the two will become
one flesh' (Mark 10:7–8), he is not on record as saying that
any of the men whom he told to 'sell all' and 'follow me'
must first ask the permission of their wives. And Christian
women and men have, like their neighbours, often
accepted this understanding of marriage, or something
very like it, in the course of history and around the world-
wide Church in our own time. But in a society which
understands marriage very differently, very few Christians
advocate a return to the biblical situation. Here, the cultural
context of the Bible is separated from what is held to be its
permanently valid 'doctrine of marriage' and the problem
about divorce is how to relate this doctrine to the new
situation where marriage is essentially love between
equals.

I now want to ask other questions about the authority of
biblical teachings which reflect the surrounding society and
its culture. I want to ask them in relation to two moral
problems to which I think Dr Stott gives the wrong
answers.

He considers the question: 'What form should women's
ministry take in a Church guided by the Bible?' (IFCT, pp.
249–54). 'A strong *prima facie* biblical case can be made for
active female leadership in the Church, including a
teaching ministry', he writes, citing the prophetesses of the
Old Testament, the reports that Jesus entrusted the good
news of his resurrection to women, the gift of the Holy
Spirit to women as well as men (Acts 2:17–18), and the
many references to women speakers and workers in the
rest of the New Testament. But he feels obliged to treat

commands to women to be silent in the public assembly as coming from apostles whom Jesus 'chose, appointed and inspired as the infallible teachers of his Church'. Paul's first letter to Corinth is taken as authoritative when it says that 'as in all the congregations of the saints, women should remain silent in the churches. They are not allowed to speak, but must be in submission, as the Law says' (14:33–34). Dr Stott has to reconcile this passage (which some scholars think is not authentically Pauline, having been added at a later date) with a passage in which Paul does recognise the practice of women talking in the congregation. For Paul tells the Corinthians that 'every woman who prays or prophesies with her head uncovered dishonours her head – it is just as though her head were shaved. If a woman does not cover her head, she should have her hair cut off' (11:5–6). Dr Stott agrees that this is a warning to Christian prophetesses, who do speak in public. His solution to this puzzle is that Paul meant that 'too talkative women should remain silent in the churches'. The first letter to Timothy also has to be respected when it says:

> I do not permit a woman to teach or to have authority over a man; she must be silent. For Adam was formed first, then Eve. And Adam was not the one deceived; it was the woman who was deceived and became a sinner. But women will be saved through childbearing – if they continue in faith, love and holiness with propriety. (2:12–15)

Here as elsewhere, Dr Stott suggests that the requirement of silence, like that of head covering, was a 'first-century cultural application' of the requirement of submission, which alone is of 'permanent and universal validity'.

The practical conclusion which he draws after considering these passages is that women may be ordained but not appointed to positions of authority over men. However, I question his logic. None of these passages gives any hint that its teaching is not thought to be of permanent and universal validity. If Paul had meant his instruction to be applicable only to talkative women, or only to Corinthians, he would have said so. But in the churches to which Dr Stott and I mostly address ourselves, women are not expected to remain silent or to cover their heads. I cannot see why in such churches some women should not be appointed to positions where they lead men. If it is never right for a woman to have authority over a man, the whole of a modern society is in rebellion against the revealed will of God. For example, it must be wrong for the United Kingdom to have a woman as its Sovereign and a woman as its Prime Minister (voted for by many Christians). If female 'headship' is right in society as a whole, the only reason why it cannot be right in the Church is that it has not yet been approved by the Pope or a Council of the Church (or so it seems to me). But Dr Stott writes: 'since I do not believe the pastoral ministry to be "priestly" in the "Catholic" sense, that is not my problem'. Yet he hesitates to say that the Church should be a model to society in giving women leadership roles. What *is* his problem, as I see it, is that he has been misled by treating the story of Adam and Eve as a story from which legislation about women's ministry in the Church can be deduced. To my mind, it would be just as sensible to try to prevent snakes from eating anything except dust. Or we might try to keep pains in childbearing undiminished on the ground that according to Genesis 3:16 they were increased as a punishment for Eve's fault and according to 2 Timothy they are able to 'save' if accepted submissively. The story of Adam and Eve is a myth. Many lessons which are of permanent and universal validity should be drawn from it, but the subjection of women to men should not be based on this myth. It is far better to be guided in church and society by Paul's most profound insight, which is that 'all of you who were baptised into Christ have clothed yourselves with Christ. There is neither Jew nor Greek, slave nor free, male nor female, for you are all one in Christ Jesus' (Galatians 3:27–28).

In *Issues Facing Christians Today* (IFCT, pp. 301–2) Dr Stott also considers the problem of homosexual relationships, concluding that 'in the light of the whole biblical revelation we should call homosexually oriented people to abstain from homosexual practices and partnerships'. He quotes and examines the story of Sodom and Gomorrah, cities which are said to have been entirely destroyed because at least some of their inhabitants had displayed a special wickedness by asking to have homosexual intercourse with two angels (Genesis 13:13; 18:20–21; 19:1–5); the story of Gibeah, where 'some of the wicked men of the city' demanded to have intercourse with a man on a journey before raping and killing that man's concubine and the city was massacred and burned down in punishment (Judges 19:22); the punishment of death for breaches of the law 'do not lie with a man as one lies with a woman' (Leviticus 18:22; 20:13); the denunciation by Paul of pagans who show that they worship and serve created things rather than the Creator by being filled with perverted homosexual lust and 'every kind of wickedness, evil, greed and depravity' (Romans 1:24–32); the teaching that 'neither the sexually immoral nor idolaters nor adulterers nor male prostitutes nor homosexual offenders (*arsenokoitai*) nor thieves nor the greedy nor drunkards nor swindlers will inherit the kingdom of God' (1 Corinthians 6:10); and the teaching that 'law is made not for the righteous but for law-breakers . . . ; for those who kill their fathers or mothers, for murderers for adulterers and perverts (*arsenokoitais*) . . .' (1 Timothy 1:9–10). But what is the significance of these passages for homosexually oriented people who wish to have stable relationships expressed in physical practices?

Dr Stott's exegesis shows that he has read and thought about the relevance of this material with careful attention to the now extensive scholarly discussion, summarised in (for example) Bishop Peter Coleman's *Christian Attitudes to Homosexuality* (1980). What the Bible shows (if I may be brief) is that practices such as raping strangers and perverted lust were roundly condemned. But the Greek word *arsenokoitai* commonly referred to men thought to be by nature heterosexual who were promiscuously active in seeking homosexual intercourse, often with post-pubertal boys and often for money, out of perverted lust; such men 'abandoned natural relations with women and were inflamed with lust for one another' (Romans 1:27). Dr Stott rightly says that 'the very notion that two men or two women could fall in love with each other and develop a deeply loving, stable relationship comparable to marriage seriously' never entered the heads of Paul and the Old Testament authors. He accepts that 'we all have a particular sexual orientation'. He quotes, without disagreeing with, the finding of Dr Kinsey that

> 4% of men (or at least of white American men) are exclusively homosexual throughout their lives, that 10% are for up to three years, and that as many as 37% have some kind of homosexual experience between adolescence and old age. The percentage of homosexual women Kinsey found to be lower, although it rises to 4% between the ages of 20 and 30. (p. 301)

These were figures in the late 1940s, when it was far less safe to admit the same-sex eroticism than it is now, and are usually reckoned to be underestimates. The question for Christians who accept that some people are exclusively homosexual throughout their lives (whether because of their genes or because of early influences on them) is therefore: Is every instance when a man lies 'with a man as one lies with a woman', or every instance of lesbian practice, to be condemned?

Obviously Christians (and almost all others) do not want to see it punished by death as the law in Leviticus laid down. But is it always to be condemned morally even within a deeply loving, stable relationship, because as Dr Stott says it is 'incompatible with God's created order'?

Dr Stott finds it 'disturbing' when it is suggested that the 'Christian rejection of homosexual practices' rests on 'a few isolated and obscure proof texts'; and I am sure that he is right to argue for his own rejection by appealing to what the

Bible taken as a whole affirms about God's purposes in creation, rather than texts of doubtful relevance and sometimes of doubtful meaning. But I am equally sure that John Boswell (*Christianity, Social Tolerance and Homosexuality*, 1980, p. 117) was correct in claiming that 'the New Testament takes no demonstrable position on homosexuality' if 'homosexuality' is understood in a modern sense; and so we must ask again what it is that the Bible would have us say now. The revelation of the creation by modern science, including medical science, must be taken into conscientious and prayerful consideration by a modern Christian. From that God-given source of truth we learn that for some people to be exclusively homosexual for a lifetime is natural. They were, as is commonly said, 'made that way'. If this is the case, then I believe that the Creator's purpose in making them that way (or in allowing them to be so made by the forces of nature as permitted by him) may be fulfilled in an adult, consenting, discreet, loving, stable partnership, within which some physical expressions of love are likely to be psychologically necessary.

I have reached this conclusion – but not because I believe that such a partnership is a fully satisfactory alternative to marriage. It seems to me inevitable that there will always be strong feelings against the relationship which is wrongly called 'gay marriage', for only the bonding of a man and a woman can produce the children who are vital to society's future and the biological make-up of the bulk of the human race obviously prepares them for procreation, childbearing and child-rearing. Nor do I believe that to be homosexual is to be gay. That minority is for ever excluded from the joys of married life and will always seem strange to the majority, particularly through the fear that children and young people will be 'corrupted' by homosexuals. (Although most homosexuals behave in such a way as to make this fear seem unreasonable, it is inevitable that the fear should be felt since many children are both innocently beautiful and bisexual in their awakening instincts.) Tragically, there seems to me no possible escape from some of the emotional problems of homosexuals, even when society does not reject them. Nor do I believe that the many people whose orientation is bisexual, even if only in adolescence or for a later period in their lives, should be encouraged to think that homosexuality and heterosexuality are equally right for them. If they fall into homosexual habits, perhaps because the prospect of forming a permanent relationship with a woman frightens them, they become the 'perverts' who are criticised in the Bible and by any philosophy which seeks the happiness of humanity. Still less am I advocating any kind of promiscuity, which is similarly condemned by the Bible and by common sense. On the contrary, the Christian acceptance of some loving, stable partnerships between homosexuals – an acceptance which does not speak of such a relationship as 'marriage' and which may apply to no more than two adult men in a hundred, and to one adult woman in every two hundred – is advocated partly in order to reduce the temptation of homosexuals to have more than one partner, incurring great psychological damage in many cases and increasing the risk of appalling diseases such as AIDS.

I hope it will be clear that the reason why I ask these questions is that I believe that Dr Stott's profoundly Christian and humane approach to social and moral problems would be strengthened, rather than weakened, if he completely renounced the fundamentalists' tendency to treat the Bible as legislation on modern issues.

# John Stott's Response to Chapter 5

My dear David,

During the first half of this century, as you well know, Evangelicals (in spite of their forefathers' outstanding record in the nineteenth century, and with some honourable exceptions) temporarily mislaid their social conscience. We, their children and grandchildren, have only begun since the Second World War to recover it. The 1982 'Consultation on the Relationship between Evangelism and Social Responsibility', to which you several times refer, was a landmark for the world-wide Evangelical constituency since, alongside some residual differences, we agreed that Christians should be committed to both evangelism and social action, and suggested some models for their integration. But Evangelicals have fallen so far behind in this area, that we have a lot of catching up to do. Some of us (myself included) are only now taking our first, faltering steps in the unfamiliar field of social ethics. It is partly because of this that there is still a lack of Evangelical consensus on a number of complex issues. But at least we recognise the need for more study and dialogue, so that, avoiding naive and artificial polarisations, we may map out the growing areas of our agreement as well as identifying continuing places of tension and disagreement.

Because of this situation in which we find ourselves, I was particularly grateful for (and encouraged by) your generally positive response to, and complimentary remarks about, both *Christian Counter-Culture: The Message of the Sermon on the Mount* and *Issues Facing Christians Today*. Thank you! I am glad that you and I have come to adopt similar positions on such topics as the nuclear deterrent, abortion and human rights. For the development of a thought-out stance on these and other questions poses particular problems for those of us who look to the Bible for guidance. We know both that the Bible addresses some issues which do not particularly concern us (like idol meats), while other issues over which we agonise (like abortion) it hardly touches, or not directly. Yet Evangelicals still believe that God intends his word to be 'a lamp to our feet and a light for our path' (Psalm 119:105), and that we need 'to pay attention to it, as to a light shining in a dark place' (2 Peter 1:19). I am not surprised, therefore, that the three questions you raise with me all relate to the use of the Bible in ethics.[1]

## The Relevance of the Old Testament

I feel the strength of your criticisms here, and am not sure how to respond to them. But it may help if I relate my comments to three different parts of the Old Testament, namely the first chapters of Genesis, the Law of Moses, and the prophetic and wisdom literature.

The early chapters of Genesis (in God's providence, I believe) lay some large and solid foundations for all Christian social ethics. I have in mind at least the following eight truths.

---

[1] I would like to make particular mention of two Evangelical books which relate to the Bible and ethics. The first is a symposium edited by Bruce Kaye and Gordon Wenham entitled *Law, Morality and the Bible*, which was published by the Inter-Varsity Press in 1978. It begins with the basic themes of grace, law, freedom and order, and then opens up the process of Christian moral reasoning. The second is a booklet by Dr Christopher Wright entitled *The Use of the Bible in Social Ethics* (Grove Booklets, 1983). In it he helpfully brings together the 'linear model' (creation—fall—redemption—new creation) and the 'triangular model' (the relations in both creation and redemption between God, humankind and the earth).

(1) God's creation is good, and is to be enjoyed by everybody with thanksgiving (Genesis 1:31; cf. 1 Timothy 4:1–5).

(2) God made human beings in his own image and likeness, which includes our distinctive rational, moral, social and spiritual faculties (Genesis 1:26–27).

(3) Human beings are invited to participate in the care of creation, to cultivate the earth and to harness its resources to the common good (Genesis 1:28–29; 2:15).

(4) Men and women share equally both in the divine image and in the earthly dominion (Genesis 1:27).

(5) The climax of the creation was not human work but human worship, together with the hallowing of one day in seven for this purpose (Genesis 2:2–3).

(6) Marriage and sex are the good gifts of a good Creator. Men and women are complementary to each other and need each other for their human fulfilment (Genesis 2:18–25).

(7) Human beings have fallen from their exalted origins, and in consequence all their relationships – to God, to each other and to the good earth – are now skewed (Genesis 3).

(8) But God has not abandoned his beloved creation. He continues to help us in his 'common grace' (Genesis 4:1). He has even planned sacrificially for our salvation, if Genesis 3:15 may still be read (as it has been traditionally) as the *protevangelium*.

I am sorry that you think my continuing belief in the historicity of Adam and Eve 'lessens the seriousness of my account of the human tragedy', for I could argue the opposite, namely that what really undermines serious discussion about our human predicament is the treating of either the sin of Adam or the salvation of Christ as mythical instead of historical. The reason I did not mention evolution is not that I do not believe in it, at least in the sub-human world. (Being myself an enthusiastic bird-watcher, I have visited two of the earth's living museums of mini-evolution, and have wondered at the thirteen species of Darwin's finch on the Galapagos Islands and at the endemic family of Hawaiian Honey creepers, for in both cases each species occupies a special ecological niche.) But I am convinced that evolution does not and cannot account for man. The gap between humans and hominids is too wide. So, whatever may be said about our anatomy and physiology being linked to the animal world, the radical discontinuity of our humanness in all its uniqueness as the image of God must be affirmed in terms of creation.

I turn from the early chapters of Genesis to the Law of Moses. It is well known that the Reformers divided the law into three parts – civil, ceremonial and moral (see Article VII 'Of the Old Testament'). The division is not watertight, and it is being criticised today because of the overlap. Nevertheless the distinction between the three is vital. The ceremonial laws are now obsolete, the dietary laws having been abolished by Jesus and the sacrifices fulfilled in his death. The civil laws are not necessarily appropriate to other nations. Some were humane, and others severe. They seem to have been necessary for the earlier stages of Israel's history, but I agree with you that they are not all of permanent or universal validity. In any case, many fell into desuetude, like stoning for adultery, and Jesus obviously approved of its discontinuance. At the same time, there is a growing Evangelical emphasis on the permanent value (whether in 'principle' or in 'pattern' is being debated) of Mosaic legislation about the land and the family. The moral law, especially as expanded and deepened by Jesus, and as illustrated in the apostolic letters (especially in their positive parallels to the law's prohibitions), is still in force as a revelation of God's will for his people (e.g. Romans 8:4).

You then press me on moral peaks versus troughs, and in particular on the slaughter of the Canaanites. Certainly I believe in progressive revelation and am a New Testament Christian. I agree with Luther who said that, although we read the Bible forwards, we can only understand it backwards. Certainly too, much of the behaviour of Old Testament characters is recorded as a warning rather than an example (e.g. 1 Corinthians 10:6–11). The activities of some of the judges, for instance, even if not specifically condemned in the text, were scandalous, not least Jepthah's reckless oath which led to his appalling deed of sacrificing his own daughter as a burnt offering. That moral standards were abysmally low in those days is hinted at by the repeated refrain that 'Israel had no king; everyone did as he saw fit' (e.g. Judges 21:25). What, then, about the Canaanite genocide? It was a ghastly business; one shrinks from it in horror. Nevertheless, the biblical text plainly attributes it to the specific command of God. What then can be said to justify it? Three things have helped me in my thinking.

First, God's command to dispossess the Canaanites was the necessary corollary to his promise that the Israelites would possess the land of Canaan. The latter could not have taken place without the former. So, if the Canaanites were not dispossessed, God's promise to Abraham, Isaac, Jacob and their descendants could not have been fulfilled, and the recurring Old Testament themes of election, covenant and promise would be undermined.

Secondly, possession of the land was postponed until 'the sin of the Amorites' had 'reached its full measure' (Genesis 15:16). The Bible views 'their detestable practices', that is, their idolatry, child sacrifice and immorality (including ritual prostitution) with such loathing that it says 'the land vomited out its inhabitants' (Leviticus 18:25). In this the righteous Judge was not guilty of discrimination. He warned Israel that if they violated the covenant, and imitated the vile practices of the nations, they themselves would be destroyed from the good land which he had given them (e.g. Joshua 23:14–16).

Thirdly, it was essential to protect God's people, who were the recipients of his special revelation, though still at a stage of immaturity (Galatians 4:1–11), from being corrupted by heathen idolatry and immorality: 'Do not bow down before their gods or worship them or follow their practices . . . Do not make a covenant with them or with their gods' (Exodus 23:24,32).

Even if this threefold case were granted, however, we must add that the annihilation of the Canaanites was *sui generis*. It was the only 'holy war' which God has ever commanded. It can provide no possible justification for war or genocide today (not least because no other nation has been a 'nation-church' or theocracy like Israel); nor, I think, does it justify Israel's later wars, some of which at least were due to their failure to take thorough possession of the land in the first place. And indeed you are right to balance the judgement of the Canaanites with other biblical teaching which reveals God's compassion and mercy to the nations.

I have left myself little room for the prophetic and wisdom literature. Both took the law for granted – the prophets appealing for the faithful observance of its moral and social requirements (e.g. 'To act justly and to love mercy and to walk humbly with your God' Micah 6:8) and denouncing their neglect, and the wise men reflecting on the application of the law to everyday life. The obligation to secure justice for the powerless (especially the alien, the widow and the orphan) shines brightly from these books, and I have already mentioned Jesus' use of the principle 'I desire mercy not sacrifice' (Hosea 6:6) to teach the paramount importance of persons, even if, in order to serve them, it means breaking the letter of the sabbath law and the convention of avoiding contact with social outcasts (Matthew 9:13; 12:7).

## Was Jesus a Legislator?

I begin my response to your second question by agreeing with you about Jesus' use of hyperbole. By no means all his teaching is meant to be read *au pied de la lettre*. On the contrary, he seems often to have taught by the surprises and shocks caused by overstatement, and by vividly dramatic imagery. Thus the command to gouge out offending eyes, and chop off offending hands and feet, was not an invitation to self-mutilation, as Origen mistakenly supposed. Nor is it conceivable that he who told us to honour our parents should later command us literally to 'hate' them. Similarly, in the same passage, the renunciation of all our possessions as a condition of discipleship must be understood as a radical inward detachment from material things, and not as a summons to give everything away (Luke 14:33).

You chide me for getting wrong 'the contrast between Jesus and the Pharisees'. But I want to plead 'not guilty'. I know the Pharisees were separatists, devout laymen who practised ritual purity. But did Jesus not criticise them because their preoccupation with purity was ceremonial rather than moral (Mark 7:1–13)? And did they not, with the scribes, reduce the law to 613 rules and regulations (248 commands and 365 prohibitions), and then sometimes claim to have kept them all? As for legalistic righteousness, 'faultless' was Paul's own description of himself during his career as a Pharisee (Philippians 3:6). Such a claim would have been impossible unless the Pharisees were referring only to an external conformity. Is that not why Jesus spoke about the heart? By their emphasis on the ritual rather than the moral, and on externals rather than the heart, they *were* in effect 'making the demands of the law less demanding', although, to be sure, they may not have realised it. We must therefore avoid like the plague any tendency to a Christian 'Pharisaism'. Christian righteousness is 'greater' than Pharisaic righteousness (Matthew 5:20) because it is deeper, a righteousness of the heart. I am sorry, therefore, that in *Basic Christianity* my exposition of the ten commandments bordered on Pharisaism. I was trying to help the reader grasp that the prohibition of murder also prohibits unrighteous anger, and that the prohibition of adultery includes the positive virtues of sexual self-control and married fidelity. I did not mean to *equate* anger with murder, and lust with adultery, for obviously they are not equally serious, but rather to highlight Jesus' teaching that it is possible to commit murder and adultery in the heart.

Thus, the call to heart-holiness in the kingdom of God is far more radical than the Pharisees' rules and regulations.

I know that most commentators reject Matthew's 'exceptive clause' about divorce (because it is in neither Mark nor Luke), and attribute it either to Matthew himself or to his community, and not to Jesus. Yet, in spite of the editorial emendations of Mark which Matthew undoubtedly made, I find it hard to believe that he would have deliberately contradicted Mark on so serious a matter; it still seems to me more likely that Mark and Luke omitted the clause because they took it for granted (adultery being punishable by death according to the law), and that Matthew preserved it in order to make sure that his readers had not overlooked it. The disciples' exclamation of dismay could well have been their reaction to Jesus' reminder that divorce was not practised or permitted 'from the beginning', and to his statement that anybody who divorces his wife (except for marital unfaithfulness) and marries another woman actually thereby commits adultery himself. Even if the stricter Rabbi Shammai had already stated this in theory, it was the more liberal policy of Hillel which seems to have controlled Jewish practice at that time.

Your other example relates to pacifism. We are agreed that the state has a responsibility to enforce the law, punish the wrongdoer and promote justice, and may use minimum necessary force in order to do so, whereas the Christian individual is forbidden to use force or take revenge. But you evidently disagree with my semi-support for Luther's notion of 'two kingdoms'. In *The Cross of Christ*, however, I elaborate this and opt not for 'two entities' (Church and state, i.e. Luther's two kingdoms), nor for 'two spheres' (private and public, which would promote a double standard of morality), but for 'two roles', personal and official. I write: 'Christians are always Christians (in church and state, in public and private), under the same moral authority of Christ, but are given different roles (at home, at work and in the community) which make different actions appropriate' (CoC, p. 303). I agree that 'not resisting evil' and 'turning the other cheek' are not absolute or legislative commands. Their fulfilment is governed by the overriding duty 'love your enemies'. Of course all personal retaliation is still forbidden us, but there may be times when the way of true love is not to turn the other cheek but to resist the evildoer, lest by not opposing evil we condone and even encourage it.

So I am agreeing with you that Jesus was not a legislator in the sense of laying down rules and sanctions. What he did was to unite the two commandments to love God and neighbour, and to add the golden rule in its positive form (Matthew 7:12), thus making sacrificial love the essence of the ethic of the kingdom. Yet love is not the only absolute; for love needs law to direct it (Romans 13:8–9). Further, we must interpret the moral teaching of Jesus in such a way as to retain the word 'obedience' in our Christian vocabulary. Jesus is recorded as having said 'If you love me, you will obey what I command' (John 14:15,21). Not superficially, but in our heart. Not in slavish conformity to an external code, but in the radical demands of the kingdom. Not with wooden literalism, but with the sensitivity of love. Nevertheless, he does call us to assume his yoke, as the Jews assumed the yoke of Torah, to learn from him as our Teacher and to obey him as our Lord (Matthew 11:29; John 13:13).

## Scripture and Culture

I remember reading a remark you made a few years ago in one of your *Church Times* book reviews. You wrote: 'I admit that a lot in the Bible . . . is culturally conditioned and therefore out of date'. I also remember thinking to myself, 'I agree with the first half of that sentence, but not with the second.' That is, all the biblical authors were culture-creatures. This being so, the Bible is not just 'often culture-bound', as you put it, but always so. One of the glories of revelation, and of the dual authorship of Scripture, is that when God wished to communicate with human beings, he condescended to speak to them in their own languages and cultural contexts. We should marvel at his humility, and not resent the problems it causes us. Because the Bible is culturally conditioned, however, having been written within the cultures of the Ancient Near East, Palestinian Judaism and the Graeco-Roman world, must we conclude that it is 'therefore out of date'? I think not. Let me try to clarify two senses in which Scripture has been called 'culture-bound', the one right and the other (I think) wrong.

The first is that Scripture includes references to many cultural practices and social customs which are now obsolete, e.g. foot-washing, greeting one another with a holy kiss, men lifting up holy hands in prayer, and women wearing veils, braiding their hair and (perhaps) keeping silence in church. In these contexts we have to learn the art of 'cultural transposition', identifying and preserving the essence of the teaching, but transposing it into contemporary cultural terms. Thus, we are still to love and serve one another even in menial ways, but, instead of washing feet, we could clean shoes or wash dishes. We can greet one another with a handshake, instead of a holy kiss, and so on. Cultural transposition is appropriate only when there are two levels of discourse – the essential teaching (which is permanent) and its cultural expression (which is transitory).

But the Bible is also said by some to be 'culture-bound' in another sense, namely that its essential doctrinal and ethical teaching is itself only a reflection of the culture within which it was written, and is therefore transient. This is an extremely serious charge. If true, it would mean that we can reject whole portions of Scripture on the ground that 'that is what they thought in those days, but we know better'. This attitude I cannot accept. It seems to me clearly in conflict with the inspiration of Scripture, that is, the process by which God himself spoke through the human authors. It also overlooks the fact that God's people were called to be different from others, not to conform to this world, but to challenge their own culture in the name of Christ.

Did the Old Testament not follow the whole ancient world, however, and condone slavery? This seems to be your position, because you write of 'the Bible's consistent acceptance of slavery'. I venture to dissent. To permit its continuance (like divorce) 'because of the hardness of your hearts' is not the same as to condone it. No. The nineteenth-century campaigners opposed slavery not on the ground that the Bible's tolerant attitude was a temporary cultural lapse, but on the ground that slavery conflicted with biblical teaching on the dignity of human beings made in the image of God. For the same reason the Old Testament law carefully regulated it, making it more humane and providing for manumission, while the New Testament went further, demanding 'justice' for slaves (Colossians 4:1) and declaring that Christian slave and slave-owner are 'brothers' (Philemon 16; 1 Timothy 6:2). Thus, principles were laid down in Scripture with which slavery was perceived with steadily increasing clarity to be incompatible.

Your second example of cultural conditioning is marriage. You set in contrast two sets of marriage customs. On the one hand, you describe what is now commonly accepted in 'modern societies' – marriage without parental consent but by state registration, based on mutual love, and often preceded by a trial period of intercourse. On the other hand, you describe marriage customs in biblical times – an arrangement between the parents, the payment of the bride price, betrothal, intercourse, wedding festivities, and no state participation. But I am not clear how you think we should relate these two sets of marriage customs to one another. My position is that both are cultural and neither is scriptural. Are we not called as Christians to confront our culture with biblical norms? So some customs should be regarded as neutral (e.g. engagement and betrothal traditions, the role of the state, wedding festivities), since the Bible makes no pronouncement about them. But the Bible does teach that marriage is God's idea rather than ours, and his general loving provision for human beings; that it involves leaving parents (still of great importance psychologically, even if young people have physically 'left home' years previously); that it is a heterosexual, monogamous and ideally lifelong partnership, expressing love and companionship; and that it is the God-given context for sexual enjoyment and the procreation and nurture of children. These aspects of marriage are creational, not cultural.

With your third example, which concerns women's ministry, I confess that I have much more difficulty. Evangelicals are deeply divided on this issue. You think I give the wrong answer, and you question my logic, and on both counts you may well be right! At the same time, I am not sure that you have altogether followed my argument, or at least that you have adequately presented it. The role and ministry of women in the Church seems to be a clear case for cultural transposition, since the two levels of discourse are apparent. Part of the essence of Paul's teaching concerns masculine 'headship', to be redefined (as you say) in terms of care rather than control, but still rooted in our created sexuality (even if we have difficulties with Paul's detailed exegesis of Genesis 2). The first-century cultural expression of this headship, however, related to such practices as veiling, coiffure, jewellery and (in my view) the requirement of silence or not teaching men. My struggle (which I have not yet resolved) is how to give women the fullest opportunities to exercise their God-given gifts, and to enable both sexes to enjoy their 'neither male nor female' equality (whose context relates to relationships not roles, to justification not ministry), without infringing the creational truths of masculinity, femininity and 'headship'.

Your fourth and last example relates to homosexual partnerships. The question here is whether our knowledge in relation to sexual inversion, the average percentages of men and women who are constitutionally homosexual or bisexual, and the possibility of stable, loving same-sex partnerships, overrides the teaching of the biblical authors who lacked this knowledge. My answer is 'no'. To say 'yes'

THE BIBLE AND BEHAVIOUR – *Response*     **271**

would mean that the more knowledge we have, the less we need and can trust the Bible. You quote John Boswell's statement that 'the New Testament takes no demonstrable position on homosexuality'. I challenge this. Jesus himself endorsed the Genesis 2:24 definition of marriage as a heterosexual partnership and the only relationship to which the 'one-flesh' experience belongs. And Paul describes both men and women, who give up 'natural relations' with the opposite sex and exchange them for relations with their own sex, as acting 'against nature' (*para phusin*, Romans 1:26–27). Now whatever is 'against nature', that is, 'contrary to the intention of the Creator' (C. E. B. Cranfield on Romans 1:26), is rightly called a 'disorder'. But you appeal to creation in another way, as being itself a 'revelation' by modern science, and as teaching that for some people the unnatural is natural, because they are 'made that way'. Consequently, you believe that 'the Creator's purpose in making them that way (or in allowing them to be so made . . .) may be fulfilled in an adult, consenting, discreet, loving, stable partnership, within which some physical expressions of love are likely to be psychologically necessary'. In response, I must honestly say that I think you develop a strange doctrine of creation and of what is 'natural'. Congenitally (i.e. 'creationally') we are all made with a variety of disorders, including many sinful and selfish tendencies. We have no liberty, however, to attribute our evil propensities to the good Creator. Nor should we declare what is 'unnatural' according to his original purpose to be 'natural' because it seems so to us.

The real motive behind your position, I feel sure, is compassion. You feel deeply for homosexual people. Although you know that a homosexual partnership cannot be 'a fully satisfactory alternative to marriage', you are haunted by the tragedy that there is 'no possible escape' from some of the emotional problems which homosexuals experience. So at least, you argue, they should be permitted the nearest equivalent to marriage that is open to them. There seem to me to be two flaws in this argument. First, if a homosexual partnership is 'against nature', and therefore creationally disordered behaviour, then to encourage people to form one is not an expression of true compassion. Secondly, your acceptance or tolerance of a same-sex partnership rests on the assumption that sexual intercourse is 'psychologically necessary'. That is certainly what our sex-obsessed contemporary culture says. But is it true? Christians must surely reply that it is a lie. There is such a thing as the call to singleness, in which authentic human fulfilment is possible without sexual experience. Our Christian witness is that Jesus himself, though unmarried, was perfect in his humanness. Same-sex friendships should of course be encouraged, which may be close, deep and affectionate. But sexual union, the 'one flesh' mystery, belongs to heterosexual marriage alone.

This is not 'fundamentalism'. Nor is it 'proof-texting' or 'random-dipping', two follies of which I repented long ago. For the Bible is not an anthology of unrelated sentences, but rather a coherent and comprehensive revelation from God. It is only by absorbing the totality of biblical teaching that we can develop a Christian mind and learn to think Christianly about the complex issues of our day. For the Christian mind is a renewed mind which refuses to be conformed to the pattern of contemporary culture, and seeks instead conscientiously to discern God's will from Scripture and then by his grace to do it (Romans 12:2).

To be continued!

Yours ever,
John

# 6   The Gospel for the World

## The Hope of the Kingdom

What is the Christian message to the world? Is it about saving the individual, or saving the society, or both? And what does it say about humanity's prospects?

Introducing the 1982 report of the International Evangelical leaders' consultation at Grand Rapids in the USA on *Evangelism and Social Responsibility*, Dr Stott looked back over a 'tension' between the emphasis on the individual and the emphasis on society – a tension which, he said, had at times amounted to a 'polarisation'. In May 1980 a conference was held in Melbourne by the Commission on World Mission and Evangelism of the World Council of Churches. There 'the necessity of proclamation was clearly recognised, but the cries of the poor, the hungry and the opposed predominated.' The following month the Lausanne Committee chaired by Dr Stott sponsored a consultation at Pattaya in Thailand. 'At Pattaya also the cries of the needy were heard (one mini-consultation focused on refugees, and another on the urban poor), but the call to proclaim the gospel to the unevangelised predominated'. And there were also disagreements between Evangelicals about what the gospel implied – disagreements so sharp that Dr Stott confessed that he went to the 1982 consultation 'with a considerable degree of apprehension'.

The report shows that some of these tensions and disagreements were overcome. To Dr Stott, it was another and dramatic demonstration of the value of international conferences. When we remain apart from one another, and our only contact with one another is the lobbing of hand grenades across a demilitarised zone, our attitudes inevitably harden and our mental images of each other become stereotyped. But when we meet face to face (or, as our American friends vividly express it, 'eyeball to eyeball'), and listen not only to each other's arguments but to the cherished convictions which lie behind the arguments, then we develop towards one another a new understanding, respect and love.

So it proved possible to agree on much and, for the rest, to disagree with charity. The 1982 meeting put first the people in the world 'still unevangelised' and reckoned that there were some three thousand million of them. But Christ's great commission to evangelise, and God's own mission 'in his love for his lost world', were seen to involve social responsibility, particularly in service and political action to help the poorest. 'We are appalled to know that about 800 million people, or one fifth of the human race, are destitute, lacking the basic necessities for survival, and that thousands of them die of starvation every day.' 'We are all agreed that salvation is a broad term, in the sense that it embraces the totality of God's redemptive purpose for such a world.' It includes new life for individuals, the new community of Christians, and 'the new world which God will one day make'. Yet 'at present only a tiny fraction of our total Christian resources is being applied to any kind of mission, evangelistic or social'. So the leaders gathered at Grand Rapids in 1982 called for a 'more costly commitment to the lost, the needy and the oppressed, for the greater glory of God, Father, Son and Holy Spirit'.

This emphasis both on evangelism and on social responsibility seems to me entirely right. Nothing less is our obligation. With shame I acknowledge that it ought to supply the motivation not only for my life but for the lives of all who call themselves Christians. But many Christians and others who would have much to contribute to this mission to the world do not think that the problems have been dealt with satisfactorily by conservative Evangelicals. Many therefore hesitate to join in tasks which are crying out to be done. And because many Evangelicals suspect that the purpose of mentioning these problems is to destroy Christianity or at least to compromise over a gospel which is for Christians 'non-negotiable', conservative Evangelicals often refuse to join with others. The Christian movement is therefore grievously divided in its mission to humanity. It is a striking feature of much Evangelical literature that it maintains a conspiracy of silence about non-Evangelical Christians who in fact greatly outnumber Evangelicals. In particular there is a tendency to ignore the Roman Catholic Church, which includes perhaps half, perhaps more than half, of the world's Christians. Seeking greater unity rather than controversy, I want to ask what, more precisely, is the gospel for society inspiring a new sense of responsibility – in other words, what is the Christian message about the kingdom of God.

The 1982 consultation devoted some study to

> history and eschatology, that is, to the relationship between *on the one hand* what we do now in the historical process and what God is doing since the last days began when the kingdom was inaugurated, and *on the other* about what God is going to do on the Last Day when he ushers in the fulness of the kingdom.

'We all agreed', the report said, 'that our Christian hope focuses on the personal, visible and glorious return of our Lord Jesus Christ, on the resurrection from the dead, and on the perfected kingdom which his appearance will bring.' But this agreement does not seem to me to meet the problems adequately. And then I want to ask what, more precisely, is the Christian message about the prospects of non-Christians. The 1982 consultation agreed that 'though created by God like God and for God, they are now living without God'. They also agreed that 'human beings without Christ are lost or "perishing", and our earnest desire in love is to reach them with the gospel before it is too late'. But this statement seems to me to deserve rejection by

Christians. An evangelism which says that the bulk of humanity is going to hell deserves, I think, its customary rejection by the bulk of humanity.

'Eschatology' is the consideration of death and other 'last things' and I find it curious that when studying the 'connection between our eschatological outlook and the attitude we adopt towards evangelism and social responsibility', these Evangelical leaders turned first to the question of the millennium. 'To begin with,' they say, 'we thought about the millennium and about its influence on Christian behaviour at different points in history.' And they considered differing millenarian views without resolving their differences. Such a sense of priorities seems strange because the only reference to the millennium in the Bible comes in Revelation 20:1–6.

This passage is clearly poetic. It tells of 'an angel coming down out of heaven' armed with a great chain and a key. He throws the dragon, who is Satan, into the Abyss and locks him in for a thousand years. It tells also of thrones 'on which were seated those who had been given authority to judge' and of the Christian martyrs who 'came to life and reigned with Christ for a thousand years'. It declares that 'the rest of the dead did not come to life until the thousand years were ended'. It is not surprising that the consultation could only register its differences in the attempt to interpret this passage, since its membership represented 'the three traditional varieties of millenarianism'. And it is inevitable that people who are not committed to any of these views ask awkward questions, believing that no amount of theological disputation is going to reach agreement about what the poetry means as a prediction of the future. The very fact that equally devout 'Bible believers' – that is, equally devout Christians who all take the poetry as detailed predictions of what is going to happen – cannot agree about what to expect shows that the poetry does not supply evidence to settle the questions which can be asked by people who do not recognise that it is poetry. I shall mention some of the questions.

The New Testament offers many assurances that the power of evil has already been defeated by the work of Christ. The Colossians are assured that they have been 'rescued from the dominion of darkness and brought into the kingdom of the son he loves' (1:13) and the Ephesians that God has 'placed all things under his feet and appointed him to be head over everything for the church' (1:22). Here salvation is an accomplished fact. How, then, can it also be said that deliverance from evil will be postponed until Satan has been imprisoned? The 1982 consultation gave the answer 'that over his redeemed people Jesus is king *de facto*, while it is only *de jure* that he is presently king over the world, his right still challenged by the usurper', Satan. But that is to contradict the conclusion of Matthew's gospel, that 'all authority in heaven and on earth has been given to me' (28:18). This is not much of an authority if it is not a fact outside the Church. And how is evil or Satan to be overthrown? In earlier parts of this tumultuously eloquent book of Revelation different images have been used before the much scrutinised and debated passage about the millennium. But talk about an angel carrying a chain and a key in order to imprison Satan is obviously mythological. Talk about 'thrones' in the plural, with saints seated on them as judges, seems to be incompatible with later talk about 'a great white throne and him who was seated on it' (20:11). Talk about the martyrs (only) coming to life seems to contradict the promises of 'Paradise' or 'eternal life' to many others, for example Christ's own promise on the cross to the dying criminal (Luke 23:43 says 'today'). Talk about Christ's reign on earth 'for a thousand years' seems to imply that he and the martyrs are still in space and time before 'earth and sky' flee from Christ, yet the processes of space and time must be halted if they are all to live for that period. Those over whom Christ and the martyrs reign are already 'like the sand on the seashore' in number before they are joined by 'all the dead, great and small'. These all now stand before the one throne, but how Christ is to be visible to 'all' (particularly if the earth that exists before 'a new heaven and a new earth' are created is round) is left mysterious. How all that vast number is to stand before a single throne is also not explained – and cannot be. It seems obvious that the reality of the Christian hope for the world cannot depend on these poetic images being capable of a literal harmonisation and explanation. And if that is the case, it seems to follow that no one detail such as the mention of a reign of a thousand years (or the mention in 7:4–8 of only 144,000 Jews being saved) should be pressed as authoritative.

The Revelation of John cannot be an accurate prediction of coming events, whatever is claimed for that book within it or elsewhere, partly because its details cannot be fitted together. It is a tremendous work of the imagination – the work of a prisoner of the Roman Empire inspired by his faith that, despite all, Christ is the conqueror. It uses imagery largely derived from the Hebrew Scriptures in order to encourage and warn the churches of Asia being addressed. Like other apocalyptic literature, what on the surface appears to be a collection of predictions is in reality a proclamation about what is going on in the present. The poetry should not be taken literally any more than we should take literally the description of Christ as carrying seven stars in his right hand (but he is still able to place that hand on the prophet's head), with a double-edged sword coming out of his mouth (but he is still able to speak). And because this is poetry, there is no way in which the study of Revelation can decide the disputes which have marked the long history of millenarianism. Are we to be premillennialists or adventists (who expect the kingdom of Christ and the martyrs to be inaugurated on earth by a cataclysmic miracle usually said to occur after an earlier miracle which by a 'rapture' has delivered the Church from the previous 'dispensation' of 'tribulation' on earth)? Or are we to be postmillennialists (who expect a gradual transition to a new age on earth as more people are converted to Christ, his Church grows and society is ruled by his teaching) – or amillennialists (who expect the kingdom to come only in heaven)? These disputes can be of considerable significance to those engaged in them. The 1984 *Evangelical Dictionary of Theology*, discussing belief in 'the Rapture of the Church', reminds us that 'those who hold this view have a narrow outlook toward the church and its mission, culture and education, and current events. Their version of Christ against culture has imparted to twentieth century evangelicals a spirit of withdrawal and of suspicion toward others'. But such convictions cannot be asserted or contradicted solely on the basis of the biblical picture of the millennium. Those who teach 'what the Bible says' with such simplicity ought to ponder a really scholarly study such as G. B. Caird's *The Language and Imagery of the Bible* (1980).

One real problem about the Christian hope for the world is that in the New Testament it appears to be bound up with the expectation that the present 'age' of the world is going to end cataclysmically and imminently. And one reason why I stress this is because it is further proof that the New Testament does not provide a history of the future. At its climax the Revelation of John voices this passionate expectation. 'The Spirit and the bride say, "Come!" And let him who hears say, "Come!" . . . He who testifies to these things says, "Yes, I am coming soon." Amen. Come, Lord Jesus' (22:17,20). At the end of his first letter to Corinth, Paul offers the same prayer – not in Greek but in Aramaic, the language of Jesus and the very first Christians: '*Marana tha*. Come, O Lord!' (16:22). Yet Jesus did not return soon. He has not yet returned. Since there has already been this immense delay, nowadays many Christians do not seriously expect him to 'return' physically during the two thousand million years that scientists say are possible for the further survival of human life on this planet. So what is left of the Christian hope?

Neither in the 1982 report nor in any of Dr Stott's own books is the problem faced squarely, so far as I can see. In *Christian Counter-Culture: The Message of the Sermon on the Mount* he mentions the view 'that Jesus was expecting the end of history to arrive almost immediately' and so 'was giving his disciples an "interim ethic", which required them to make total sacrifices like leaving their possessions and loving their enemies – sacrifices appropriate only for that moment of crisis'. But he does not pause to argue against that view (CCC, p. 27). His bestseller, *Basic Christianity*, contains no specific discussion of the idea of the kingdom of God. But the New Testament makes it quite clear that if we are Christians looking for 'the heart of the gospel', we shall find it in the proclamation of the kingdom, for that is absolutely basic in the teaching of Jesus. The rest is commentary. So the key questions are what 'the kingdom' meant then – and what it should mean in our time.

In the earliest documents of Christianity to have survived, the hope that the kingdom of God would come soon is vivid and urgent. In or around AD 51 Paul wrote in his first letter to the Thessalonians:

> According to the Lord's own word, we tell you that we who are still alive, who are left till the coming of the Lord, will certainly not precede those who have fallen asleep. For the Lord himself will come down from heaven . . . with the voice of the archangel and with the trumpet call of God, and the dead in Christ will rise first. After that, we who are still alive and are left will be caught up together with them in the clouds to meet the Lord in the air. (4:15–17)

This passage shows clearly that the coming (*parousia*) of Christ in glory was expected within Paul's lifetime. The second letter to the Thessalonians explicitly denies that 'the day of the Lord has already come' and suggests that some, believing that it is imminent, have given up work (2:2; 3:6–15). Paul urged Christians to support themselves by their labours but to do so in a detached spirit:

> What I mean, brothers, is that the time is short. From now on those who have wives should live as if they had none; those who mourn, as if they did not; those who are happy, as if they were not; those who buy something, as if it were not theirs to keep; those who use the things of this world, as if not

engrossed in them. For this world in its present form is passing away. (1 Corinthians 7:29–31)

Among all the letters attributed to Paul, only the letter to the Ephesians fails to refer to his hope that his Lord was about to return to earth, to consummate the new age which had already begun. Paul is our chief and sufficient witness that the early Christians regarded themselves as a people living during the End.

The earliest of the gospels sums up the message of Jesus: 'The time has come. The kingdom of God is near. Repent and believe the good news!' (Mark 1:15). When Jesus has predicted his own death, according to this gospel he is still emphatic that some of his contemporaries will live to see his promise fulfilled: 'I tell you the truth, some who are standing here will not taste death before they see the kingdom of God come with power' (9:1). The gospels of Matthew (16:28) and Luke (9:27) have parallel passages, slightly changed in order to fit into their own editorial tendencies. Mark attaches the promise that the words of Jesus 'will never pass away' to these words: 'I tell you the truth, this generation will certainly not pass away until all these things have happened' – things which include the coming of the 'Son of Man in clouds with great power and glory' (13:30,26). The instructions to the Twelve for their first mission continue the note of urgency which makes Mark's swift gospel so electric: they are not to take food or money (6:8). In a fuller version of these instructions, Matthew's gospel promises: 'You will not finish going through the cities of Israel before the Son of Man comes' (10:23). To many scholars this suggests that Jesus then hoped for his glorification as the 'Son of Man' within a few weeks, although it does not say exactly that. (Possibly although not probably it may record a tradition that a 'Son of Man' other than Jesus was expected – or that the mission to the whole of Israel, which would be quite an undertaking, would still be incomplete when the 'Son of Man' did come at an unspecified date.) And whatever may be the right exegesis of this or that passage, there is widespread agreement among scholars that Jesus announced the dawn of the kingdom of God and hoped for high noon within the lifetime of his hearers. He was in his own eyes that kingdom's last envoy. The urgency of that message echoes in the cry: 'Follow me, and let the dead bury their own dead' (Matthew 8:21–22).

Luke's gospel has often been interpreted so as to support the idea that the kingdom of God is a spiritual matter, the rule of God in the heart (which may be extended to the whole of society by the influence of individuals). That was the favourite theme of Liberal Protestantism, associated in the history of theology with the great names of Ritschl and Harnack. The key passage is Luke 17:20–21 – 'Once, having been asked by the Pharisees when the kingdom of God would come, Jesus replied, "The kingdom of God does not come with your careful observation, nor will people say, 'Here it is' or 'there it is,' because the kingdom of God is . . ."' The New International Version prefers as the translation of *entos humon* 'within you', but gives as an alternative 'among you' which the New English Bible prefers. The NEB adds two other possible translations: 'the kingdom of God is within your grasp' and 'suddenly the kingdom of God will be among you'. The last suggestion seems to be the one most in keeping with the passage as a whole and with the rest of the gospel (supplemented by Acts). For this saying of Jesus is addressed not to the disciples but to the Pharisees. It talks about the future ('the time is coming . . .') and it declares that what is to come will be visible to all, 'like the lightning, which flashes and lights up the sky from one end to the other'. And at his last supper with his disciples Jesus says that he will not share the Passover feast with them again 'until it finds fulfilment in the kingdom of God' (Luke 22:16,18).

Promises and warnings about God's kingdom are the most frequent theme of the parables of Jesus. Obviously his teaching challenges his hearers to reach a spiritual decision in response to this news, and to enter a new level of spiritual life when they have made that decision; but the news is of a future (near or delayed) consummation of God's royal activity which breaks into human history. That is the most common meaning of the idea of the kingdom of God in the surviving Jewish literature of this age and it is certainly how the hearers of Jesus would have immediately understood the phrase. The Lord's Prayer itself enshrines the fact that the kingdom has not yet 'come'. All this was placed unforgettably before students of theology by Albert Schweitzer's survey of German scholarship translated into English as *The Quest of the Historical Jesus* (1910). That is an imperfect and now dated book, but a good example of the continuing conviction of most scholars that the proclamation of Jesus was thoroughly eschatological is B. F. Meyer's *The Aims of Jesus* (1979), with its translation (on p. 208) of Luke's version of the Lord's Prayer (11:2–4):

> Father!
> Let your name be hallowed! Let your reign come!
> The bread of tomorrow give us today,
> and forgive us our debts as we now forgive our debtors,
> and do not let us fall victim to the ordeal!

However, modern scholars usually, and in my view rightly, agree that Schweitzer exaggerated the extent to which the message of Jesus and the first Christians depended for its whole force on the hope that the kingdom of God would come in its fullness swiftly. There is no evidence of a profound and widespread breakdown of faith when the first generation of Christians realised that it would probably not be the last generation on earth. Even the initial enthusiasm did not absolutely fix the date of the End: 'about times and dates we do not need to write to you, for you know very well that the day of the Lord will come like a thief in the night' (1 Thessalonians 5:1–2). Writing to the Philippians about five years later, Paul expects and longs to die but his final promise is that 'my God will meet all your needs according to his glorious riches in Christ Jesus' (4:19). And God meets the ultimate need of a life stronger than death, for 'we know that if the earthly tent we live in is destroyed, we have a building from God, an eternal house in heaven, not built by human hands' (2 Corinthians 5:1). The gospel of John has almost entirely translated the idea of the future kingdom of God into the idea of eternal life through a spiritual communion with Christ. Its central emphasis is on the glory revealed, and the life given, in the crucifixion and resurrection and in the coming of the Holy Spirit. The latest document to be included in the New Testament admits that scoffers will say, 'Where is this "coming" he promised?' But it shows a tranquil confidence like that of Paul and John: 'With the Lord a day is like a thousand years, and a thousand years are like a day' (2 Peter 3:4,8). And the gospels themselves contain an element of agnosticism about the future within a faith in the fulfilment of God's purposes. Thus Mark includes a saying of Jesus which, being agnostic, is unlikely to have been invented by the Christians: 'no-one knows about that day or hour, not even the angels in heaven, nor the Son, but only the Father' (13:32). Matthew's version of the instructions for the first mission of the Twelve includes not only the verse on which Schweitzer relied (suggesting that the Son of Man was expected to come in glory during that mission) but also material which points to a long mission. They are to expect to be handed over to the local councils, flogged in the synagogues and tried before 'governors and kings as witnesses to them and to the Gentiles' (10:17–18). Later in the same gospel we read predictions of wars and rumours of wars, famines and earthquakes, the lapse of many from the faith and the hatred of 'all nations' for those who are left, and the preaching the gospel 'in the whole world', before the End comes (24:3–14). All these will be 'signs' of the coming kingdom and the idea that the kingdom will be announced by such signs is also prominent in Mark's gospel. Yet elsewhere the idea that the kingdom will come suddenly, while people are going about their ordinary business, is no less prominent.

Scholars assess the connection between these various

expectations and the main thrust of the actual teaching of Jesus variously. It seems probable that the material incorporates teachings given after his death, so that we cannot know exactly what the historical Jesus thought. But it seems certain that the only surviving evidence about the beliefs of Jesus and the first Christians contains both the hope that the End which had already begun would come fully soon and the faith that if it did not God could still be trusted to consummate his royal activity in a final triumph. They humbly believed that 'it is not for you to know the times or dates the Father has set by his own authority' (Acts 1:7). They consoled themselves for any delay with the great thought that the End had already dawned. Matthew's gospel itself includes the saying of Jesus: 'If I drive out demons by the Spirit of God, then the kingdom of God has come upon you' (12:28).

From the New Testament as a whole I draw the conclusion that the connection between our eschatological outlook and the attitude we adopt towards evangelism and social responsibility, which Evangelical leaders seek, ought not to depend on taking any one picture of the End either literally or by itself. I may be forgiven for repeating or summarising some words which I wrote in *Jesus for Modern Man* (1975), agreeing with scholars who have found a central idea of permanent validity expressed symbolically in the hopes of the first Christian century. (I am specially indebted to Norman Perrin, *The Kingdom of God in the Teaching of Jesus*, 1963, and *Jesus and the Language of the Kingdom*, 1976.)

Taken together, the gallery of pictures of the End which we find in the New Testament suggests a vision of life as a whole, disturbing, haunting, and dominated by the reality of God. Here is a vision of life as *aionios*, the New Testament word which refers to the life of the 'age to come', whether in time or out of it. In response we must be spiritually detached from the familiar things of this world – from the happiness as well as from the misery that this world offers – because we now realise that we do not depend on these things in the long run. As individuals we must depend entirely on the eternal God for any hope of a joy greater than the power of death and the power of the evil in the world and in our hearts. But since every individual is to a large extent shaped and corrupted by the surrounding society, we must long for the liberation of society as a whole, so that the will of God is done on earth as in heaven (the definition of the kingdom of God given by Jesus himself). The faith that God is already active in the affairs of the world, leading to the hope that he will one day take over the government of it, provides the only final remedy for the innumerable and inescapable disillusionments of politics and of personal life. This belief that God's victory will ultimately not be frustrated by our defeats gives the only really effective consolation for our many corporate and individual blunders.

Many modern people ask why it was within the purpose of God that Jesus of Nazareth should hope for the quick coming of the kingdom. Why was his vision so intense that his Father's will would soon be done in the towns and villages of Galilee and Judea as in heaven? Why did he teach his followers to hope with a similar passion, even if it meant being punished by a disappointment as bitter as his own when he wept over Jerusalem? To glimpse an answer is to see also why so many Christians have ardently expected the 'second coming' of their beloved Lord to come soon. They have interpreted the events of their own age as signs of that coming, comparing them with the signs which seem to be predicted in the poetry of the gospels and the Revelation of John. They have hoped – and they have been disappointed. Yet the faith which gave rise to those hopes had deeper foundations which (as the continuation of Christianity witnesses) have never crumbled. As Bruce Chilton summed up the long scholarly discussion in *The Kingdom of God in the Teaching of Jesus* (1984, p. 23), Jesus 'was impelled to preach by his certainty that God would reveal himself powerfully; the kingdom announcement affirmed vividly but simply that God would act in strength on behalf of his people'.

In order to be human Jesus had to belong to some group whose world-view he would accept in part and reject in part, according to his education and experience – and the group in which he lived was the Jewish, and in particular the Galilean, people at a time when hopes of the coming kingdom were many and varied. And we may guess that, even had he been born into a less expectant community, a man with such a vision of God would always experience in the depths of his soul the hope that in his time this loving Father would triumph. To him, belief in God would be no comfortable convention but a light in darkness. He would always hope that the light would soon shine fully on him and on all. Because the earth, made so lovely by God, had been so thoroughly polluted by the crimes and follies of mankind, he would always wish to set it on fire (Luke 12:49).

## Hell

Must the message of Christians include hell fire if it is to be faithful to the message of Jesus? The Lausanne Covenant of 1974 is the most authoritative statement of Evangelical belief in recent years. While it avoids the crudity of taking the pictures of hell fire literally, I am going to suggest that it gives an answer to this question which falls short of what the Bible taken as a whole affirms and what the Christian conscience can now accept. It certainly deserves quotation and reflection.

'We affirm that there is only one Savior and only one Gospel,' the Covenant says, 'although there is a wide diversity of evangelistic approaches'. It continues:

We recognize that all men have some knowledge of God through his general revelation in nature. But we deny that this can save, for men suppress the truth by their unrighteousness. We also reject as derogatory to Christ and the Gospel every kind of syncretism and dialogue which implies that Christ speaks equally through all religions and ideologies. Jesus

Christ, being himself the only God-man, who gave himself as the only ransom for sinners, is the only mediator between God and man. There is no other name by which we must be saved. All men are perishing because of sin, but God loves all men, not wishing that any should perish but that all should repent. Yet those who reject Christ repudiate the joy of salvation and condemn themselves to eternal separation from God. To proclaim Jesus as 'the Savior of the world' is not to affirm that all men are either automatically or ultimately saved, still less to affirm that all religions offer salvation in Christ. Rather it is to proclaim God's love for a world of sinners and to invite all men to respond to him as Savior and Lord in the wholehearted personal commitment of repentance and faith. Jesus Christ has been exalted above every other name; we long for the day when every knee shall bow to him and every tongue shall confess him Lord. (ELC, p. 9)

Dr Stott has written an approving commentary on that tightly packed paragraph and I have considered it carefully. My own main comment has to be deep regret that the Covenant seems to support (without clearly stating) the old belief that all those who do not accept Jesus Christ as Lord and Saviour before they die are 'lost' or 'perishing' because doomed to hell.

Dr Stott comments that the natural knowledge which men have of God 'actually condemns them' because 'their rejection of the truth which they know then leads them to idolatry, to immorality and to the judgement of God'. For him, 'it is false to suppose that sinners can be saved through other systems' apart from the Christian gospel. He bases this comment on the first chapter of Paul's letter to the Romans. But I have to ask whether it is a comprehensively just verdict on all non-Christian religion, a subject on which the Bible offers many more generous views. And I have to answer that it is an insulting travesty of much sincere seeking, devotion and holiness to be found among Muslims, Hindus, Buddhists and other non-Christians. To say that such religious systems produce only idolatry and immorality is to indulge in the kind of prejudice which

Christians always resent when it is directed against their own religion. And to deny that God can save those countless millions through their response to the religious traditions into which they have been born is, I think, to deny either God's power or his love. I much prefer the more informed and thoughtful treatment in a book such as Hans Küng's *Christianity and the World Religions* (in English, 1987). It is to me highly significant that the Lausanne Covenant contained no reference to the position of the Jews (an omission for which Dr Stott handsomely apologised in his commentary). For the Jews are the people who have always reminded the Christians that God does not deal savingly only with the Church or only with those who have accepted Christ as Lord and Saviour. They are the perpetual stimulus to deepen thought about 'non-Christians'. A passionate longing for their salvation, and a final conviction that it would come, were what made Paul write some of his most profound passages to the Romans.

Those who drafted this paragraph of the Lausanne Covenant curiously failed to understand what is almost always intended when Christians engage in serious religious dialogue with the adherents of other religions. 'Dialogue' is praised and practised by Dr Stott himself, as in this book. It is not the same as 'syncretism', defined in the *Oxford English Dictionary* as 'the attempted union or reconciliation of diverse or opposite tenets or practices, especially in philosophy or religion'. 'Dialogue' can be entered by people who know that many of their own beliefs are 'diverse or opposite' but who still hope to learn from each other about the one God who is greater than all religious systems. In particular it can be entered by Christians or non-Christians who fully recognise how nonsensical it would be to say that Christ 'speaks equally' through Christianity as through, say, Buddhism. Indeed, Evangelicals know this. The very next paragraph of the Lausanne Covenant says that the kind of dialogue 'whose purpose is to listen sensitively' is 'indispensable to evangelism' and Dr Stott has himself offered a discussion of 'dialogue' which is, up to a point, positive:

> Dialogue is a token of genuine Christian love, because it indicates our steadfast resolve to rid our minds of prejudices and caricatures which we may entertain about other people; to struggle to listen through their ears and look through their eyes so as to grasp what prevents them from hearing the gospel and seeing Christ; to sympathise with them in all their doubts, fears and 'hang-ups'. (CMMW, p. 80)

The international consultation on 'Gospel and Culture' which Dr Stott chaired in 1978 recommended 'missionary humility'. Since 'different cultures have strongly influenced the biblical revelation, ourselves and the people to whom we go', Christian evangelists need 'the humility to begin our communication where people are not where we would like them to be' (WR, p. 16). My only criticism of these more positive statements is that they do not admit that Christians have much to learn from the rest of humanity. I have argued in *The Futures of Christianity* (1987) that the glad acceptance of Christ as Saviour and Lord, as the One who is able to bring us to the Father as no other teacher can, is entirely compatible with a willingness to learn from other teachers. In the past Christians gladly learned from Greek philosophers and Roman poets. In our time Christians can be taught about community life under God by Jews, about devotion to God by Muslims or Hindus, about detachment from the passions by Buddhists, about the sacredness of nature by animists, and about goodness by atheists. Having learned these and many other truths from traditions outside the Church, we can find that they are already taught in the Bible – but evidently the Bible was not able to teach us perfectly. Having found that these truths fit into the truth taught by Christ, we can say that Christ – or, using Greek, the *Logos* – is in the other religions and philosophies; but I agree that there is a danger that this way of talking may empty the word 'Christ' of all connection with the historical, biblical Christ, causing intellectual confusion as well as spiritual damage.

It is not a hopeful beginning to any dialogue to think that 'it is our solemn duty to affirm that those to whom we announce the gospel and address our appeal are "perishing"' (CMMW, p. 111). This is likely to be heard as an announcement that the living non-Christians and the ancestors are all doomed to hell unless they consciously believe in Jesus Christ as Lord and Saviour before dying. And that is, of course, what many evangelists and missionaries have said very clearly and loudly. But in common with many other Christians nowadays I accept the teaching of the Second Vatican Council where the bishops, after an eloquent emphasis on the missionary task of the Church as the 'People of God', declared:

> Those also can attain to everlasting salvation who through no fault of their own do not know the gospel of Christ or his Church, yet sincerely seek God and moved by grace, strive by their deeds to do his will as it is known to them through the dictates of conscience. Nor does divine Providence deny the help necessary for salvation to those who, without blame on their part, have not yet arrived at an explicit knowledge of God, but who strive to live a good life thanks to his grace. Whatever goodness or truth is found among them is looked upon by the Church as a preparation for the gospel. She regards such qualities as given by him who enlightens all men so that they may finally have life. (*Lumen Gentium* II. 16)

I notice with grateful joy that the Lausanne Covenant repudiates the Calvinist but unbiblical notion that it is the will of God that some or many are predestined to everlasting punishment in hell. It is true that Paul speculated that there might be 'objects of [God's] wrath – prepared for destruction' (Romans 9:22). But that speculation was brief, undeveloped and in its effects tragic. It is far less significant in the Bible than the insight, which seems to me luminously true, that 'God our Saviour . . . wants all men to be saved and to come to a knowledge of the truth' since he is 'the Saviour of all men, and especially of those who believe' (1 Timothy 2:3–4; 4:10).

I also rejoice that Lausanne spoke about 'eternal separation from God' rather than about 'everlasting punishment'. The latter idea may conjure up the unchristian picture of

God as the Eternal Torturer – as in the notorious sermon on 'Sinners in the Hands of an Angry God' preached by Jonathan Edwards in 1741. The idea (without the lurid details) was still taught in, for example, the 1984 *Evangelical Dictionary of Theology*. 'It is not always realized', Leon Morris wrote there,

> that Jesus spoke of hell more often than did anyone else in the New Testament. And nowhere is there a hint of any possible reversal of judgement . . .
> And against the strong body of NT teaching that there is a continuing punishment of sin we cannot put one saying which speaks plainly of an end to the punishment of the finally impenitent. Those who look for a different teaching in the NT must point to possible inferences and alternative explanations. (pp. 369–70)

The phrase which Lausanne bravely preferred to 'everlasting punishment' is connected with Dr Stott's consistent preference for 'perish' to refer to the end of those who reject God. So far as I know, he has never made it clear whether or not this means that he holds the belief that the wicked are ultimately annihilated – the doctrine known as 'conditional immortality'. But this doctrine certainly seems to be implied in the idea that some may be 'separated eternally' from the Creator who is the only Source of life. It also seems to be implied in the very word 'perish', for it is indeed difficult to imagine a perpetually inconclusive process of perishing. And annihilation seems to me (as to many others) the only alternative to heaven which is compatible with the faith that God is love.

The prospect of 'eternal separation' is restricted by the Lausanne Covenant to those who condemn themselves because they 'reject Christ'. That avoids the teaching that one 'mortal' sin earns the same punishment as a lifetime of total wickedness. By this teaching God was alleged to condemn the guilty to hell without adhering to the elementary principle of justice that the gravity of the punishment must fit the gravity of the crime. And it avoids any suggestion that people may be 'sent to hell' against their wills. Since Christ has been unknown to most of the human race, and since when known he has seldom been presented worthily by Christians, Lausanne may have intended to say that anyone 'eternally separated' from God would be a person who after death consciously, deliberately, systematically, totally and permanently rejects a fully worthy presentation of Christ that has been completely understood. If so, it may be hoped that the category which Leon Morris called the 'finally impenitent' will be unpopulated.

I ask whether this interpretation would be endorsed by Dr Stott. He says alarmingly that

> the doctrine of God as a universal Father was not taught by Christ nor by his apostles. God is indeed the universal Creator, having brought all things into existence, and the universal King, ruling and sustaining all that he has made. But he is the Father only of our Lord Jesus Christ and of those whom he adopts into his family through Christ. (OOW, p. 99)

This God whose attitude to non-Christians is said to be *not* fatherly (for I have to ask: what else can Dr Stott's denial mean?) is said to dismiss all human efforts to obey him outside the gospel of his grace in Christ. 'Whenever teachers start exalting man, implying that he can contribute anything to his salvation by his own morality, religion, philosophy or respectability, the Gospel of grace is being corrupted' (OOW, p. 27). 'Outside Christ man is dead because of trespasses and sins, enslaved by the world, the flesh and the devil, and condemned under the wrath of God', for Dr Stott maintains that 'it is not universal reconciliation that Christ achieved or that Paul proclaimed; it is rather a nearness to God and to each other gratefully experienced by those who are near Christ, indeed "in" him in a vital, personal union' (GNS, pp. 79, 98).

Elsewhere I find him more persuasive. For example he considers Luke's report of the answer of Jesus to the question, 'Are only a few people going to be saved?' The answer was: 'Make every effort to enter through the narrow door, because many, I tell you, will try to enter and will not be able to' (13:23–24). This saying is linked with Matthew 7:13–14: 'Enter through the narrow gate. For wide is the gate and broad is the road that leads to destruction, and many enter through it. But small is the gate and narrow the road that leads to life, and only a few find it.' But it is also linked with the final vision of the Bible that the redeemed before God's throne will be not 'only a few' but 'a great multitude that no-one could count' (Revelation 7:9). Dr Stott comments disarmingly:

> How to reconcile these two concepts I do not know. Nor am I clear how this passage relates to the perplexing problem of those who never hear the gospel . . . The whole picture seems to relate only to those who have had the opportunity of decision for or against Christ; it simply leaves out of view those who have never heard. We shall be wise, therefore, not to occupy our minds with such speculative questions . . . (CCC, p. 196)

I greatly respect the humility shown by Dr Stott here. But even here I have to ask questions on behalf of the vast majority of humankind. Was it the teaching of Jesus, when that teaching is studied as a whole, that the majority of those who try to enter the door into eternal life will never be able to do so? Did he claim certainty that some will never be able to enter? And did he say nothing at all about those who have never really heard his message? These are not merely 'speculative questions'. These are questions about whether the gospel about Jesus is in any sense good news for the mass of humanity.

I do not wish to affirm that all are 'automatically' saved, which is what the doctrine of 'universalism' has often been understood as affirming. I of course respect some of the theologians who have taught universalism in various shapes (from Origen to Barth), but their doctrine appears to deny human free will. The Bible emphatically affirms that because he desires their free response to his love God has given people the freedom to reject him. No other belief seems possible if one believes in the God who discloses his love in the Bible, although as Dr Stott movingly writes in his commentary on the Lausanne Covenant that 'the prospect is almost too dreadful to contemplate; we should be able to speak of hell only with tears'. What I do wish to affirm is not a prediction of something that is bound to happen but a hope. It is the hope that all will be saved ultimately. I disagree passionately with Dr Stott's opinion, in his commentary on Lausanne, that 'some *will* refuse to repent and believe . . . and so *will* condemn themselves to eternal separation from God' – and with his belief that 'those who are lost *will* accept all the blame themselves' (the italics are mine). For according to Christianity God is both all-powerful (or sovereign) and all-loving. If he is all-powerful, will he not exert his infinite power to the utmost to save all the perishing? If he is all-loving, will he not save any soul with a glimmer of a belief that the rejection of Christ would deserve blame? I would rather be an atheist than believe in a God who accepts it as inevitable that hell (however conceived) is the inescapable destiny of many, or of any of his children, even when they are prepared to accept 'all the blame'.

But I need not be an atheist, for I am sure that Stephen Travis was right to conclude his examination of the biblical evidence: 'None of this literature exhibits a speculative interest in the process of judgment or in the nature of existence beyond final judgment' (*Christ and the Judgment of God*, 1986, p. 167). And as I read the Bible I see a picture of the real God – the God whose love for all is like a patient parent's (only infinitely more loving and more patient). I recognise of course that the Bible offers many warnings which could not be more solemn. As Stephen Travis observed, '"punishment" language affirms that God's treatment of human sin is not arbitrary or capricious' just as 'references to reward underline particularly the reliability of God to keep his promises to his servants' (p. 168). And I recognise that these warnings about punishment apply to my own sins and to the sins of the world (which seem to have been specially abundant during the twentieth century). But the Bible gives us also the picture of the God who hopes even on Calvary, as he sees into the hearts of the executioners and knows that they do not know what they are doing. As I read the New Testament, it is the story of the growing insight given by the eye-opening Holy Spirit. When Jesus saw how a Pharisee 'despised' a woman who had 'lived a sinful life in that town', he challenged him: 'Do you *see* this woman?' (Luke 7:44). Jesus gave an example by seeing the faith of several Gentiles who asked him for healing – and Peter saw in a dream that the strange cargoes in the harbour at Joppa belonged to a Gentile world which was clean (Acts 10:9–23). When some Gentiles had become Christians, and despised Jews because it was the strict keeping of the Law of Moses that now seemed contempt-ible, Paul eventually saw that Israel remained God's beloved people. Now in the twentieth Christian century we are, I believe, challenged to *see* the non-Christian world: to *see* the African, the Indian, the Chinese, the Japanese, the secularised . . . with the eyes of the Father.

The second letter to the Thessalonians contains some of the most terrible warnings:

> When the Lord Jesus is revealed from heaven in blazing fire with his powerful angels, he will punish those who do not know God and do not obey the gospel of our Lord Jesus. They will be punished with everlasting destruction and shut out from the presence of the Lord and from the majesty of his power on the day he comes to be glorified in his holy people and to be marvelled at among all those who have believed. (1:7–10)

In another letter which is early (and which unlike 2 Thes-salonians is indisputably the work of Paul himself), the apostle is ready to threaten with hell those who offer the Galatians 'a different gospel' – 'let him be eternally con-demned!' (1:6–9). But in his first letter to the Corinthians Paul's imagery points to the total triumph of the God displayed on the cross of Christ. The cross is 'foolishness to those who are perishing' (1:18) but it seems to be highly significant that Paul does not say that they are already perished or as good as lost. 'As in Adam all die,' he writes, so in Christ all will be made alive. But each in his own turn: Christ, the firstfruits; then, when he comes, those who belong to him. Then the end will come, when he hands over the kingdom to God the Father after he has destroyed all dominion, authority and power. For he must reign until he has put . . . everything under his feet . . . so that God may be all in all. (15:22–28)

Paul proceeds to refer, apparently with approval, to the practice of being 'baptised for the dead' – that is, giving sacramental expression to the belief that the non-Christian dead can share the salvation which Christians have experienced. When a notorious sinner has been excommunicated for incest ('hand this man over to Satan'), Paul still hopes for his salvation (5:5).

In his letter to the Romans, after his supremely powerful reminder that the wrath of God condemns the sins of the pagan world, for 'God gave them over in the sinful desires of their hearts' (1:24), Paul declares about the death of Christ: 'the result of one act of righteousness was justification that brings life for all men' (5:18). In chapter 11 he urges those who have tasted it to 'continue in God's kindness' lest they be 'cut off' but he holds out the hope that those who have experienced God's sternness, 'if they do not persist in unbelief', will be 'grafted in'. Finally the hope kindles into a vision that 'the full number of the Gentiles' and 'all Israel' will be saved, 'For God has bound all men over to disobedience so that he may have mercy on them all' (11:32).

The later letter to the Ephesians begins with the announcement of God's 'good pleasure, which he purposed in Christ, to be put into effect when the times will have reached their fulfilment – to bring all things in heaven and on earth together under one head, even Christ', who 'fills everything in every way' (1:9–10,23). And the letter to the Colossians proclaims God's intention 'to reconcile to himself all things, whether things on earth or things in heaven' (1:20). I have studied Dr Stott's exegesis of these passages, arguing that they refer not to 'all things' in this present universe but to a future universe which will be created around such people as are finally saved. However, I am not persuaded that this nervousness about a tendency to universalism is necessary.

A text that is constantly quoted by those who deny that non-Christians can be saved is John 14:6: 'I am the way and the truth and the life. No-one comes to the Father except through me.' But the context shows that the fourth gospel is here concerned with the intimacy of trust in God as Father, for life or death, which is the special privilege of the disciples. It is possible to treasure this text and the experienced reality which lies behind it – as I most emphatically do – without using it to write off most of the spiritual quest of humanity.

Another text often cited comes from Acts (4:10,12): 'It is by the name of Jesus Christ of Nazareth, whom you crucified but whom God raised from the dead, that this man stands before you healed . . . Salvation is found in no-one else, for there is no other name under heaven given to men by which we must be saved.' This one text, which arises out of a story of the healing of a crippled beggar, is sometimes thought to settle the eternal destiny of all but a fraction of mankind. I am one of those who believe (with the Second Vatican Council) that it does no such thing. It seems ludicrous to suggest that the problem of the non-Christians is settled by these few words, found in an account of a speech said to have been delivered by Peter to the Sanhedrin in Jerusalem with only one other Christian (John) present about half a century before the Acts of the Apostles was written. For the problem is about centuries and continents about which Luke and Peter knew nothing or next to nothing. It would be equally ridiculous to use later texts in Acts as solving the problem although they show slightly more awareness of it. When Peter has ordered the baptism of Cornelius and other Gentiles, he declares that Christ is 'the one whom God appointed as judge of the living and the dead' and that 'everyone who believes in him receives forgiveness of sins through his name'. But he also says: 'I now realise how true it is that God does not show favouritism but accepts men from every nation who fear him and do what is right' (Acts 10:34–48). And Paul in Athens says that God has dealt with every nation 'so that men would seek him and perhaps reach out for him and find him, though he is not far from each one of us' (Acts 17:24–28). I do not find Dr Stott's comment on these passages adequate. 'It is clear,' he writes, 'that although in some sense "acceptable" to God, Cornelius before his conversion had neither "salvation" nor "life"' and he adds that the Athenians' search for God was futile, since 'what these truths and the Athenians' knowledge of them did was not to enable them to find God but rather to make their idolatry inexcusable' (CMMW, p. 67). These ungenerous suggestions do not seem to do justice to the tension in the mind of the author of Luke's gospel and the Acts of the Apostles – the tension between two loves, for the sinners and for the Saviour.

In one form or another this tension is often found in Christian thought. An example is provided by the first letter of John. There it is written that 'everything in the world – the cravings of sinful man, the lust of his eyes and the boasting of what he has and does – comes not from the Father but from the world' (2:16). 'He who has the Son has life; but who does not have the Son of God does not have life' (5:12). But it is also written that 'everyone who loves has been born of God and knows God . . . No-one has ever seen God; but if we love one another, God lives in us and his love is made complete in us' (4:7,12). It is true that, as Dr Stott insists in his commentary (EJ, p. 164), John concentrates on 'reciprocal Christian love'. But he does not explicitly confine the love he writes about to love between Christians, perhaps recalling that he who 'has the Son' has the teaching of Jesus about the good Samaritan. I have to add that Dr Stott's own views do not seem to reckon fully with the teaching of Jesus. In his parables (for example) Jesus repeatedly compared the characters and actions of non-Christians (his Jewish hearers) with the nature and activity of the Father. He was sharply observant, discriminating and realistic, but also generous, in his estimate of the spiritual condition of the people among whom he lived, prayed and suffered. He saw into people's hearts. And he did not leave the impression that the end of the road for the good Samaritan would be hell.

Dr Stott rightly says that 'perishing is a terrible word, but Jesus himself used it' (ELC, p. 10). In this connection he quotes Matthew 18:14 and Luke 13:3,5. He invites us to consider also John 3:14–16: 'The Son of Man must be lifted up, . . . that everyone who believes in him may have eternal life. For God so loved the world . . . that whoever believes in him shall not perish but have eternal life.' So let us give our profoundly serious attention to the evidence about Jesus.

He is said to have warned his hearers that 'unless you repent, you too will all perish' like the Galileans massacred by Pilate or those killed by the fall of a tower in Siloam (Luke 13:1–5). This cannot mean that literally all impenitent sinners will be either massacred or crushed by falling masonry. Jesus appears to be teaching that although the victims of these disasters were not worse sinners than all the others, their deaths should be taken as a general warning to all the others. Such warnings are often found in the gospels, where Jesus divides people into two groups – the sons of the kingdom and of the evil one; the sons of light and the sons of this world; the wise and the foolish; the sheep and the goats; those who 'enter life' and those who are in danger of hell. Obviously such warnings should not be dismissed. But the gospels do not leave the impression that Jesus was so certain that most (or any) of his hearers would end up in hell that he spent his whole time warning them about it. On the contrary, one of the most eloquent parts of his recorded teaching is his total silence on the subject of hell when his enemies are about to commit the supreme sin of crucifying him. He did *not* warn them that they were separating themselves eternally from the life and mercy of the Father. On the brink of eternity he was not a hell-fire preacher. On Calvary the whole emphasis is that 'God so loved the world'.

The references to hell are most numerous in Matthew's gospel. The first two are plainly hyperbole, for the Jesus whose character is presented to us by the gospel as a whole cannot have meant that his Father would throw into hell anyone who once used the expression 'you fool!' or who looked at a woman lustfully (5:22,21–30). 'Be afraid of the One who can destroy both soul and body in hell' (10:28) probably is the authentic teaching of the One who taught that sins needed to be forgiven. But according to Matthew Jesus was not concerned to teach in detail about hell. He warned whole cities that they would be judged corporately (11:20–24) but also that an individual would be acquitted because of his good words (12:37). How a good person living in a bad city was to escape was not explained; nor how the punishment of Korazin and Bethsaida is to be greater than the punishment of Tyre and Sidon, and Capernaum's fate worse than Sodom's. His main warnings about the possible end of the wicked came in parables. Naturally they used different imagery. The wicked in these stories might be burned (13:30; 25:46), tortured (18:34), cut in pieces (24:51) or thrown into darkness (8:12; 22:13; 25:30). These images are taken in the Lausanne Covenant to mean 'eternal separation from God'. They lose none of their terrible solemnity if they are so interpreted.

Jesus as we meet him in the gospels offers his hearers the most fateful of all choices. His horror at the thought that anyone may make the wrong choice is a profound emotion which repeatedly breaks forth into grim eloquence – and, as he sees Jerusalem, into tears. He whose longing to see the reign of the Father complete 'on earth as in heaven' leads to hopes that the End is imminent is so moved by the possibility of the rejection of the Father and his kingdom that burning images of hell are set alight in urgent warnings. These are, like the pictures of the imminent kingdom, pictures – but not 'only pictures'! Their imagery clothes the fear of an end about which it can be said: 'it would be better for him if he had not been born' (Matthew 26:24).

The image that has burned itself into the horrified

imagination of many centuries is 'their worm does not die, and the fire is not quenched' (Mark 9:48). This is a quotation from Isaiah 66:24. It is derived from the rubbish dump in the valley of Hinnom outside the city wall of Jerusalem – *ge Hinnom* or 'Gehenna', the word translated as 'hell'. And it is significant that the prophet who saw in the bonfire and the maggots the destiny of the wicked (remembering that the valley had been polluted by human sacrifices) was himself not clear about who would end up in Gehenna. Some would survive to 'look upon the dead bodies of those who rebelled' – and these would not be few, as the prophet hoped 'all mankind will come and bow down' before God.

At one point the Lausanne Covenant seems to share that hope of a universal salvation. 'We long for the day when every knee shall bow to him and every tongue shall confess him Lord'. This quotation of Philippians 2:10–11 is in keeping with the vision that praise will be sung 'to him who sits on the throne and to the Lamb' from 'every creature in heaven or on earth and under the earth and on the sea, and all that is in them' (Revelation 5:13). To hold to such hopes for all humanity is, I believe, thoroughly in keeping with the Christian's other duty, which is to take the warnings with a complete seriousness. But if so – if this blend of hope and fear is what the New Testament taken as a whole affirms – it seems necessary to believe that an opportunity will be given after death, in the condition pictured in the Bible as *Sheol* or *Hades*. This so-called 'Hades Gospel' has usually been rejected by Evangelicals, often because of abuses in the medieval Church (surviving despite some reforms into Roman Catholicism in our own time). The Church was believed to be authorised to dispense from a 'treasury of merits'. The merits of Christ and the saints could be drawn on in order to shorten the days spent by souls in punishment in 'Purgatory' – in exchange for a specified number of payments to the clergy for Requiem Masses, the building of St Peter's, Rome, and so forth. Protestants have, I believe, been completely right to protest against that clerical racket. But it does not follow that the whole of the 'Hades Gospel' should be rejected. We may take another look at the Revelation of John. Although magicians, the sexually immoral, murderers, idolaters and 'everyone who practises falsehood' are excluded from the ultimate City of God, there are also images of inclusion. Inside that city is 'the river of the water of life' running with its cleansing power 'down the middle of the great street of the city'. The tree of life grows by that river 'and the leaves of the tree are for the healing of the nations'. 'The nations will walk by its light, and the kings of the earth will bring their splendour into it' (21:24–22:15). That was written at a time when no nation and no king was even nominally Christian.

Is this 'Hades Gospel' found in the teaching of Jesus? It may reasonably be held to be implied in the exultant cry of the Jesus of the fourth gospel – 'I, when I am lifted up from the earth, will draw all men to myself' (John 12:32) – but the authenticity of that saying from a historical point of view must be questionable along with the rest of the gospel. Our question is complicated by the evidence that the historical Jesus concentrated on the proclamation of the kingdom of God 'on earth as in heaven', not on teaching about heaven. But specially since the full coming of that kingdom has been delayed for considerably longer than Jesus and the early Christians hoped for, we may find a pointer to the ultimate population of heaven in the prominent tradition that Jesus and his disciples practised table-fellowship with tax-collectors, prostitutes and other Jewish 'sinners'. There is also the prophecy about the Gentiles: 'many will come from the east and the west, and will take their places at the feast with Abraham, Isaac and Jacob in the kingdom of heaven' (Matthew 8:11, paralleled in Luke).

That prophecy retains the warning image of the darkness. 'There will be weeping and gnashing of teeth' not for the wicked as classified by conventional morality and piety but for those orthodox Jews or 'subjects of the kingdom' who have in practice rebelled against God the King. It is a terrible warning for orthodox Christians as well. But there is prominently in the teaching of Jesus a parable which stands in contrast with the parable of the rich man and Lazarus where the conventional Jewish imagery about life after death is used ('Abraham's side', literally 'bosom', is eternally separate from hell, where the bad man is 'in agony in this fire' and 'a great chasm has been fixed' between him and the ex-beggar in Luke 16:19–31). In contrast, in the parable of the sheep and the goats (Matthew 25:31–46) Jesus is surprising. He does much more than praise the faith of those who have accepted him before death as Lord and Saviour and have shown it by good works of love. He does, it is true, teach that 'it will be necessary for public evidence to be produced, namely the outworking of our faith in compassionate action', as Dr Stott notes (FC, p. 115). In this parable, however, Jesus teaches also that he will at last be recognised by many who never thought that they knew him before they met him as judge after death. This is a parable told not about the disciples but about 'all the nations' (Matthew 25:32). So it offers the world a great hope. It contains a warning that the unloving will have to 'depart from me . . . into the eternal fire' for 'eternal punishment' – but it says that this fire has been 'prepared for the devil and his angels', not for human beings (25:41). And it promises 'eternal life' to all the 'righteous' who feed the hungry, answer the needs of the thirsty and the strangers, clothe the naked, care for the sick and visit the prisoners. So it seems that after death anyone who has helped Lazarus can, after all, take the road to eternal life. Here is another image of inclusion and it comes in Matthew's gospel as the finale of the teaching of Jesus before he goes to his death.

## The Gospel for Humanity

What, then, is essential for Evangelicals in evangelism? 'To evangelise,' says the Lausanne Covenant, 'is to spread the good news that Jesus died for our sins and was raised from the dead according to the Scriptures, and that as the reigning Lord he now offers the forgiveness of sins and the liberating gift of the Spirit to all who repent and believe.' Together with many others who do not call themselves conservative Evangelicals, I believe that gospel with all my heart. But negatively I plead that Evangelicals should not insist on some interpretations of that gospel which seem to them to be both biblical and true, but which do not thus persuade their fellow-Christians. So I plead with deep respect that Evangelicals should not insist on the doctrines which I have criticised – that the Bible is infallible or inerrant; that the cross propitiates God's wrath because Jesus is our substitute under God's punishment; that all the miracle stories in the Bible have to be accepted literally; that the Bible has to be treated as legislation about morality and information about the future; that some *will* (not could) perish eternally and that masses of, or all, non-Christians will be among them. And positively I ask that Evangelicals should say something good about humanity's future in the hands of the Creator who is also revealed as the Father.

The message of Jesus is good news for all, demanding to be shared because it is such happy news. As Luke's gospel expresses it, this is a salvation 'prepared in the sight of all people' (2:31). Here is good news for the poor, for the sick, for women and for others who are oppressed. It is good news for sinners. It announces that people who love their enemies are 'sons of the Most High, because he is kind to the ungrateful and wicked' (6:35). 'Forgive, and you will be forgiven' (6:37). If the loving God who deserves love is loved, and if the merciful Samaritan is imitated, that is the Law. God's government is like the small seed which becomes a plant and like a pinch of yeast that makes a loaf. For God never gives up. The lost sheep, the lost coin, the lost son, the lost criminal is found. And those who hear this good news have great joy, praising God.

# John Stott's Response to Chapter 6

My dear David,
What draws me to you is your passion, exhibited in the fearlessness of your thinking and the depth of your feeling. As you know, many times I do not agree with you (nor do you with me). But you think. You ask the questions which many of us prefer to sweep under the carpet. And you feel. Your heart goes out to human beings in all their need and pain. I wish the same could be said of all of us Evangelicals. Some of us neither think nor feel. We go on defending our pet convictions (shibboleths?), without either facing or feeling their implications. Our mouth is larger than our head or our heart. Even though, in this chapter as in the previous five, there remain some wide differences between us, you have challenged me to keener thought and deeper feeling, in other words, to be a more authentic human being and Christian. For this I thank you.

## Eschatology and the Kingdom

The 'last things' (death, the parousia, the resurrection, the last judgement and the final destinies of heaven or hell), which are together the focus of eschatology, have always fascinated Christian minds. Yet you are right to reproach Evangelicals for developing at times an unhealthy pre-occupation with them. We have tended both to be too literalistic in our interpretations, and to forget that New Testament teaching in this area is not given to satisfy our curiosity but rather to stimulate our holiness, service, witness and hope.

Let me first take up your criticism of our excessive literalism (which is sometimes an over-reaction to the excessive scepticism of other schools of thought!), and of the dogmatism which often accompanies it. Actually, I think you indulge in a little hyperbole as you poke fun at us. Your chiding becomes chaffing. And ridicule is a dangerous weapon, not altogether conducive to dialogue! I myself regret that some Evangelical societies and institutions include in their basis of faith a particular eschatological viewpoint, and so make it a test of orthodoxy. For I believe that both the interpretation of prophecy and the nature of the millennium belong to the *adiaphora*, in which we should accord one another liberty of opinion.

Not all Evangelicals are nincompoops, however, who 'take the poetry as detailed predictions of what is going to happen'. Most of us recognise that the Book of Revelation is full of symbolism (including its numerology, like multiples of twelve symbolising the Church, e.g. the twenty-four elders and the 144,000), and that some of its imagery could be called 'mythological' (lambs and dragons, for example). The popular interpretations of the book (the 'preterist', 'futurist' and 'historicist') all understand it as containing references to particular historical events which belong respectively to the past (the first century), the future (the end of the age) and the span of church history in between. A fourth school of interpretation, which has been gaining ground among Evangelicals during this century, avoids this historical particularity and preserves the best of all three other schools. It is clumsily called the 'successivo-parallelist', was expounded by William Hendriksen in his *More Than Conquerors* (1962) and popularised in this country by Michael Wilcock's *I Saw Heaven Opened: The Message of Revelation* (1975). It sees the book as a series of highly dramatic visions, each of which recapitulates the story of the 'interadventual period' (the whole era stretching between Christ's two comings), and culminates in the End.

According to this view, the essence of the message of
Revelation concerns the age-long conflict between the lamb
and the dragon, the Church and the world, Jerusalem the
holy city and Babylon the great city (a conflict which has
had many historical manifestations and will have yet
more), together with the assurance of Christ's victory. As
H. B. Swete wrote years ago, 'the whole book is a *Sursum
Corda*', exhorting us to rejoice that Christ is both reigning
now and coming soon.

As for the millennium, since you give a wholly inadequate account of the 'amillennial' position, allow me to
remedy this defect! Amillennialists do not just 'expect
the kingdom to come only in heaven'. We notice that in
Revelation 20 the one-thousand-year period (symbolic of a
long but unspecified time) has three main characteristics.
First, Christ is reigning (incidentally not 'on earth', the
locale of his rule being nowhere mentioned). Secondly,
certain people (including witnesses, martyrs and those
'given authority to judge') come to life, reign with Christ
and serve as 'priests' (verses 4,6). Thirdly, the dragon
(Satan) is bound and locked up 'to keep him from deceiving
the nations any more' (verse 3). What strikes us is that in the
rest of the New Testament these three activities characterise
the present age, that is, the whole interadventual period.
First, having been exalted by the Father, Jesus Christ is
seated and reigning at his right hand now, all authority
having been given him. Secondly, his people have been
raised and exalted with him, are seated with him, sharing
his reign (e.g. Ephesians 2:6; Colossians 3:1–3), and are
called 'kings and priests' (1 Peter 2:5–9; Revelation 1:6,
5:10). 'This is the first resurrection,' John comments, because it refers to our being raised with Christ now, and not
to the resurrection of the body, which will take place only at
the end of history (verse 5). Thirdly, Satan is bound, having
been overthrown by Christ at his first coming. He likened
Satan to 'a strong man, fully armed', and himself to 'someone stronger', who overpowers him, binds him and then
robs his house (Luke 11:21–22). If it be objected that Satan

does not appear to be bound, we answer that this is a problem of the whole New Testament, and not just of Revelation 20. For the New Testament plainly affirms that Jesus has defeated, dethroned and disarmed the devil, with all the evil principalities and powers (e.g. Colossians 2:15; Hebrews 2:14). Probably the best way to understand the binding of Satan in Revelation 20 is to note its purpose, which is 'to keep him from deceiving the nations'. Both postmillennialists and amillennialists explain this as referring to the missionary advance of the Church following the resurrection, as a result of which people of all nations are being delivered from their deceptions and gathered into Christ's Church (Matthew 28:18–20). Isn't this kind of reconstruction reasonable? And does it not escape your strictures on literalism and on turning the Revelation into 'information about the future'?

You then move on to a discussion of the kingdom, its nature and its coming. We are agreed, I think, that it came with Jesus. He said 'the time has come [been fulfilled]' (Mark 1:15) and 'the kingdom of God has come upon you' (Matthew 12:28), and he challenged people to 'receive' or 'enter' it then and there (e.g. Mark 10:14–15). At the same time he taught that its full manifestation lay in the future, as is clear from the petition 'may your kingdom come' and from several of his parables. By both apocalyptic imagery ('coming in the clouds of heaven') and simile ('like the lightning, which flashes and lights up the sky from one end to the other', Luke 17:24) he indicated his belief that his coming would be a global, divine and cataclysmic climax to history, and he warned people against trying to localise it ('Lo here! Lo there!').

Is it certain, however, that (leaving aside what his personal hope or expectation may have been) he definitely predicted that the end was on the threshold and would come very soon? This was basic to Schweitzer's thesis, of course, and is probably held by a majority of commentators. You yourself seem to contemplate with equanimity the idea that Jesus was mistaken in this matter, and even

that 'in order to be human' he was obliged to adopt a
world-view which would inevitably include error. You
seem reluctant to consider the alternative, that it may be the
scholars who are wrong and not Jesus. My presupposition
is that Jesus was not mistaken, and there are many conservatives who share this confidence. Indeed, the evidence
that he erred is far from compelling. To begin with, he
confessed that he himself did not know 'that day or hour'
(Mark 13:32); it is therefore antecedently unlikely that he
would teach what he did not know. To be sure, ignorance
can lead to error. What is significant, however, is that he
was not ignorant of his ignorance. He knew the limits of his
knowledge. So the reason why his teaching was inerrant is
that, however great his ignorance in certain areas may have
been, he remained within the sphere of his knowledge and
spoke only what his Father gave him to speak (e.g. John
7:16; 8:28; 12:49; 14:10).

Returning to the question of his coming, the three texts
which you and others have quoted as evidence of his
mistake are all capable of satisfactory alternative explanations. The synoptists certainly understood his 'some who
are standing here will not taste death before they see the
kingdom of God come with power' (Mark 9:1 and parallels)
as referring to the transfiguration (the 'some' being Peter,
James and John), since they proceed immediately to the
story of this manifestation of his glory. His statement in the
mission charge to the Twelve that 'you will not finish going
through the cities of Israel before the Son of man comes'
(Matthew 10:23) could quite naturally mean that he would
catch them up or overtake them before their mission was
accomplished, for it seems probable that, like the Seventy
(or Seventy-two) whom he commissioned later, he 'sent
them . . . ahead of him to every town and place where he
was about to go' (Luke 10:1).

The most difficult text is the third, namely his statement
in the apocalyptic discourse that 'this generation will certainly not pass away until all these things have happened'
(Mark 13:30). The critical question is to what events he was

alluding by 'all these things'. The exegetical problem of Mark 13 and its parallels is of course that he was answering the disciples' two questions 'when will these things happen?' (which referred to the destruction of the temple, verses 2–4) and 'what will be the sign that they are all about to be fulfilled?' (which could refer to the signs preceding the End, for so Matthew interpreted it, 24:3). At all events these two strands, relating to both immediate and ultimate events, are interwoven in the discourse, and because of the customary foreshortening of prophetic vision they are sometimes telescoped into each other.

My own belief is that Jesus was deliberately contrasting 'all these things' which would happen within the lifetime of that generation (namely the events leading up to AD 70, verse 30) with 'that day and hour' which only the Father knew (namely the day of his coming, verse 32). The other point which needs to be made is that Jesus' emphasis (even in spite of the heralding signs, including the evangelisation of the nations, which would have taken some time) was on the unexpected and surprise nature of his return (like a burglar, Matthew 24:43; Luke 12:39), on account of which they must watch and be ready: 'Be on guard! Be alert! You do not know when that time will come' (Mark 13:33). Indeed this is the 'element of agnosticism about the future' which you yourself concede.

If Jesus did not teach that he would return within their lifetime, did the apostles teach it? Certainly some of their hearers *thought* they did, like the *ataktoi* in Thessalonica who were playing truant from work in expectation of his imminent return (1 Thessalonians 4:11–12; 5:14; 2 Thessalonians 3:6–7). And the references to 'times and dates' (Acts 1:7; 1 Thessalonians 5:1) suggest that there was debate about the matter in the early Church, just as 2 Peter 3 shows that there was need later to explain the supposed delay. But what about the repeated cry, 'Behold, I am coming soon!' (Revelation 3:11; 22:7,12,20), and the excited response 'Amen. Come, Lord Jesus' or '*Marana tha*. Come, O Lord' (Revelation 22:20; 1 Corinthians 16:22), and Paul's 'we who are still alive', 'we will not all sleep' and 'the time is short' (1 Thessalonians 4:15; 1 Corinthians 15:51; 1 Corinthians 7:29)? Well, of course, it is possible for you to press these (as others do) into being Paul's definite (and mistaken) teaching that the parousia would take place in his lifetime. But would you not then be guilty of the very literalism of which you keep accusing me? If I am right that Jesus did not teach it, it seems to me unlikely that the apostles did. If I am also right that Jesus' emphasis was on the unexpectedness of his return and on the consequent need for watchfulness, then it seems to me likely that this was the apostles' emphasis too. I believe God's purpose is for every generation of Christians to live in eager anticipation of the parousia; the promise 'I am coming soon' well expresses and secures this expectation. It is an aspect of the Christian 'hope' which has always been precious to Evangelicals.

## Judgement and Hell

It is with great reluctance and with a heavy heart that I now approach this subject. You quote the Grand Rapids report which describes the unevangelised millions as human beings who, 'though created by God like God and for God . . . are now living without God'. This is a phrase which I have myself often used, because it seems to me to sum up the poignant tragedy of human lostness. And when it is extended to the possibility that some who live without God now may also spend eternity without him, the thought becomes almost unbearable.

I want to repudiate with all the vehemence of which I am capable the glibness, what almost appears to be the glee, the *Schadenfreude*, with which some Evangelicals speak about hell. It is a horrible sickness of mind or spirit. Instead, since on the day of judgement, when some will be condemned, there is going to be 'weeping and gnashing of teeth' (Matthew 8:12; 22:13; 24:51; 25:30; Luke 13:28), should we not already begin to weep at the very prospect? I thank God for Jeremiah. Israelite patriot though he was, he was charged with the heartbreaking mission of prophesying the destruction of his nation. Its ruin would only be temporary; it would not be eternal. Nevertheless, he could not restrain his tears. 'Oh that my head were a spring of water and my eyes a fountain of tears! I would weep day and night for the slain of my people' (Jeremiah 9:1; cf. 13:17; 14:17).

It is within this prophetic tradition of tragedy, of sorrow over people's rejection of God's word and over the resultant inevitability of judgement, that Jesus wept over the impenitent city of Jerusalem. He cried out: 'If you, even you, had only known on this day what would bring you peace . . . !' (Luke 19:41–42; cf. Matthew 23:37–38). In this too Paul had the mind of Christ. He wrote of the 'great sorrow and unceasing anguish' he felt in his heart for his own race, the people of Israel. His 'heart's desire and prayer to God' was for their salvation. He was willing even, like Moses before him, to be himself 'cursed and cut off from Christ' if only thereby his people might be saved (Romans 9:1–4; 10:1; cf. Exodus 32:32). He had the same deep feelings for the Gentiles. For three whole years in Ephesus, as he reminded the church elders of that city, 'I never stopped warning each of you night and day with tears' (Acts 20:31; cf. 20:19; Philippians 3:18).

I long that we could in some small way stand in the tearful tradition of Jeremiah, Jesus and Paul. I want to see more tears among us. I think we need to repent of our nonchalance, our hard-heartedness.

## (a) What is hell?

You raise two main questions in relation to hell. The first concerns what is meant by it, and the second who may be condemned to go there. We both agree that the imagery

which Jesus and his apostles used (the lake of fire, the outer
darkness, the second death) is not meant to be interpreted
literally. In any case it could not be, since fire and darkness exclude each other. You comment positively on the
Lausanne Covenant's expression 'eternal separation from
God'; it is a conscious echo both of Jesus' words 'depart
from me' (Matthew 7:23; 25:41) and of Paul's 'shut out from
the presence of the Lord' (2 Thessalonians 1:9). We surely
have to say that this banishment from God will be real,
terrible (so that 'it would be better for him if he had not been
born', Mark 14:21) and eternal. The New Testament
contains no hint of the possibility of a later reprieve or
amnesty. The biblical phraseology includes, in contrast to
'eternal life' and 'eternal salvation', 'eternal judgement'
(Hebrews 6:2 and possibly Mark 3:29), 'everlasting contempt' (Daniel 12:2), 'eternal punishment' (Matthew 25:46),
'everlasting destruction' (2 Thessalonians 1:9) and 'eternal
fire' (Matthew 18:8; 25:41). And the imagery supporting
this phraseology includes the pictures of the door being
shut (Matthew 25:10–12) and the great chasm being fixed
(Luke 16:26).

You press me, however, to go beyond this. You rightly
say that I have never declared publicly whether I think hell,
in addition to being real, terrible and eternal, will involve
the experience of everlasting suffering. I am sorry that you
use in reference to God the emotive expression 'the Eternal
Torturer', because it implies a sadistic infliction of pain, and
all Christian people would emphatically reject that. But will
the final destiny of the impenitent be eternal conscious
torment, 'for ever and ever', or will it be a total annihilation
of their being? The former has to be described as traditional
orthodoxy, for most of the church fathers, the medieval
theologians and the Reformers held it. And probably most
Evangelical leaders hold it today. Do I hold it, however?
Well, emotionally, I find the concept intolerable and do not
understand how people can live with it without either
cauterising their feelings or cracking under the strain. But
our emotions are a fluctuating, unreliable guide to truth

and must not be exalted to the place of supreme authority in determining it. As a committed Evangelical, my question must be – and is – not what does my heart tell me, but what does God's word say? And in order to answer this question, we need to survey the biblical material afresh and to open our minds (not just our hearts) to the possibility that Scripture points in the direction of annihilation, and that 'eternal conscious torment' is a tradition which has to yield to the supreme authority of Scripture. There are four arguments; they relate to language, imagery, justice and universalism.

First, *language*. The vocabulary of 'destruction' is often used in relation to the final state of perdition. The commonest Greek words are the verb *apollumi* (to destroy) and the noun *apòleia* (destruction). When the verb is active and transitive, 'destroy' means 'kill', as when Herod wanted to murder the baby Jesus and the Jewish leaders later plotted to have him executed (Matthew 2:13; 12:14; 27:4). Then Jesus himself told us not to be afraid of those who kill the body and cannot kill the soul. 'Rather,' he continued, 'be afraid of the One [God] who can destroy both soul and body in hell' (Matthew 10:28; cf. James 4:12). If to kill is to deprive the body of life, hell would seem to be the deprivation of both physical and spiritual life, that is, an extinction of being. When the verb is in the middle, and intransitive, it means to be destroyed and so to 'perish', whether physically of hunger or snakebite (Luke 15:17; 1 Corinthians 10:9) or eternally in hell (e.g. John 3:16; 10:28; 17:12; Romans 2:12; 1 Corinthians 15:18; 2 Peter 3:9). If believers are *hoi sōzomenoi* (those who are being saved), unbelievers are *hoi apollumenoi* (those who are perishing). The phrase occurs in 1 Corinthians 1:18, 2 Corinthians 2:15; 4:3, and in 2 Thessalonians 2:10. Jesus is also recorded in the Sermon on the Mount as contrasting the 'narrow . . . road that leads to life' with the 'broad . . . road that leads to destruction' (Matthew 7:13; cf. also Romans 9:22; Philippians 1:28; 3:19; Hebrews 10:39; 2 Peter 3:7; Revelation 17:8,11; the word used in 1 Thessalonians 5:3 and 2 Thessalonians 1:9 is *olethros*, which also means 'ruin' or 'destruction'). It would seem strange, there-fore, if people who are said to suffer destruction are in fact not destroyed; and, as you put it, it is 'difficult to imagine a perpetually inconclusive process of perishing'. It cannot, I think, be replied that it is impossible to destroy human beings because they are immortal, for the immortality – and therefore indestructibility – of the soul is a Greek not a biblical concept. According to Scripture only God possesses immortality in himself (1 Timothy 1:17; 6:16); he reveals and gives it to us through the gospel (2 Timothy 1:10). And by the way, 'annihilation' is not quite the same as 'conditional immortality'. According to the latter, nobody survives death except those to whom God gives life (they are there-fore immortal by grace, not by nature), whereas according to the former, everybody survives death and will even be resurrected, but the impenitent will finally be destroyed.

The second argument concerns the *imagery* used in Scrip-ture to characterise hell, and in particular that of fire. Jesus spoke of 'the fire of hell' (Matthew 5:22; 18:9) and of 'eternal fire' (Matthew 18:8; 25:41), and in the Revelation we read about 'the lake of fire' (20:14–15). It is doubtless because we have all had experience of the acute pain of being burned, that fire is associated in our minds with 'conscious tor-ment'. But the main function of fire is not to cause pain, but to secure destruction, as all the world's incinerators bear witness. Hence the biblical expression 'a consuming fire' and John the Baptist's picture of the Judge 'burning up the chaff with unquenchable fire' (Matthew 3:12, cf. Luke 3:17). The fire itself is termed 'eternal' and 'unquenchable', but it would be very odd if what is thrown into it proves indestructible. Our expectation would be the opposite: it would be consumed for ever, not tormented for ever. Hence it is the smoke (evidence that the fire has done its work) which 'rises for ever and ever' (Revelation 14:11; cf. 19:3).

Four objections are raised to this understanding of 'the lake of fire'.

(1) There is the vivid picture of hell as a place where 'their worm does not die, and the fire is not quenched' (Mark 9:48). It is a quotation from the last verse of Isaiah (66:24), where the dead bodies of God's enemies are consigned to the city's rubbish dump to be eaten by maggots and burned. It is not necessary to apply this as Judith did, however, namely that God would take vengeance on the hostile nations, 'to put fire and worms in their flesh' so that 'they shall weep and feel their pain for ever' (Judith 16:17). Jesus' use of Isaiah 66:24 does not mention everlasting pain. What he says is that the worm will not die and the fire will not be quenched. Nor will they – until presumably their work of destruction is done.

(2) At the end of the so-called parable of the sheep and goats, Jesus contrasted 'eternal life' with 'eternal punishment' (Matthew 25:46). Does that not indicate that in hell people endure eternal conscious punishment? No, that is to read into the text what is not necessarily there. What Jesus said is that both the life and the punishment would be eternal, but he did not in that passage define the nature of either. Because he elsewhere spoke of eternal life as a conscious enjoyment of God (John 17:3), it does not follow that eternal punishment must be a conscious experience of pain at the hand of God. On the contrary, although declaring both to be eternal, Jesus is *contrasting* the two destinies: the more unlike they are, the better.

(3) But did not Dives cry out because he was 'in agony in this fire' (Luke 16:23–24,28)? Yes, he did. But we must be cautious in interpreting a parable (if it was that) which speaks of 'Abraham's bosom' as well as hell fire. Moreover, these two states were experienced immediately after Dives and Lazarus died (verses 22–23). The natural interpretation would be that Jesus was referring to the so-called 'intermediate (or interim) state' between death and resurrection. I myself believe that this will be the time (if indeed we shall be aware of the passage of time) when the lost will come to the unimaginably painful realisation of their fate. This is not incompatible, however, with their final annihil-

ation. Similarly, the 'torment' of Revelation 14:10, because it will be experienced 'in the presence of the holy angels and of the Lamb', seems to refer to the moment of judgement, not to the eternal state. It is not the torment itself but its 'smoke' (symbol of the completed burning) which will be 'for ever and ever'.

(4) But does the Book of Revelation not say that in the lake of fire 'they will be tormented day and night for ever and ever'? Yes, that sentence occurs, but only once (20:10), where it refers not only to the devil, but to 'the beast and the false prophet', just as the noun for 'torment' had been used of 'the harlot Babylon' (Revelation 18:7,10,15), though without the addition of the words 'for ever and ever'. The beast, the false prophet and the harlot, however, are not individual people but symbols of the world in its varied hostility to God. In the nature of the case they cannot experience pain. Nor can 'Death and Hades', which follow them into the lake of fire (20:13). In the vivid imagery of his vision John evidently saw the dragon, the monsters, the harlot, death and hades being thrown into the lake of fire. But the most natural way to understand the reality behind the imagery is that ultimately all enmity and resistance to God will be destroyed. So both the language of destruction and the imagery of fire seem to point to annihilation.

The third argument in favour of the concept of annihilation concerns the biblical vision of *justice*. Fundamental to it is the belief that God will judge people 'according to what they [have] done' (e.g. Revelation 20:12), which implies that the penalty inflicted will be commensurate with the evil done. This principle had been applied in the Jewish law courts, in which penalties were limited to an exact retribution, 'life for life, eye for eye, tooth for tooth, hand for hand, foot for foot' (e.g. Exodus 21:23–25). Would there not, then, be a serious disproportion between sins consciously committed in time and torment consciously experienced throughout eternity? I do not minimise the gravity of sin as rebellion against God our Creator, and shall return to it shortly, but I question whether 'eternal conscious torment' is compatible with the biblical revelation of divine justice, unless perhaps (as has been argued) the impenitence of the lost also continues throughout eternity.

The fourth and last argument relates to those texts which have been used as the basis for *universalism*. I am not a universalist, and you tell me that you are not either. So there is no need for me to say more than that the hope of final salvation for everybody is a false hope, since it contradicts the recorded warnings of Jesus that the judgement will involve a separation into two opposite but equally eternal destinies. My point here, however, is that the eternal existence of the impenitent in hell would be hard to reconcile with the promises of God's final victory over evil, or with the apparently universalistic texts which speak of Christ drawing all men to himself (John 12:32), and of God uniting all things under Christ's headship (Ephesians 1:10), reconciling all things to himself through Christ (Colossians 1:20), and bringing every knee to bow to Christ and every tongue to confess his lordship (Philippians 2:10–11), so that in the end God will be 'all in all' or 'everything to everybody' (1 Corinthians 15:28).

These texts do not lead me to universalism, because of the many others which speak of the terrible and eternal reality of hell. But they do lead me to ask how God can in any meaningful sense be called 'everything to everybody' while an unspecified number of people still continue in rebellion against him and under his judgement. It would be easier to hold together the awful reality of hell and the universal reign of God if hell means destruction and the impenitent are no more.

I am hesitant to have written these things, partly because I have a great respect for longstanding tradition which claims to be a true interpretation of Scripture, and do not lightly set it aside, and partly because the unity of the world-wide Evangelical constituency has always meant much to me. But the issue is too important to suppress, and I am grateful to you for challenging me to declare my present mind. I do not dogmatise about the position to which I have come. I hold it tentatively. But I do plead for frank dialogue among Evangelicals on the basis of Scripture. I also believe that the ultimate annihilation of the wicked should at least be accepted as a legitimate, biblically founded alternative to their eternal conscious torment.

### (b) Who will go to hell?

You now ask me a second equally difficult and delicate question. Whatever the nature of hell may be, who will go there? Do Evangelicals believe that hell will be the fate of 'the bulk of humanity', in which case the gospel does not appear to be 'good news for the mass of humanity'?

Again, you are right to put this searching question to Evangelicals. You then quote paragraph three of the Lausanne Covenant which is entitled 'The Uniqueness and Universality of Christ'. It contains the stark statement that 'those who reject Christ repudiate the joy of salvation and condemn themselves to eternal separation from God'. I stand by this, as I believe would the whole Evangelical community. It reminds me of a similar clause in the Congress Statement of Keele 1967: 'A persistent and deliberate rejection of Jesus Christ condemns men to hell' (I.11). Both assertions are clear and definite because they refer only to people who have heard of Christ but have rejected him, consciously, deliberately, persistently. Such people are not just condemned; they condemn themselves.

But neither the Lausanne Covenant, nor the Keele Statement which preceded it, said anything about the final destiny of those who had never heard of Christ, never received a 'worthy presentation of him' and so never had a reasonable opportunity to respond to him. What will be their fate? What does the New Testament authorise us to say about them? My answer includes four parts, of which the first three are (for Evangelicals at least) non-controversial, while the fourth leads us into the precarious area of wondering and speculating.

First, *all human beings*, apart from the intervention and mercy of God, *are perishing*. Yes, I deliberately used and use the present continuous tense, as Paul did when he referred to the *apollumenoi*. The word describes their present, not their future, state. They are, in Jesus' phrase, on the broad road that leads to destruction, but they have not reached that destination, and they need not. The door of opportunity is still open. They may yet hear and believe. Nevertheless, at the moment they are not saved and therefore must be described as 'perishing'. Is this too harsh? Those who think so I would want to direct to pages 89–110 of *The Cross of Christ*, in which I have written about both the gravity of sin and the majesty of God. All divine judgement seems and sounds unjust until we see God as he is and ourselves as we are, according to Scripture. As for God, Scripture uses the pictures of light and fire to set forth his perfect holiness.

He dwells in unapproachable light, dazzling, even blinding in its splendour, and is a consuming fire. Human beings who have only glimpsed his glory have been unable to bear the sight, and have turned away or run away or swooned. As for ourselves, I often want to say to my contemporaries what Anselm said to his, 'You have not yet considered the seriousness of sin'. True, Scripture recognises both our ignorance ('they do not know what they are doing') and our weakness ('he remembers that we are dust'), but it dignifies us by holding us accountable for our thoughts and actions. Think of God's endlessly repeated refrain in the Old Testament: 'I spoke to you, but you refused to listen'. Jeremiah kept calling it 'the stubbornness of your evil heart'. Think too of the words of Jesus: 'You refuse to come to me to have life' (John 5:40), and 'how often I have longed to gather your children together . . . but you were not willing' (Matthew 23:37). It was the wilful blindness and wilful disobedience of people that he condemned. And is not this the essence of

Paul's argument in Romans 1–3? I accept your rebuke that to apply the end of Romans 1 (where God gives people up to idolatry and immorality) to earnest adherents of other faiths, when Paul applied it to the moral decadence of his own day, is 'an insulting travesty of much sincere seeking, devotion and holiness'. But I cannot surrender Paul's conclusion, which is that Jews and Gentiles, the religious and the irreligious, the morally educated and uneducated, because they have all failed (yes, wilfully) to live up to what they have known to be true and good, are all guilty before God and without excuse.

How then do we explain the phenomenon of religious and righteous people who belong to other faiths and ideologies? It is part, I think, of the paradoxical nature of our humanness, that is, that we are both breath of God and dust of earth, godlike and bestial, created and fallen, noble and ignoble. That seems to be why we both seek God (Acts 17:27) and run away from him, both practise righteousness and suppress the truth in our unrighteousness (Acts 10:22; Romans 1:18), both recognise the claims of the moral law upon us and refuse to submit to it (Romans 8:7), both erect altars in God's honour and need to repent of our ignorance and sin (Acts 17:23, 30).

You are too inclined, I think, to praise the good you see in others, and I may be too inclined to blame the evil. But the reason in my case is that I believe I know myself. To be sure, I welcome and affirm all those noble gifts of God which are part of his image in me (rationality and curiosity, moral aspirations, the primacy of love, artistic creativity, the urge to worship), but it is this very glory which highlights the shame – the vanity, obstinacy, selfishness, envy, impatience, malice, and lack of self-control. My perceptions of God and of myself, however distorted, convince me that in myself I am completely unfit to spend eternity in his presence. I need to be 'made fit' (NIV, 'qualified') to share in the saints' inheritance in light (Colossians 1:12). Without those white robes made clean in the blood of the Lamb, I could never stand before God's throne (Revelation 7:9–10).

'Hell-deserving sinner' sounds an absurdly antiquated phrase, but I believe it is the sober truth. Without Christ I am 'perishing', and deserve to perish.

Secondly, *human beings cannot save themselves* by any religious or righteous acts. Christians cannot. Nor can non-Christians. Self-salvation is out. In this connection we need to think about Cornelius, because he is the person often chosen to exemplify the upright seeker whom God 'accepts' on account of his sincerity and decency. Certainly Luke describes him before his conversion as righteous, generous, pious, and widely respected in the local community. He prayed, attended synagogue and gave alms. Not yet, however, had he received salvation. The overriding lesson Peter learned from the story was that God has no racial favourites (10:34). He 'accepts' people from every nation 'who fear him and do what is right' (10:35), in the sense that, irrespective of Cornelius' Gentile status, God heard his prayer and made provision for him to hear the gospel (10:30–33). But only later did God 'accept' him in a saving sense when he gave him the Holy Spirit (15:8). It was then that he was 'saved' (11:14; 15:11), that he was granted 'repentance unto life' (11:18), and that God 'purified his heart by faith' (15:9). God honoured his reverent spirit, his prayers and his uprightness, and led a messenger of the gospel to him. But his salvation came through his penitent, believing response to the gospel, not through his previous religion and righteousness. I don't think this conclusion can be avoided. Principled exegesis requires it. We have to say that Cornelius did not win salvation by good works or religious observances; and if Cornelius could not, nor can anybody else.

Thirdly, *Jesus Christ is the only Saviour*. The uniqueness to which Christians bear witness does not refer to Christianity in any of its numerous empirical manifestations, but only to Christ. He has no peers, no rivals, no successors. And his uniqueness is most evident in relation to the incarnation, the atonement and the resurrection. He is the one and only God-man, who died for our sins and was then raised from the dead to authenticate his person and work. And it is this threefold, historical uniqueness which qualifies him to be the Saviour of the world, the only mediator between God and humankind (1 Timothy 2:5). No one else has these qualifications. I confess to being sad that in your chapter you tried to wriggle out of the plain, natural and obvious meaning of John 14:6 and Acts 4:12. As the way, the truth and the life, no one can come to the Father except through Jesus Christ's mediation. And 'salvation is found in no-one else, for there is no other name under heaven . . . by which we must be saved'. If there is only one Saviour, there can be only one way of salvation.

That brings me to the fourth point. Here we need to ask questions rather than make statements. If we grant that human beings left to themselves are perishing, and that they cannot save themselves, and that Jesus is the only qualified Saviour – which are the three truths which Evangelicals are at all costs determined to safeguard – what condition has to be fulfilled in order that they may be saved? How much knowledge of Jesus do people have to have before they can believe in him? And how much faith do they have to exercise? Those who genuinely hear the gospel must repent and believe, of course. But what about those who have not heard it? They cannot save themselves, as we have seen, and Christ is the only Saviour. Is there then any way in which God will have mercy on them, through Christ alone, and not through their own merit? A variety of answers have been given to these questions.

(1) There is the quotation you give from Vatican II's *Lumen Gentium*, on which I also have reflected. It seems to promise salvation to those who 'seek God', and who give evidence of the sincerity of their search by 'striving' to do his will and live a good life. At the same time, it includes a number of caveats, which seem to be designed to avoid the impression of salvation by good works. It emphasises that their ignorance of the gospel must be 'through no fault of their own' and 'without blame on their part'. It contains two

references to God's grace and one to his providence. And it not only attributes people's goodness and truth to the *Logos*, but calls these things 'a preparation for the gospel'. Does that mean that like Cornelius they will be given the privilege of hearing it? And why does the Statement begin that such people only '*can* [not *do*] attain to everlasting salvation who . . . sincerely seek God . . .'? In other words the statement has many ambiguities. A statement of John Paul II at the beginning of his papal ministry is quite unambiguous, however. In his encyclical *Redemptor Hominis* (1979) he wrote: 'Man – every man without any exception whatever – has been redeemed by Christ, and . . . with man – with each man without any exception whatever – Christ is in a way united, even when man is unaware of it' (para. 14).

That kind of unconditional universalism must, however, be firmly rejected by those who look to Scripture for authoritative guidance.

(2) Others turn to the sheep and goats passage in Matthew 25, as you do. They point out that Jesus refers to 'the nations' being judged and to the surprise of both groups when they find out that they are accepted or rejected, and why. We certainly must not interpret it as teaching salvation by works, or we would be turning the whole New Testament on its head. There is also a continuing debate over the identity of Jesus' 'brothers'. If it can be shown to mean human beings in general, with whom Jesus identifies himself, then we would have to insist that the nations are not accepted or rejected according to their works, but according to their attitude to Jesus which is revealed in their works. But in Matthew's gospel Jesus' 'brothers' are his disciples who do his Father's will (12:48–50). As he sends them out into the world to preach, people will either welcome or reject them, and in their attitude to Jesus' brothers their attitude to him will be made known (10:5–15).

(3) A third approach is to say that God knows how people would have responded if they had heard the gospel, and

will save or judge them accordingly. For Jesus said to the cities of Korazin, Bethsaida and Capernaum: 'If the miracles that were performed in you had been performed in Tyre and Sidon, they would have repented long ago in sackcloth and ashes' (Matthew 11:21). What is true of cities, could also be true of individuals.

(4) Others have speculated that God gives everybody a vision of Jesus, and therefore an opportunity to repent and believe, at the moment of their dying. But no evidence is available to support this, either from Scripture or from death-bed experiences.

(5) A more common suggestion is that God will give everybody an opportunity in the next life to respond to Jesus. I think this possibility appeals to you. You refer to it as the 'Hades Gospel'. Some have tried to base it on Peter's statement that Jesus 'went and preached to the spirits in prison' (1 Peter 3:19). But 'the spirits' were almost certainly (see E. G. Selwyn's famous commentary) demonic, not human, and Jesus' preaching was an 'announcement' of his victory, not a proclamation of the gospel with an invitation to respond. You, however, seem to suggest that the Corinthian practice of being 'baptised for the dead' (1 Corinthians 15:29) supplies some hope that after death people will be able to share in Christ's salvation. But was Paul not using an *argumentum ad hominem* here? One cannot say with any confidence that he approved of the practice. Besides, as I'm sure you know, Robertson and Plummer in their old ICC commentary on 1 Corinthians (1911) mention that thirty-six explanations of the practice have been collected! Although the guess that people will be given in the next world an opportunity to believe is an attractive one, it remains a guess and lacks biblical warrant.

(6) Sir Norman Anderson, in speech and writing, has often suggested that some people who have never heard of Christ may be brought, by a sense of their sin, guilt and inability to save themselves, to cry for mercy to the God they but dimly perceive; that God does have mercy on them; and that he saves them on the basis of Christ's

atoning work, through faith, even though they have not heard of him. This proposal has two particular merits. First, it preserves the three safeguards outlined above, especially that we cannot save ourselves and that Christ is the only Saviour. Secondly, it can claim some biblical warrant, since Old Testament believers were saved by God's grace through faith, even though they knew little if anything about the coming Christ. Norman Anderson writes: 'The believing Jew was accepted and blessed not because of the prescribed animal sacrifices he offered, nor even his repentance and abandonment of himself to God's mercy, but because of what God himself was going to do in his only Son at the cross of Calvary' (*Christianity and World Religions: The Challenge of Pluralism*, 1984, p. 153).

Speaking now for myself, although I am attracted by Sir Norman Anderson's concept, and although there may be truth in it and even in some of the other suggestions, I believe the most Christian stance is to remain agnostic on this question. When somebody asked Jesus, 'Lord, are only a few people going to be saved?', he refused to answer and instead urged them 'to enter through the narrow door' (Luke 13:23–24). The fact is that God, alongside the most solemn warnings about our responsibility to respond to the gospel, has not revealed how he will deal with those who have never heard it. We have to leave them in the hands of the God of infinite mercy and justice, who manifested these qualities most fully in the cross. Abraham's question, 'will not the Judge of all the earth do right?' (Genesis 18:25) is our confidence too.

Like yourself, however, I am imbued with hope. I have never been able to conjure up (as some great Evangelical missionaries have) the appalling vision of the millions who are not only perishing but will inevitably perish. On the other hand, as I have said, I am not and cannot be a universalist. Between these extremes I cherish the hope that the majority of the human race will be saved. And I have a solid biblical basis for this belief. True, Jesus said that those who find the narrow road that leads to life were 'few' (was he referring to the little remnant of his own day within the nation of Israel?). But we need to remember that God is the Creator of all humankind, and remains infinitely loving, patient and compassionate towards all whom he has made. Yes, and he is also everybody's 'Father', both in the sense that they 'live and move and have their being' in him, deriving the richness of their human life from his generosity (Acts 17:25–28), and in the sense that he continues to yearn for his lost children, as in the parable of the prodigal son. (It is the intimacy of a father-child relationship which according to the New Testament is given only to those whom God has reconciled to himself through Jesus Christ.) We have to remember too that God does not *want* anybody to perish but *wants* everybody to be saved (2 Peter 3:9; 1 Timothy 2:4); that Jesus expressed his compassion for society's outcasts (the 'publicans and sinners' and the prostitutes), refused to reject them, but deliberately made friends with them; that his own forecast was that 'many' would come from the four points of the compass and the four corners of the earth to join the Jewish patriarchs in God's kingdom (Luke 13:29); and that the final vision of the redeemed in the Book of Revelation is of 'a great multitude that no-one could count' (7:9), a huge international throng, in whom God's promise to Abraham will at last be fulfilled that his seed (his spiritual posterity) would be as innumerable as the stars in the sky, the dust of the earth and the grains of sand on all the seashores of the world.

That is the hope I cherish, and that is the vision that inspires me, even while I remain agnostic about how God will bring it to pass. Meanwhile, there is an urgency to make the gospel known. This is 'our obligation', as you rightly say near the beginning of your chapter. We are charged to share the good news with 'all the nations'. This must include the Jews, for the gospel is 'the power of God for the salvation of everyone who believes: first for the Jew, then for the Gentile' (Romans 1:16). And our supreme motivation in world evangelisation will not primarily be obedience to the great commission, nor even loving concern for those who do not yet know Jesus, important as these two incentives are, but first and foremost a burning zeal (even 'jealousy') for the glory of Jesus Christ. For God has exalted him to the highest place, and desires everybody to honour him too.

## The Gospel for Today

Once more I have gone on too long. But you have raised so many issues and asked so many questions! I must now be brief in responding to the main topic of your final chapter: What is the gospel for the world? What is the gospel for today?

I feel confident that you and I would want to begin our reply in relation to Jesus Christ. It would be impossible to share the good news without talking about Jesus. So we focus on God's love in the gift of his Son to live, die and rise again, and on his further gift to those who trust in him of a new life of forgiveness and freedom in the Spirit, of a new community of brothers and sisters to which he joins us, and one day of a new world of perfect righteousness and peace. But how shall we formulate this good news, especially in our increasingly pluralistic society, in a way that communicates and resonates with people? There seem to me two extremes to avoid.

The first is *total fixity*. Some Christians (including some of us Evangelicals) are in bondage to words and formulae, the prisoners of a gospel stereotype. They wrap up their message in a neat little package, almost labelled and price-tagged as if destined for the supermarket. Then, unless their precise *schema* and their favourite phraseology are used, they declare that the gospel has not been preached. For many Evangelicals it used to be 'the precious blood of Jesus'. Now for some it is being born again or justified by faith, and for others the kingdom of God (which you yourself call 'the heart of the gospel' and 'absolutely basic',

although the apostles did not concentrate on it as much as
Jesus did, especially to Gentile audiences). For yet others
the 'in-word' is human liberation. What these folk seem
not to have noticed is the diversity of gospel formulation
within the New Testament itself. Also, in their determination to recite their set piece, they tend to be insensitive both
to the leading of the Spirit and to the existential situation.
There is of course only one apostolic gospel, as Paul emphasised (e.g. 1 Corinthians 15:11), so that he could call down
God's judgement on anybody (NB himself included) who
preaches 'a different gospel' (Galatians 1:6–9). Yet the
apostles presented it in a wide variety of ways – now
sacrificial (the shedding and sprinkling of Christ's blood),
now messianic (the breaking in of the new age or of God's
promised rule), now mystic (receiving and enjoying eternal
life, being 'in Christ'), now legal (the righteous Judge
pronouncing the unrighteous righteous), now personal
(the Father reconciling his wayward children), now salvific
(the heavenly liberator coming to the rescue of his oppressed people, and leading them out in a new exodus) and
now cosmic (the universal Lord claiming universal dominion over the powers). And these seven are only a selection!

The opposite extreme to avoid is *total fluidity*. I remember
hearing Bishop David Brown of Guildford, shortly before
he died, saying to a group on evangelism convened by the
British Council of Churches: 'You don't even know what
the gospel is until you enter each particular situation. You
have to enter the situation first, and then you *discover* the
gospel when you're there.' Now I think I know what he was
driving at, namely that he wanted a gospel in context and
not a gospel in vacuum, and that we need to relate the
gospel sensitively to each situation. But I think his claim
that the gospel remains unknown until we have entered
each situation was a serious overstatement. For what the
advocates of total fluidity seem not to have noticed is that,
alongside the New Testament's rich diversity of gospel
formulation, there is an underlying unity which binds the
different formulations together. As A. M. Hunter put it

some years ago, 'There is . . . a deep unity in the New Testament, which dominates and transcends all the diversities' (*The Unity of the New Testament*, 1943, p. 109).

Now both extremes express important concerns. The first ('total fixity') emphasises that the gospel has been revealed and received. We did not invent it, and therefore we may not tamper with it. The second ('total fluidity') emphasises that the gospel has to be contextualised, that is, related to each particular person or situation. Otherwise it is irrelevant. Somehow, it seems to me, we have to learn to combine these two proper concerns. We have to wrestle with the dialectic between the ancient and the modern, God's word and our world, the given and the open, content and context, Scripture and culture, revelation and contextualisation. We need more integrity (faithfulness to the New Testament) and more sensitivity (awareness of the particularity of each person or group). Not one without the other, but both.

In theory I think you and I will be agreed about this, even if in practice we come to different conclusions about the gospel.

Yours ever,
John

# Epilogue by John Stott

My dear David,

Our dialogue is nearly over, but in conclusion I would like to share with you one or two general reflections. To begin with, it still grieves me somewhat that, in order to respond to your criticisms, I have had to be so defensive. Several times I have remembered the famous remark of Buffon, the eighteenth-century French naturalist, who used his knowledge of animals to comment on the behaviour of people: 'Cet animal est très méchant: quand on l'attaque, il se défend'! At the same time, I hope my concern has not been self-defence so much as what Paul called 'the defence and confirmation of the gospel' (Philippians 1:7,16).

I think that during our dialogue what is meant by the question, What is essential for Evangelicals? has been clarified. It is what Evangelicals believe is necessary to be an Evangelical in particular, not a Christian in general. Although we believe in principle that to be a Christian is, or should be, to be an Evangelical, yet my concern in attempting to answer your questions has been to define and justify our distinctives and not to disenfranchise you or anybody else.

What, then, is the ultimate difference between us? In the course of our discussion we have often been in agreement – sometimes in areas which have surprised me. So wherein lies our basic disagreement? It seems still to belong to those two subjects of traditional debate – authority and salvation. Indeed, the fundamental questions in every religion are the same: By what authority do we believe and teach what we believe and teach? By what means can sinful men and women be reconciled to God, or 'saved'?

Have we made any progress in our exchanges on authority? Repeatedly I have appealed to Scripture, and you to rationality. Of course the contrast is not as stark as that. For in appealing to Scripture I have insisted on the vital importance of the mind and the Church's tradition in the elucidation of Scripture, while you in appealing to rationality have also argued from Scripture, and in particular from the teaching and example of Jesus. Nevertheless, even when these necessary modifications have been made, the final court of appeal for you is rationality and for me is Scripture. Sometimes you objectify your authority, as when you write in chapter 4 of 'the climate of educated opinion', 'modern knowledge', 'contemporary culture' and in chapter 3 of 'the world which we have entered either through education or through daily experience'. At other times you have been more subjective, referring to your mind and conscience, 'what the Christian conscience can now accept' (chapter 6) and your experience (especially as a human parent). In either case, is it unfair to say that your final criterion for truth is 'modern opinion', whether yours or others'? It certainly seems to me like that, and explains why you feel able to set aside biblical teaching, e.g. on the cross, on miracles and on homosexuality. Is your position very different from that of Thomas Maurer who wrote:

> There is no greater misuse of the Bible than to make it our taskmaster, a body of writing to which we are enslaved. I can see no validity whatsoever to the claim that something written two or three thousand years ago has any special relevance to my way of living and thinking. I happen to buy most of what Jesus said, but not because it's in the Bible or because he said it, but rather because I find it existentially valid. And I have to be candid enough to say that there are a few things Jesus said that I can't buy. (quoted from *Is Gay Good? Ethics, Theology and Homosexuality* by Richard Lovelace in *Homosexuality and the Church*, 1978, p. 44)

I grant that this is an extreme statement which you would probably not endorse. For theological liberalism, I realise, covers a broad spectrum of positions. There are many truths to which you yourself (like the 'liberal Evangelicals' of an earlier period) are committed, but which the latter-day radicals reject. Nevertheless, what you write provokes me to ask a series of questions: How are we to evaluate modern knowledge and educated opinion? Will the next generation view them as favourably as you do? How are the Christian mind and conscience to be informed and directed? Do not these subjectivities need the objectivity of Scripture to control them? You will perhaps respond that Evangelicals are subjective too, because our authority is not in practice 'Scripture' but, as I have said, 'Scripture as correctly interpreted'. Does that not put our opinion as interpreters above the Scripture itself? And in that case are not both Evangelicals and liberals in the end subjectivists, finding our criterion of judgement inside rather than outside ourselves? Honestly, no! For although our authority is 'Scripture as correctly interpreted', the qualifying clause is a parenthesis, so that the emphasis is not on our interpretation but on the Scripture which is being interpreted. Consequently, in Christian debate both sides can appeal back from an interpretation of Scripture to Scripture itself. This is exactly what Jesus did in his controversies with the Jewish authorities. Both they and he accepted the supreme authority of Scripture; their disagreement was over its true interpretation.

If Evangelicals continue to insist, however, that Scripture has authority even over 'modern knowledge' and 'educated opinion', are we not heading straight for another confrontation comparable to the Church *versus* Galileo or the Church *versus* Darwin, in which yet again the Church will have to beat a humiliating retreat? My response is again 'honestly, no'. The mistake, I suggest, would be to contrast 'science' and 'Scripture', since these, being respectively (in our view) human formulation and divine revelation, are not comparable. What we should be comparing instead is nature with Scripture, and science with theology. For 'science' is the systematic study of the natural order, while 'theology' is the systematic study of the biblical revelation. I do not feel able to accept your phrase 'the revelation of science', since it seems to me dangerous to elevate science (as a human study) to the level of revelation. What I do accept is that nature and Scripture are both divine revelation ('general and special', 'natural and supernatural', to use the traditional terms), since God has revealed himself both in the world he has made and in Christ and the biblical witness to Christ. Science is the fallible human interpretation of nature, while theology (or 'tradition', which is theological reflection) is the fallible human interpretation of Scripture. You and I believe (I think) that in nature and Scripture there are certain given things, *data* (although they relate to largely different spheres), which, if they truly come from God, cannot contradict one another. The contradictions have not been between nature and Scripture, but between science and theology, that is, between different human interpretations of God's double revelation. If, therefore, we are to learn lessons from the past, it is neither for conservatives to deny the evidence of nature, nor for liberals to deny the evidence of Scripture, but for all of us to re-examine our interpretations of both. Through such a reciprocal challenge, and through humble and patient listening to one another, it should be possible to find an increasing integration of word and world, Scripture and nature, theology and science. It will involve what I have sometimes called the pain of 'double listening', as we listen above all to the word of God, although in the light of contemporary questions and opinions, but also to the voices of the modern world, although in submission to God's word.

Turning from authority to salvation, the basic difference between us seems to be that you see the sincerity, devotion and uprightness of adherents of other religions or none, and ask why God should not accept them, while I see the sinful rebellion of all human beings (in addition to their value and dignity as creatures made in God's image), and hear the uncompromising words of Scripture 'there is no-one righteous, not even one' and 'no-one will be declared righteous in God's sight by observing the law' (Romans 3:10,20). Such an emphasis on human sin and inability is not morbid, or at least it does not need to be. On the contrary, it is the way to health because it is the indispensable preliminary to trusting in Christ. He did not come to call the righteous (i.e. the self-righteous) to repentance, but sinners. Was not the purpose of the law to be our *paidagōgos*, condemning and imprisoning us in sin, in order 'to lead us to Christ' who alone can rescue us (Galatians 3:23–25)? And is not the ministry of the Holy Spirit first to convince us of our sin and then to bear witness to Christ as the Saviour of sinners (John 15:26; 16:8)?

So then, behind our differences in relation to both authority and salvation there lies a divergent understanding of our human being and condition. Both the Catholic and the liberal traditions have tended to exalt human intelligence and goodness and therefore to expect human beings to contribute something towards their enlightenment and their salvation. Evangelicals, on the other hand, while strongly affirming the divine image which our humanity bears, have tended to emphasise our human finitude and fallenness and therefore to insist that without revelation we cannot know God and without redemption we cannot reach him.

That is why Evangelical essentials focus on the Bible and the cross, and on their indispensability, since it is through these that God's word to us has been spoken and God's work for us has been done. Indeed, his grace bears a trinitarian shape. First, in both spheres the Father took the initiative, teaching us what we could not otherwise know, and giving us what we could not otherwise have. Secondly, in both the Son has played a unique role as the one mediator through whom the Father's initiative was taken. He is the Word made flesh, through whom the Father's glory was manifested. He is the sinless one made sin for us that the

Father might reconcile us to himself. Moreover, the word God spoke through Christ and the work God did through Christ were both *hapax*, completed once and for all. Nothing can be added to either without derogating from the perfection of God's word and work through Christ. Then thirdly, in both revelation and redemption the ministry of the Holy Spirit is essential. It is he who illumines our minds to understand what God has revealed in Christ, and he who moves our hearts to receive what God has achieved through Christ. Thus in both spheres the Father has acted through the Son and acts through the Spirit.

It is this horizon of trinitarian grace which, more than anything else, makes humility appropriate, the humility which acknowledges our dependence on grace. Is this not why Jesus made the little child our model? We have to humble ourselves like a little child, he said. And since children are often far from humble in their behaviour, it must have been the humility of their status to which he referred. For children are rightly named 'dependants'. Everything they know has been taught them; everything they possess has been given them. So Jesus taught that God reveals his truth not to 'the wise and learned' but to 'little children' (Matthew 11:25), and that the kingdom is given only to little children and to those adults who become like them (Mark 10:13–15). This is not to denigrate human beings, or to inculcate irresponsibility. For the same Scripture, which tells us to resemble little children in the humble way in which we learn and receive, forbids us to behave like children in other ways. Jeremiah was rebuked for wanting to abdicate the responsibility to work by declaring himself 'only a child' (Jeremiah 1:6–8). And the Corinthians were rebuked for wanting to abdicate the responsibility to think: 'Stop thinking like children. In regard to evil be infants, but in your thinking be adults' (1 Corinthians 14:20). We are to think hard, using our God-given minds, but to do so humbly, acknowledging our dependence on his grace in revelation. We are also to work hard, 'struggling with all his energy, which so powerfully works' in us (Colossians 1:29), but to do so humbly, acknowledging our dependence on his grace in redemption.

Technologically and scientifically it may be accurate to speak of 'man come of age'. Morally and spiritually it is not. Like little children we still depend utterly on divine grace both to teach us what we do not know and to give us what we do not have. Such dependence on grace brings glory to God – Father, Son and Holy Spirit. Indeed 'from him grace, to him glory' seems to summarise what is 'essential for Evangelicals'. 'Where, then, is boasting? It is excluded'; 'let him who boasts boast in the Lord' (Romans 3:27; 1 Corinthians 1:31).

I thank you again, David, for initiating this dialogue, and for giving me the opportunity to respond to what you have written. For myself I believe that some useful clarifications have emerged. You have my continuing, warm good wishes.

Yours as ever,
John

# Questions

## Chapter 1

1  What is your experience of Evangelicals?
2  How would you define 'Evangelical'?
3  How would you define 'liberal Christianity'?

## Chapter 2

4  Is the Bible 'infallible' or 'inerrant'?
5  What was the attitude of Jesus to the Scriptures?
6  What is the authority of the Bible for Christians?

## Chapter 3

7  Is John Stott's interpretation of the cross taught by the New Testament?
8  Can it be communicated as today's gospel?
9  Can the centrality of the cross be maintained with the kind of interpretation that David Edwards offers?

## Chapter 4

10  How literally should we accept the miracle stories of the Bible?
11  How does our attitude to miracles affect our understanding of God and salvation?
12  Should we expect miracles today?

# Chapter 5

13 What is the authority of the Old Testament in ethics?
14 Was Jesus a legislator?
15 If the Bible reflects surrounding cultures, how can it guide us in our moral problems?

# Chapter 6

16 Should Christians today mean by the 'kingdom of God' exactly what Jesus meant?
17 Are 'non-Christians' or 'non-believers' 'perishing'?
18 How can Christians avoid both 'total fixity' and 'total fluidity' in evangelism?

# Epilogue

19 Is it the essential difference between the Evangelical and the liberal Christian that the one appeals to Scripture and the other to rationality?
20 To what authority does the Catholic or Orthodox Christian appeal?
21 What is essential for Evangelicals, what for liberals, and what for Christians?

# Books referred to in the text

| | | |
|---|---|---|
| Abraham, William J. | *The Divine Inspiration of Holy Scripture* | (Oxford University Press, 1981) |
| Abraham, William J. | *Divine Revelation and the Limits of Historical Criticism* | (Oxford University Press, 1982) |
| Anderson, Norman | *Christianity and World Religions: The Challenge of Pluralism* | (Inter-Varsity Press, 1984) |
| Athanasius, St (trans. & ed. R. W. Thomson) | *Contra Gentes and De Incarnatione* | (Clarendon Press, 1971) |
| Atkinson, Basil | *Old Paths in Perilous Times* | (1933) |
| Aulen, Gustaf | *Christus Victor* | (SPCK, 1931) |
| Bailey, Kenneth | *The Cross and the Prodigal* | (Concordia, 1973) |
| Barclay, Oliver | *Whatever Happened to the Jesus Lane Lot?* | (Inter-Varsity Press, 1977) |
| Barr, James | *Fundamentalism* | (SCM Press, 1977; revised 1981) |
| Barr, James | *Holy Scripture: Canon, Authority, Criticism* | (SCM Press, 1983) |
| Barr, James | *Escaping from Fundamentalism* | (SCM Press, 1984) |
| Barrett, C. K. | *Jesus and the Gospel Tradition* | (SPCK, 1967) |
| Barrett, C. K. | *The First Epistle to the Corinthians* | (A. & C. Black, 1971) |
| Barton, John | *The Oracles of God* | (Darton, Longman & Todd, 1986) |
| Baxter, Christina | *Stepping Stones* | (Hodder & Stoughton, 1987) |
| Black, Matthew and H. H. Rowley (eds) | *Peake's Commentary on the Bible* | (Nelson Van Nostrand Reinhold, 1982) |

| Blamires, Harry | *Where Do We stand?* | (SPCK, 1980) |
|---|---|---|
| Blocher, Henri | *In the Beginning* | (Inter-Varsity Press, 1984) |
| Bloesch, Donald | *The Future of Evangelical Christianity* | (Doubleday, 1983) |
| Blomberg, Craig | *The Historical Reliability of the Gospels* | (Inter-Varsity Press, 1987) |
| Boice, J. M. (ed.) | *The Foundation of Biblical Authority* | (Pickering & Inglis, 1978) |
| Boswell, John | *Christianity, Social Tolerance and Homosexuality* | (Chicago University Press, 1980) |
| Brown, Colin | *Miracles and the Critical Mind* | (Paternoster Press/Wm B. Eerdmans, 1984) |
| Brown, Colin | *That You May Believe* | (Paternoster Press/Wm B. Eerdmans, 1985) |
| Brown, Raymond | *The Birth of the Messiah* | (Geoffrey Chapman, 1977) |
| Calvin, John (trans. F. L. Battles) | *The Institutes of the Christian Religion* (1559 edition) 2 vols | (Westminster Press, 1960) |
| Calvin, John (trans. F. L. Battles) | *The Institutes of the Christian Religion* (1536 edition) | (Collins Flame, 1986) |
| Capon, John | *Evangelicals Tomorrow* | (Collins, 1977) |
| Carnley, Peter | *The Structure of Resurrection Belief* | (Oxford University Press, 1987) |
| Carson, D. A. | *Matthew* (Expositor's Bible Commentary) | (Zondervan, 1984) |
| Carson, D. A. and J. D. Woodbridge (eds) | *Scripture and Truth* | (Inter-Varsity Press, 1983) |
| Carson, D. A. and J. D. Woodbridge (eds) | *Hermeneutics, Authority and Canon* | (Inter-Varsity Press, 1986) |
| Catherwood, Christopher | *Five Evangelical Leaders* | (Hodder & Stoughton, 1984) |
| Chilton, Bruce | *The Kingdom of God in the Teaching of Jesus* | (SPCK, 1984) |
| Chilton, Bruce | *A Galilean Rabbi and His Bible* | (SPCK, 1984) |

| Cole, Alan | *Mark* (Tyndale New Testament Commentaries) | (Inter-Varsity Press, 1961) |
|---|---|---|
| Cranfield, C. E. B. | *The Epistle to the Romans* (International Critical Commentary) 2 vols | (T. & T. Clark, 1975/79) |
| Cullmann, Oscar | *The Christology of the New Testament* | (SCM Press, 1959; revised 1963) |
| Daube, David | *The New Testament and Rabbinic Judaism* | (Athlone, 1956) |
| Dillistone, F. W. | *The Christian Understanding of Atonement* | (SCM Press, 1968) |
| Dodd, C. H. | *According to the Scriptures* | (Nisbet, 1952) |
| Dunn, James D. G. | *Jesus and the Spirit* | (SCM Press, 1975) |
| Edwards, David | *Jesus for Modern Man* | (Collins Fount, 1975) |
| Edwards, David | *Christian England* 3 vols | (Collins Fount, 1982/84/85) |
| Edwards, David | *God's Cross in Our World* | (SCM Press, 1963) |
| Edwards, David | *The Last Things Now* | (SCM Press, 1969) |
| Edwards, David | *A Key to the Old Testament* | (Collins Fount, 1978) |
| Edwards, David | *Bishops and Beliefs* | (Modern Churchmen's Union, 1986) |
| Edwards, David | *The Futures of Christianity* | (Hodder & Stoughton, 1987) |
| Edwards, David | *Religion and Change* | (Hodder & Stoughton, 1967) |
| Elwell, Walter A. (ed.) | *Evangelical Dictionary of Theology* | (Marshall Pickering, 1985) |
| England, Edward (ed.) | *David Watson: A Portrait by His Friends* | (Highland Books, 1985) |
| France, R. T. | *Jesus and the Old Testament* | (Tyndale Press, 1971) |
| France, R. T. | *Matthew* (Tyndale New Testament Commentaries) | (Inter-Varsity Press, 1985) |
| France, R. T. and D. Wenham (eds) | *Gospel Perspectives* vols 1–3 | (Sheffield Academic Press, 1980/81/83) |

| Fuller, R. H. | *Interpreting the Miracles* | (SCM Press, 1963) |
| Geisler, Norman | *Inerrancy* | (Zondervan, 1980) |
| Green, Michael | *The Empty Cross of Jesus* | (Hodder & Stoughton, 1984) |
| Harris, Murray | *Raised Immortal* | (Marshalls, 1984) |
| Harvey, A. E. | *Jesus and the Constraints of History* | (Duckworth, 1982) |
| Hendriksen, William | *More Than Conquerors* | (Tyndale Press, 1962) |
| Hengel, Martin | *The Cross and the Son of God* | (SCM Press, 1986) |
| Henry, Carl F. | *The Uneasy Conscience of Modern Fundamentalism* | (1947) |
| Henry, Carl F. | *Confessions of a Theologian* | (Word Books, 1986) |
| Hooker, M. D. | *Jesus and the Servant* | (SPCK, 1959) |
| Hooykaas, R. | *Religion and the Rise of Modern Science* | (Scottish Academic Press, 1972) |
| Hunter, A. M. | *The Unity of the New Testament* | (SCM Press, 1943) |
| Jeremias, Joachim | *New Testament Theology: The Proclamation of Jesus* | (SCM Press, 1971) |
| Kantzer, Kenneth | *Evangelical Roots* | (Nelson, 1978) |
| Käsemann, Ernst | *Commentary on Romans* | (SCM Press, 1980) |
| Kaye, Bruce & Gordon Wenham (eds) | *Law Morality and the Bible* | (Inter-Varsity Press, 1978) |
| Kidner, Derek | *Genesis* (Tyndale Old Testament Commentaries) | (Inter-Varsity Press, 1967) |
| King, John | *The Evangelicals* | (Hodder & Stoughton, 1969) |
| Knox, John | *The Death of Christ* | (Abingdon Press, 1959) |
| Kummel, W. G. | *The New Testament: The History of the Investigation of its Problems* | (SCM Press, 1973) |
| Kummel, W. G. | *Introduction to the New Testament* | (SCM Press, 1975) |
| Kummel, W. G. | *The Theology of the New Testament* | (SCM Press, 1974) |

| Küng, Hans | *Christianity and the World Religions* | (Collins, 1987) |
|---|---|---|
| Küng, Hans | *Infallible?* | (Collins, 1971) |
| Ladd, George Eldon | *I Believe in the Resurrection* | (Hodder & Stoughton, 1975) |
| Lane, William | *The Gospel of Mark (New International Commentary on the New Testament)* | (Eerdmans, 1974) |
| Lapide, Pinchas | *The Resurrection of Jesus* | (SPCK, 1983) |
| Lewis, C. S. | *Miracles: A Preliminary Discussion* | (Geoffrey Bles, 1947) |
| Lewis, C. S. | *Surprised by Joy* | (Geoffrey Bles, 1955) |
| Lindsell, Harold | *The Battle for the Bible* | (Zondervan, 1977) |
| Lovelace, Richard | *Homosexuality and the Church* | (Revell Books, 1978) |
| Lyttelton, George | *Observations on the Conversion and Apostleship of St Paul (1769)* | |
| MacKay, Donald | *The Clockwork Image* | (Inter-Varsity Press, 1974) |
| Marsden, George M. | *Fundamentalism and American Culture* | (Oxford University Press, 1980) |
| Marshall, I. Howard | *Luke: Historian and Theologian* | (Paternoster Press, 1970) |
| Marshall, I. Howard | *The Gospel of Luke* | (Paternoster Press, 1978) |
| Marshall, I. Howard | *Biblical Inspiration* | (Hodder & Stoughton, 1983) |
| Marshall, I. Howard (ed.) | *New Testament Interpretation* | (Paternoster Press, 1977) |
| Martin, David and Peter Mullen (eds) | *Strange Gifts?* | (Basil Blackwell, 1984) |
| Martin, Ralph | *Mark: Evangelist and Theologian* | (Paternoster Press, 1972) |
| Meyer, Ben F. | *The Aims of Jesus* | (SCM Press, 1979) |
| Montagu, Ashley | *Man's Most Dangerous Myth: The Fallacy of Race* | (1974) |
| Morris, Leon | *The Apostolic Preaching of the Cross* | (Tyndale Press, 1965) |

| Morris, Leon | *The Gospel of John* (New International Commentary on the New Testament) | (Wm B. Eerdmans, 1971) |
|---|---|---|
| Morris, Leon | *The Atonement* | (Inter-Varsity Press, 1983) |
| Moule, C. F. D. | *Miracles* | (Cambridge University Press, 1965) |
| Moule, C. F. D. | *Essays in New Testament Interpretation* | (Cambridge University Press, 1982) |
| Neill, Stephen | *Christian Faith Today* | (Penguin Books, 1955) |
| Packer, J. I. | *Fundamentalism and the Word of God* | (Inter-Varsity Press, 1958) |
| Packer, J. I. | *Keep in Step with the Spirit* | (Inter-Varsity Press, 1984) |
| Packer, J. I. | *Under God's Word* | (Lakeland, 1982) |
| Packer, J. I. | *Knowing God* | (Hodder & Stoughton, 1973) |
| Packer, J. I. | *Freedom, Authority and Scripture* | (Inter-Varsity Press, 1981) |
| Padilla, C. Rene (ed.) | *The New Face of Evangelicalism* | (Hodder & Stoughton, 1976) |
| Paul VI, Pope | *Credo of the People of God* | (Catholic Truth Society, 1968) |
| Perrin, Norman | *The Kingdom of God in the Teaching of Jesus* | (SCM Press, 1963) |
| Perrin, Norman | *Jesus and the Language of the Kingdom* | (SCM Press, 1976) |
| Pinnock, Clark | *A Defense of Biblical Infallibility* | (1967) |
| Pinnock, Clark | *The Scripture Principle* | (Hodder & Stoughton, 1985) |
| Planck, Max | *A Scientific Autobiography* | (Williams & Norgate, 1950) |
| Ramm, Bernard | *After Fundamentalism* | (Harper & Row, 1983) |
| Rashdall, Hastings | *The Idea of Atonement in Christian Theology* | (Macmillan, 1919) |
| Richardson, Alan | *The Miracle-Stories of the Gospels* | (SCM Press, 1941) |
| Robertson, A. and A. Plummer | *A Critical and Exegetical Commentary on the First Epistle of Paul to the Corinthians* | (T. & T. Clark, 1911) |
| Robinson, J. | *Twelve More New Testament Studies* | (SCM Press, 1984) |

| | | |
|---|---|---|
| Roszak, Theodore | *Where the Wasteland Ends* | |
| Roszak, Theodore | *The Making of a Counter-Culture* | (Faber, 1969) |
| Rowley, H. H. | *The Faith of Israel* | (SCM Press, 1965) |
| Sanders, E. P. | *Paul and Palestinian Judaism* | (SCM Press, 1977) |
| Sanders, E. P. | *Jesus and Judaism* | (SCM Press, 1985) |
| Schweitzer, Albert | *The Quest of the Historical Jesus* (1910) | (SCM Press, 1981) |
| Selwyn, E. G. | *The First Epistle of St Peter* | (Macmillan, 1947) |
| Smalley, Stephen | *John: Evangelist and Interpreter* | (Paternoster Press, 1978) |
| Smart, James D. | *The Interpretation of Scripture* | (SCM Press, 1961) |
| Smart, James D. | *The Strange Silence of the Bible in the Church* | (SCM Press, 1970) |
| Smart, James D. | *The Past, Present and Future of Biblical Theology* | (Westminster Press, 1979) |
| Stanton, Graham | *The Interpretation of Matthew* | (SPCK/Fortress Press, 1983) |
| Stott, John R. W. | *Fundamentalism and Evangelism* | (Evangelical Alliance, 1956) |
| Stott, John R. W. | *Make the Truth Known* | (UCCF, 1982) |
| Stott, J. R. W., I. Cundy & B. Kaye (eds) | *Obeying Christ in a Changing World* | (Collins Fount, 1977) |
| Stott, John | *The Evangelical-Roman Catholic Dialogue on Mission* | (1987) |
| Swete, H. B. | *The Apocalypse of St John* | (Macmillan, 1906) |
| Taylor, Vincent | *Forgiveness and Reconciliation* | (Macmillan, 1941) |
| Theissen, Gerd | *The Miracle Stories of the Early Christian Tradition* | (T. & T. Clark, 1983) |
| Thiselton, Tony | *The Two Horizons* | (Paternoster Press, 1980) |
| Toland, John | *Christianity Not Mysterious* (1696) | |
| Vermes, Geza | *Jesus the Jew* | (Collins, 1973) |

| Warfield, Benjamin B. | *Counterfeit Miracles* (1918) | (Banner of Truth, 1972) |
|---|---|---|
| Wenham, David | *Gospel Perspectives* vol 4 | (Sheffield Academic Press, 1984) |
| Wenham, David (ed.) | *Gospel Perspectives* vol 5 | (Sheffield Academic Press, 1984) |
| Wenham, David and Craig Blombery (eds) | *Gospel Perspectives* vol 6 | (Sheffield Academic Press, 1986) |
| Wenham, John W. | *Christ and the Bible* | (Inter-Varsity Press, 1973) |
| Wenham, John W. | *Easter Enigma* | (Paternoster Press, 1984) |
| Whiteley, D. E. H. | *The Theology of St Paul* | (Basil Blackwell, 1974) |
| Wilcock, Michael | *I Saw Heaven Opened: The Message of Revelation* | (Inter-Varsity Press, 1975) |
| Wimber, John with Kevin Springer | *Power Healing* | (Hodder & Stoughton, 1986) |
| Wimber, John with Kevin Springer | *Power Evangelism* | (Hodder & Stoughton, 1985) |
| Wright, Christopher | *The Use of the Bible in Social Ethics* | (Grove Booklets, 1983) |
| Young, Frances | *Sacrifice and the Death of Christ* | (SPCK, 1975) |
| Youngblood, Ronald (ed.) | *Evangelicals and Inerrancy* | (1984) |
| Ziesler, John | *Pauline Christianity* | (Oxford University Press, 1983) |

# INDEX

# INDEX